THE COLOR OF PAIN

THE COLOR OF PAIN

A Novel

MELISA E. ARNOLD

Olympus Story House

THE COLOR OF PAIN

© Melisa E. Arnold

For what is the color of pain, you ask?
Is it multi-hued like a morning rainbow?
Is it black or white, no grey shades to mask?
Or is it as blue as the oceans below?
Does it match the cerulean skies above?
Warm, comforting, like a baby's blanket?
Some say it's like the bright color of love,
Or like that elusive scent you just can't forget.

I think the color of pain can be seductive,
As we strive our hardest not to succumb,
To the lure of death; we still desire to live
To feel no more, desiring to go numb.
Wanting a cure to ensure that agony leaves
And pain be replaced by warm sensations,
That suffering stops, then we believe . . .
We're the only one feeling such emotions

But wait, shh, just listen! The color of pain
May be necessary, for us to appreciate
Such suffering, we don't want to feel again
Knowledge imparted to us, not too late,
Yet still effective enough, so we can learn
Our limits, the farthest edge, the extreme
And with dogged perseverance, we'll earn
The realization that the color of pain feels like a dream!

ACKNOWLEDGMENT

All glory to God from whom all blessings flow...I praise Him for all He has done, and continues to do!

A few years ago, I was discussing with Belizean friends how it feels to be in a new country, far away from home. I was lamenting the fact that I've never really felt that I "belong" even though I've spent more than half my life in America. I arrived in California from Belize, Central American in the mid-1970's, the age of Afros, bell-bottoms, platform shoes—yeah, that glorious time! I arrived with my "nose open", as the older folks would say, ready to be wowed by my new country of residence. I felt like I was on the cusp of a great discovery, but somehow, America didn't quite live up to my expectations.

As friends and I discussed, we were kindred spirits who lamented the fact that we and other peers were somewhat disappointed by life in our new country. One of my friends mentioned that this was the second time that he'd been so displaced because, after having grown up in Belize, he'd moved to England at the age of five, returned at the age of sixteen, then had been uprooted again to join his own single mother in America. We pondered the idea that parents often thought they were giving us everything, that they struggled mightily to provide for us financially, and that should be enough. Like many Belizean parents, they were not overly affectionate; they showed us "love" by providing for us proudly, without government assistance or handouts, but we were left out in the cold when it came to our parents' expression of love for us, whether verbal or physical.

Through our shared angst, I decided to create this book, telling the story from our point of view, weaving in many of my own observations, especially since we'd lived in Belize up to our mid-teenage years: Hence, *"The Color of Pain"* was born. While it's a work of fiction, it's semi-autobiographical, because many of the situations are real, and reflect a general sense of our growing-up experience in Belize, and in our Garifuna culture. The story is told with a feminine slant, as I'm the scribe, but I've tried to incorporate the teenage angst we lived through, feelings we thought were common to any Belizean teenagers, male or female.

I hope that my Belizean and expatriate Belizean-American peers will be able to relate to many experiences in "The Color Of Pain", and that those from other parts of Belize can also get a flavor of how life growing up in the southern district of Stann Creek, specifically, Dangriga Town.

Please let me know what you think of this effort at misseebiz1@gmail.com, misseebiz1@yahoo.com, my website www.melisaearnoldauthor.com or melisaea1 (Instagram).

Regards,
Melisa E. Arnold

PROLOGUE

Present-Day Dangríga
Stann Creek District
Belize, Central America

F riday night, and the plain pine coffin stood on three unpainted sawhorses in the middle of the floor. Mourners murmured among themselves as they gathered under the white tent and stood directly in front of the coffin looking down at the almost angelic face of the deceased. A copper penny had been placed on top of each of the deceased's eyelids in true Garífuna fashion. The toes of the new white socks had been attached together with a shiny safety pin; that too was a Garífuna tradition, origin unknown. The copper pennies were vaguely representative of the "toll" that the dead would have to pay to get a pass from Saint Peter into heaven. Yes, you couldn't always tell, but Garífunas, one of which the deceased was, believed in heaven, hell, and an afterlife. Sure, they dabbled in *Obeah*, the Belizean-African system of spells, hexes, curses, and magic, and they regularly participated in *Dugú*, a voodoo-like healing ritual, in the *Dabúyabah* (Temple) to appease the spirits, but they wanted to make absolutely sure the deceased paid their way into heaven. They, functioning in the shadowy, dual world of Christianity and spiritualism, wanted to make sure that all bases were covered, just in case the deceased needed help to get to meet their maker.

Directly to the right of the coffin sat a woman in a wheelchair, a tragic figure, her head bent and sobbing or at times wailing and cursing at God, blaming Him for the loss of the deceased. An average, nondescript gentleman stood awkwardly behind her, talking soothingly to her, rubbing her shoulders and back, trying in vain to comfort her. Another male, this one a stranger, stood near the inside entrance of the tent, shuffling from one foot to the other, twisting a beat-up brown fedora between gnarled hands. He seemed ill-at-ease, reeking of marijuana and rum; he too was sobbing pitifully. Some people whispered to each other, wondering who he was, what his connection to the deceased was, and why he was there, but nobody was brave enough to ask him. The few who knew who he was would not satisfy the curiosity of those clueless to his identity.

To complete the tableau of mourners, near the front, just to the left of the coffin, was a young girl of about fifteen or sixteen years of age, beautiful but clearly wracked with sorrow, with head bowed as she shrieked in agony. You could tell from looking at her that she was hugely pregnant, like she was about eight-and-a-half months along. Many of those present wondered whether she would last through the funeral or if she would have to be rushed to the hospital even before the night was over. She was quite literally "ready to pop" and deliver her baby, but some were reassured because they saw that Mamma Graciela, the local midwife known for her magic fingers and calm demeanor, even in breech-birth situations, was in the crowd. They were confident that she would be able to handle things or whatever complications would arise.

A local band kept a lively flow of Punta music and other favorites going; people were nodding their heads and shaking their bodies to the sounds, even the non-Garífunas: Kriols, Indians, Spanish, or *gi-yows* as they were called. Papa Deuce had his card table set up in a corner and was doing a brisk business at four different tables at a dollar buy-in; one table was dedicated to the dice game "under or over," the second to five-card Pitty Pat, the third to checkers, and the fourth to a cutthroat game of dominoes, or "bones." The domino table drew the largest crowd as gleeful players loudly yelled "Domino!" as they slapped winning tiles to the appropriate end of the domino board.

The louder the slap at the placing of that final tile, the more in-your-face the win and temporary bragging rights until that winner was taken down by the next challenger, and so on. Marty, the most recent winner, taunted Louis as he slammed the winning domino tile down.

"Hey, Lou, get up, let mi tek the next player on, so I can knock them out too. Know what? Can't wait to beat all challengers, so go on home right now. Tell your wife to get ready for me. A winner's on his way to rock her world tonight. I want her to wear the best lingerie she's got . . . Yeah, the red one!

Louis was absolutely furious; he looked like he wanted to grab Marty and choke him, but the crowd roared their approval. There was no entertainment better than the strut and shenanigans of gamers!

Adding to the air of entertainment was a Garífuna choir, who sang traditional favorites and other hymns designed to comfort the family of the deceased. In true Garífuna style, this wake was about partying and was far removed from the thought of honoring the dead or comforting the bereaved. Teenagers hooked up near the outdoor bathrooms, but none of them was brave enough to try to go all the way for fear that one of the very watchful grannies would see something and go tell their parents. Everyone knew that wakes were occasions to see and be seen—typically, the wilder the action at the wake, the more promising the drama would be at the actual funeral service and burial ceremony in a few days. There were "professional" mourners in place who wailed and lamented over the coffin, exhorting the dead to relay messages to their own previously-departed loved ones and to deliver them when they got to heaven. These mourners would really show their skill on funeral day and would be quite a sight to behold! You'd never seen mourners until you saw these folks in action.

Caribbean and Belizean rum and Lighthouse, Belikin, Heineken, and Guinness beer and Stout flowed in abundance. Local home-brewed wine made from blackberries, rice, cashews, potatoes, sugarcane, and other homegrown staples was the drink of choice for the ladies and some teenagers bold enough to take a sip. Belizeans were known for being particularly skilled at making local home-brewed wine from just about anything; all one had to do was to be patient and wait for the wine to ferment and be declared ready for drinking. Some of these winebrewers would give the finest French bottlers or American winemakers such as Gallo Brothers, Woodbridge (Mondavi), or Beringer a serious run for their money! It appeared that everyone was having a wonderful time indeed. The forced gaiety of the revelers contrasted starkly with the tragic figures near the coffin, the mother-to-be, and the stranger standing near the entrance. As they wailed and moaned, you could really feel their pain; it was obvious that they found the partiers a bit much to take. They would've been content for everyone to leave so they could be alone in their private grief.

Pastor Jacobs circulated determinedly among the bereaved, promising salvation, resurrection, and anything else that sounded appropriate for the occasion. He wasn't really sure how much of an impact he was having, but he persevered anyway, while keeping a disapproving eye on the noisy revelers and the tippling teenagers, helping ensure that things remained under control at all times. He left most of the teenager-monitoring to the parents, some of whom were badly in need of monitoring themselves. Just looking at the debauchery gave him an idea regarding what the subject of Sunday's sermon would be: fire and brimstone and hell would definitely be topics on his agenda!

A large fan lazily stirred the air in the stiflingly hot tent, and people sat around inside and out eating delectable favorites like *hudút,* beaten or smashed green plantains served in coconut milk gravy; rice and beans; stewed chicken; johnnycakes; powder buns; ham sandwiches; pinole, or corn porridge; *beemeh cackileh,* or sweet rice; cassava bread; fish; chicken, pork, or beef tamales; and other delicacies. For the nondrinkers, *hee-u,* a cassava-ginger concoction, and large pots of coffee and tea liberally flavored with sugar and condensed milk (a common sweetener in the Caribbean and Third World countries like Belize) washed the food down perfectly. Older women opened plastic bags brought from home in their purses and surreptitiously scooped food into them so they could reheat and serve it to their families for breakfast next morning. The "mothers" of the community had this particular move down to a fine science: they were known for going to wakes under the guise of offering comfort when all knew that their real goal was to load up on free treats to take home. These women were by no means destitute; they just considered acquisition of food from wakes their big score. As they boasted, there was "no shame in their game" even though they knew that people knew them for what they truly were and, as a matter of fact, had caught on to them a long time ago.

It was now about twelve midnight, but the party showed absolutely no signs of stopping. Soon, some of the older, concerned family members and friends would have to start suggesting that the attendees at the wake leave so that the deceased's family could get some rest and get ready for a second or possibly third night of revelry. Eventually, they would just have to put the alcohol away, turn the lights off, and force the mourners to leave the premises. The coffin would be closed temporarily, and people would rotate in shifts to ensure that the dead would never be left alone at any point throughout the night. They must never be allowed to make that transition while all alone.

PART I

June 1963
Belize City, British Honduras

CHAPTER 1

Cathlean Alvarez arrived at Phillip Goldson Airport in the sweltering heat of British Honduras. She couldn't believe that she used to live here and hadn't ever been bothered by the heat before. Right now, she felt like a used, wrung-out washrag as she stood near the pavement awaiting a taxi. "God," she said to herself, "I must remember I'm not in England anymore. Is the proper term 'pavement' or 'sidewalk'?" Neither seemed appropriate for the hard, mud-ravaged, piece of sandy strip on which she stood. She wanted to make sure she used the proper terminology; she knew she didn't want to offend anyone because she remembered that British Hondurans returning from abroad were looked at questioningly or mocked if they used the wrong words for things they called by a different name before leaving home. Nobody "put you back in your place" quite as effectively as a British Honduran; it behooved you to remember that, or if you dared to forget, you did so at your own risk.

Cathlean sucked her teeth as she waited impatiently as a "taxi" pulled up in front of her. It was unclear whether this was a taxi at all; it had started out as a traditional yellow-gold, but apparently, the painter had run out of paint and had finished up with whatever colors were available: about half of the cab's body was yellow, the rest a mixture of brown, white, and cream. Frankly this was really a multicolored vehicle, where not one color dominated but all blended and bled into each other. The driver who jumped out of the "taxi" was as much of a mess as his car; grey and matted dreadlocked hair hung untidily from under a cap with the bill turned sideways. He was tall, wore "flooding" khaki pants way too short for him, a dingy white shirt, and dusty black loafers with the heels worn down flat to the ground.

The thing that really stood out on this character was his gold tooth, the only one visible when he smiled in welcome. He helped her to load up her numerous pieces of Louis Vuitton luggage, then tipped his cap to Cathlean saying, "Hello, ma'am, hello. Mi name's Tooth. I'm sure you can see why heh, heh, heh. Let me take you home. I see you just came in from England. How was the weather when you left? Cold, rainy? You don't need to worry 'bout that here, ma'am. It's very hot. I hope you enjoy yo' trip!" He said this while loading up the luggage and ushering her into the car, all seemingly without taking a breath.

"Well, you have any children, Miss Lady? Guess what, I got eighteen. My mum always says children are a blessing. Guess I'm blessed eighteen times!" He guffawed, proud of himself, "Only problem with eighteen blessings is that I have to take care of all of them. Now how you t'ink I do that on a cabdriver's salary? Well, God provides, God provides. But, you—you sure are a pretty one. What's your name? Oh, did I tell you to call me Tooth?" He grinned, his gold tooth glistening in the bright tropical sunlight. "So, what're you doing here?"

Cathlean had to take a few minutes to think about all the questions Tooth was throwing at her. His rapid-fire speech took some getting used to, especially since she'd been gone the last five years and had become unused to the accent and speech patterns. Once she got over Tooth's appearance and digested what he had said, she was horrified to hear that he had eighteen children. She thought to herself, *Eighteen children. I really hope he takes care of all of them like he says.*

She gingerly pulled the legs of her pristine white linen pantsuit up as she climbed into the passenger seat. Before sitting, she brushed some unidentifiable crumbs off her seat, settled in, and tried to buckle the seat belt until she realized that the clasp was broken and not at all functional. Tooth closed the rear passenger door and pulled together the wire twine hanging off the door; once he was satisfied it was secure, he jumped behind the wheel and took off with a jerk.

"So, you still didn't tell me your name. You home for good? Damn, maybe you can be my nineteenth baby's mum, what do you say to that?" He laughed, a deep belly laugh for one so thin, enjoying his own joke.

"My name's Cathlean. I grew up here, but I've been gone for a few years. I have a five-year-old son named Alex who lives in Dangríga with my sister, Salomie. I'm going to surprise them. They don't know I'm coming." She looked at the traffic and scenery going by and couldn't help but say, "My, my, so much traffic here now. It wasn't like this before I left. I believe that's called progress, Tooth."

"Yes, ma'am, but don't worry. It's only a hundred miles, so we should have you home in about two-and-a-half hours. Just sit back and relax. Sleep if you want to, Cathlean, or I'll just keep talking if you don't mind. I hope your boy remembers you. You ever talk to him? You say he's five years old? That's a good age."

"Well, I hope he remembers me. My sister always sends me photos. I think he's doing fine since I left him. But you . . . eighteen children. How do you take care of that many children? You're crazy!"

"Oh, I'm very creative," he boasted. "I divide my money up so everyone gets a piece. At least you have only one child. What's his name again?"

"Alex. I won't ask you your children's names because I think you'll have a problem remembering all of them. Alex's father has other children too. Last I heard, he has about ten of them."

Tooth chuckled, saying, "Gial, I 'membah all their names. Let's see, the oldest is Bertha, she's 16, Margaret's 14, Ellie's 13, my first son Carl is 13 too—yes I had two women pregnant at the same time. I'm fertile like that," he said with a wink. "Misty and Michael are 12-year-old twins, Dylan's 11, Monty 10, Phillippa is 9½—can't forget the half—Sarah's 9, Bobby 8. Then I took a break and had triplets: Keanu, Kevin, and Kyrie, two boys and a girl, who are 6. Chloe is 5, Muriel 4, Marlton's 3, the baby, Leroy, is one year old. I bet you didn't t'ink I knew all their names and ages. I'm rich in children . . . you got some catching up to do. I'm slowing down but could go for one more with you!"

Oh, he's so gross. I can't believe he fathered eighteen children with that nasty-looking tooth, she thought to herself. She said, "Well, I have one. Can't wait to see him. I know that he and my sister will be happy to see me when I show up. I can't wait to hug my Alex." Upon saying that, she leaned back on the seat, dismissing Tooth as some no-count dullard even though she would've been shocked to know that he held several advanced degrees and was in fact very intelligent. As a matter of fact, he chose to be a taxi driver so he could be his own boss, self-employed, and also because he genuinely enjoyed talking to people as he drove them around. He took every opportunity he could to impart his wisdom and philosophy of life to a mostly unappreciative but captive audience.

CHAPTER 2

Looking out on the left-hand side of the car as they traversed the Stann Creek District, Cathlean could see and smell orange blossoms from the many trees lined up neatly in numerous citrus groves and orchards dotting the countryside. On the right side of the highway, she observed orange trees growing profusely, loaded with fruit turning slightly yellow, ready for picking. She even spied a few workers with baskets and machetes as they harvested the oranges for market, either to be sold locally or internationally to America and Europe. Cathlean remembered her parents and their friends laboring for many long backbreaking years at Alta Vista and Pomona, at the Stann Creek Valley, as they harvested citrus sold in open trade internationally, especially in America, where it was labeled with "American-grown" stickers. She shook her head at the deception perpetrated on Americans, who really thought they were having U.S.-grown fruit with their breakfast. Free trade and free enterprise back then, as it still often is, were synonymous with fraud and deception. In the end, it was all about profits to big corporations, mostly foreign ones, which really galled Belizeans; for the most part, they felt powerless to do anything about the situation but complain and quietly nurse their hatred of the interlopers in their hearts.

Cathlean tuned out Tooth's incessant chatter, turned away from him, and must have dozed off, because the next thing she knew, he was waking her up saying that they were in Dangríga. He wanted to know the address to which Cathlean was going, so she quickly rattled it off, anxious now to get there right away. Soon, Tooth pulled up in front of an unattractive two-story house of indeterminate color; Cathlean, undeterred, pointedly ignored its appearance, impatient to see her only child.

Tooth pulled into the muddy, unpaved driveway, and with grand flair, he untied the wire from the passenger door. "We're here, and right on time, too!" he exclaimed, extending his arm so Cathlean could grab it to help herself out of the car. She climbed out very slowly and hesitantly; all of a sudden, she felt nervous and uncharacteristically unsure of herself.

"Ah, Mr. Tooth," she said, opening her purse and batting her eyes flirtatiously at him. "Sir, can you wait right here? I'll be back soon. Can you please wait?" It wasn't the first time she would flirt with a man to get what she wanted. She was especially used to getting her way with not-so-handsome men like Tooth. Quite frankly, he was an ugly specimen of manhood, the type that Cathlean and her friends used to call "mothers-love," meaning he had a face that only a mother could love.

For a second or two, she wondered if she was losing her touch because Tooth looked her over from head to toe, his eyes lingering overly long on her low-cut blouse displaying her overflowing cleavage, then back up to her face. His own face had an expression that said that he knew he was being played, but he looked her up and down once more, then stuck a toothpick between his lips, his tongue skillfully moving it back and forth near his one single tooth. He narrowed his eyes at her, licked his dry, ashy lips, and stated, "Just plain old Tooth will do, don't need no Mister. Look, Miss Lady, I don't wait for people, but because you look good and can be my nineteenth baby's mamma, go ahead. Go see your little bwai, but hurry back now, I have to go . . ."

Cathlean didn't hear the rest of what he said; she sashayed across the mud-caked yard, stepping around a few scrawny chickens and a goat tethered to a skinny, barkless tree. She pushed up her plump breasts, smoothed her hands down her sides and hips, and put an extra sway in her hips as she strutted precariously on her high-heeled strappy sandals. She glanced over her shoulder as she turned the doorknob; Tooth was standing near his car with a glazed, lust-filled look on his face. Honestly, the man was drooling, his spittle hanging off his bottom lip, his gold tooth glistening. "Do you need a bib, Tooth?" she called out with a knowing laugh.

Tooth shook his head as if coming out of a deep fog. "Ha, ha, that's funny. Go on, go do your t'ing, I'll be here when you get back, and, good luck to you, you hear me?"

Now why would I need luck to see my own child? she wondered. *That man's crazy.* She shook her head as she turned the door handle, pushing at the door with her hip as she walked in. "Hullo? Is anyone home? Hullo?" She stepped in and saw a man and woman sitting at a table directly in front of her. Their backs were turned toward her so they didn't see her, but they turned quickly, eyes swiveling toward her. The woman jumped up knocking over a toddler who'd been sleeping on her lap. He woke up, fussed a little, then stayed on the floor, where he fell back asleep.

"Who, what, C-C-Cathy? Oh, it's you, it really is you! Manny, look who it is, my sister Cathlean from England. Girl, why didn't you call? Whatchu doing here, and how did you get here?" The questions tumbled incoherently from her lips as she ran over to embrace Cathlean. However, when she was standing directly in front of Cathlean, she stopped short. "I want to hug you, but I don't want to dirty your nice white clothes. Let me look at you. You really look good, sis. Life must be treating you good."

Cathlean stood at arm's length from her sister, her expression a sneer of disgust. She wondered to herself, *Who is this stranger? She looks so old . . . What happened to her?* Her eyes took in the man, who was still seated. *I see she still has that sorry excuse for a man. Oh, I'm so glad I'm here to rescue Alex from this mess.* Words failed her as she looked around at the plain, dirty walls and bare floor and the sparsely decorated house, wondering what her sister had done with all the money that she sent her every month during the years she'd been gone. Finally she said out loud, "Hullo, Salomie. I'm happy to see you. I didn't call because I wanted to surprise you and Alex. Where is he? I need to see him right away, so get him for me. Where is my son?" She could hear her voice rising.

Salomie held herself back. She could see and hear the disdain, the judging and condemnation in her younger sister's eyes. She suddenly felt old, frumpy, and unattractive, but she would not let Cathlean see how hurt she was; instead, she pointed to three muddy, shirtless boys playing near the backdoor. "There's your boy, Alex," she said, grinning widely.

Cathy looked at them, thinking they desperately needed a bath to wash off the multiple layers of caked-on mud. "Which one is he, and why is he so dirty? I know I send you money to feed and clothe my child. Why is he shirtless and wearing raggedy, torn shorts? I need to touch and hug my son, so please tell me quickly, which one is he?"

Salomie pointed at the dirtiest of the three boys. He looked at Cathlean questioningly, her head cocked sideways. Of the other two, one was about seven to eight years old, the other about three; Cathlean knew

6

she had to be looking at her son. He, with a frown on his face, looked like he was trying to place her. Then he said, "Mummy? Are you my mummy? Oh, you came for me!" He appeared to be thinking of launching himself at Cathlean but she stepped back quickly, saying, "Go take a bath. You two, go with him. All three of you need to bathe right now!" Alex hung his head in shame and disappointment, but he and the two boys turned and left the room, leaving the toddler and the three adults frozen in place. The door quietly swung shut behind them.

Cathlean turned to her sister with bloody murder in her eyes. "How could you?" she snarled. "What did you do with the money I sent to take care of my child? My God, he appears malnourished. I think you've been taking care of yourself and your own family with my money. Your boys look healthy, and Mr. Man here sure doesn't look like he's struggling. I hope he's working now, or is he still waiting for his ship to come in?" She sneered as her scornful eyes turned from her sister to Manny. "What happened to you, Salomie?"

Salomie stepped back hastily from the verbal assault, but Manny jumped up quickly, knocking the chair over as he prepared to defend Salomie. "Hey, look here, Cathlean, you can't come talking to my girl like that. She took care of Alex and did a damned good job of it, while you were off having a grand time in England! Miss High-and-Mighty, I'm so glad you descended from on high to visit us little poor people in Dangríga. You really should just take your boy and—"

He couldn't finish as Cathlean turned on him like a whirling dervish. "I know you are not talking to me, you sorry-ass excuse for a man! All the years I've been in England sending money to my sister, she shouldn't have taken care of you with it. That's my sweat and labor you've been enjoying. Guess you still haven't married her, since she's still your 'girl.' Are you working, or are you still waiting for that big job to fall into your lap?" She shouted at the top of her voice, feeling herself losing control.

Manny started stammering out a response, or some words to defend himself, but Cathlean shut him down with one hate-filled look. If looks could kill, surely he would have been laid out where he stood, and the undertaker could be called in to prepare him for burial. He saw the look of utter disdain on Cathlean's face, so he hastily plopped himself back down in his chair. He wasn't a fool; he may not have liked Cathlean, but he enjoyed dressing and smelling nice and eating three square meals per day. If he, Salomie, and their boys lost their meal ticket, he'd have to go out and get a job! He shuddered at the thought. Miss High-and-Mighty Cathlean was no better than Salomie, but she sure sent plenty of money to take care of him and his family. He looked over at Salomie, then quickly turned his head away. She looked at him with a pleading expression in her eyes, but he picked up his glass of beverage, and put it to his mouth, waiting to see what would happen next.

Cathlean looked sadly from him to Salomie. "See, sis, this is your 'man,' but he can't even try to defend you. What a sorry excuse he is. As a matter of fact, I'll call him 'Sperm' from now on, just that, because that's all he is . . . 'Sperm.' What happened? You know you can do better for yourself. As soon as Alex is ready, I'm taking him away from here. Let's see what you do then." She looked down the hall but saw nobody coming. "Alex, son, come on. Are you ready? It's time to go now." She could feel her heart thumping wildly, like it was coming out of her mouth; she was so very angry. So much for her surprise—seemed like both the surprise and the joke were on her!

As she waited for Alex, all she could think of was the fact the he'd been conceived as a result of sexual abuse by her "uncle," one of her mum's common-law husbands. She may have been forced to leave British Honduras and live in England as an absentee mum, but really, was it her fault? She made up for it by regularly sending money for Alex's care. Salomie should be living like a queen as she raised Alex and her own children in style, but was she? No, Sperm appeared in her life at some point, changing everything when he became the most important person to Salomie.

Cathlean vowed that now that she was back, she was going to be Alex's mummy once more. Maybe if she stopped giving money to Salomie and family, Sperm would leave, and she and her sister would become close again. She could only hope, but right now, she needed to get her child and leave immediately before she could give Salomie and Sperm the satisfaction of falling apart in front of them. Besides, Tooth was waiting for her. Tooth! Oh no, he'd be upset; she wondered why he hadn't come after her, but when she looked at her watch, she realized that she'd only been in the house for about twenty minutes. She felt so wrung out from the highs and lows of the emotional rollercoaster she was on that she felt like she'd been here at least a few hours already!

She looked out the window, and pulling the curtain back shouted at Tooth "Hold on, I'll be right there!" He waved at her, not looking particularly upset but not too pleased either. Cathlean turned as she heard footsteps coming down the hallway; Alex poked his head into the room, looking and smelling clean. He was wearing a T-shirt and jean shorts, but he had nothing on his feet. "Boy, come give me a hug, then go put your shoes on right now. You're going with me." Alex approached cautiously; as he got closer, Cathlean reached out and hugged him very tight as she tried to lift him off his feet. "Ooh, you're so heavy. Soon I know I won't be able to lift you at all. Mummy's home for good, here to take care of you now. Let's get ready to go, son."

"Can my cousins go with us?" Alex asked worriedly, his world as he knew it going into a tailspin.

"Not this time. Maybe they can visit us soon. No, please don't cry. It'll be fine, I promise you."

Alex turned dejectedly and headed toward a room on the other side of the bathroom. His aunt came out holding a small suitcase in one hand and a pair of beat-up leather sandals in the other. They didn't quite fit when Alex put them on, leading Cathlean to believe that they actually belonged to his older cousin, but suddenly, she was tired of fighting and arguing, so she held her peace and glared at Salomie one last time.

CHAPTER 3

Cathlean held Alex's hand, pulling him along as they headed for the door. He was sniffling, his cousins were crying, and there was a lot of last-minute commotion, but she kept her eyes forward so she wouldn't have to see if Sperm was standing there with Salomie watching her leave. As Salomie tried to hand Cathlean a small suitcase, Cathlean said, "No, keep the clothes and suitcase. I don't want it. Maybe your kids can use it. I'm buying Alex new clothes. Bye-bye kids, see you around. Salomie, I will call you with my address once I get settled. Let's go, Alex." She headed toward the car as Tooth jumped out. "Sorry that took a while, Tooth. I'll make it up to you."

"Well, hi, young man, name's Tooth. I know yours is Alex. Cathlean, not a good surprise? Sorry."

"Let's not talk about it, please. Just take me to a cheap hotel where they have long-term-stay rates. I need something where I can have a bunk bed for my Alex and something comfortable for me."

Tooth must've picked up on the mood; he could see that things hadn't gone well. He saw the unshed tears in Cathlean's eyes, so he simply pushed Alex into the backseat, then fastened the front passenger door with the twisted wire like before. Alex, crying silently, kept looking back at his aunt's house as Tooth backed out of the driveway and jerkily pulled away. Wisely, Tooth kept quiet as he negotiated Commerce Street toward downtown Dangríga. Then he remembered that Cathlean wanted a cheap hotel, so he turned abruptly, and after much bouncing and jostling, he pulled up in front of the Dangríga Arms, its flashing sign advertising cheap rooms at daily, weekly, monthly rates.

It was a new hotel built after Cathlean had left Dangríga, so she didn't recognize anything about it; as a matter of fact, she realized that she was either too distraught to recognize any landmarks or that she'd really been away too long. She did not know where she was, but having been blessed with smarts and a good sense of direction, she vowed that she would re-learn her way around town in little to no time. She and Alex climbed out the car while Tooth, who appeared to have a big heart and some intelligence, went in to help arrange for rooms for the newly-reunited mother and son.

Cathlean and Alex quickly settled into a routine while trying hard to adjust to each other. Alex, always a shy, quiet child, became even more withdrawn even though there were a couple of children near his age who lived in the hotel and some others who lived in the neighborhood. Cathlean's immediate concern was to move out of the hotel as soon as she could because, even though the rate of conversion was about three Belizean dollars to a British pound, she was quickly running out of funds. She was going to have to get herself a job as fast as possible.

In addition to looming financial woes, Cathlean was becoming very bored with domestic life. The party girl and flirt missed her fast-paced life in England; she needed to see and be seen, especially by the males of the community. She started leaving Alex with one of her neighbors so she could go to the clubs and party until the wee hours of the morning. She came to the conclusion that motherhood wasn't her thing—overnight or instant motherhood, absolutely not—but she was stubborn and was determined that she would not seek Salomie and Sperm's help.

From her late-night clubbing, Cathlean quickly befriended like-minded women whose sole purpose in life was to snag themselves a man who would take care of their every need. Her new best friends convinced her to leave the Dangríga Arms Hotel, and move in with them in their "Booty Bunker." Oh yeah, Cathlean was thrilled! The Booty Bunker was the place to hang out; she could stay out late, sleep in until noon or so, and not have to worry about taking care of Alex because of her friends' younger sister, Karla, who lived with them and was the resident cook, housekeeper, and caregiver to Alex and other children in the home. For a small fee, Karla made sure that Alex and all the other children were bathed, fed, and taken to school every day. She even helped them with their homework at night.

This was the life for Cathlean. She was in a win-win situation—she could play mummy to Alex, hang out at night, do exactly what she wanted, and never have to ask her own family for help. The fact that Cathlean was considered a "foreigner" from England didn't hurt her case either; she was beautiful, sexy, smart, and people were fascinated with her, her proper speech, and her British accent. They competed with each other to spoil and cater to her, but whenever they didn't, she just pouted until she got her way. Men, women, and children were charmed by her, and she made much of her effect on people. She saw everyone as a potential conquest, especially those of the male persuasion.

CHAPTER 4

A about six months after Cathlean moved into the Booty Bunker, so named by its residents whose only goal in life was to party, "work" to earn money from men, and to generally just check out of life, legitimate responsibilities, and expectations forced on them by society. She and a couple of her friends were having a serious conversation, the subject of which was the usual: men. "Well, I'm not going to deal with any man who can't take care of me and buy me nice things," said Betty, as she walked back and forth, breasts jiggling, pounding one fist in the palm of her hand to emphasize her point. "I always say his sex game can be weak—hell, it can be non-existent for all I care, but he better give up the money. That's all I want from him, and I don't care if he knows it."

"Well, you know me, ladies," said Bridgette, the oldest of the party girls. "I got sick, old parents, so I need a man to give me money to take care of them. My mum's a diabetic, and her medical supplies cost way too much money. Dad's heart is wearing down, and he's getting weaker every day, but you know he's got to have his cigarettes and rum every day. What can I do? I think that's what keeps him going. They took care of me and my children when I needed them, so I need to take care of them now. You know my brother and that ungrateful sister of mine won't do it. If a man can give me money for that, shoot, he can get some action from me any day, all day, or as long as he can keep goin'!" She hugged her friends as she laughed, thinking how amazingly easy it was to get what she wanted from men. She wasn't worried about aging; she knew she looked good, still had what it took to attract anyone she wanted to, along with the erotic skills to keep him, but pretty soon her looks would fade. What then? There was no retirement plan or old-age home for hookers who no longer "worked." She shrugged her shoulders carelessly; oh, well, she'd cross that bridge when she got to it, but she'd keep doing her thing now and make her money for as long as she could.

Cathlean laughed at her friends' antics. Then she said, pausing for full dramatic effect in true Cathlean fashion, "Well, ladies, I understand where you're coming from, but none of these British Honduran men can do anything for me. Their game is weak, they're broke, and if they think I want to stand in line behind all their women to get my share of what's in their pockets, they're sadly mistaken. And what's with them having all these children . . . Hullo, have they heard of condoms or some kind of birth control? There's no dick that good that will make me have a child for a man who already has twenty children and has no money to take care of them."

"You know, a few months ago, this man named Tooth picked me up from the airport, and while we were traveling to Dangríga, he told he has eighteen children! Eighteen children, and this man is butt-ugly and has only one tooth, a gold one at that! Girls, he was a mess! I know I'm not that desperate. I need somebody to take care of me and be a father to my little boy, but none of those broke, drunk, too-many-children-having excuses for a man fit the bill. What I need is a foreigner, like one of those we see at the club every night. Better yet, I need a white man who can save me and my son from this life." Nodding her head, she said, "Yes, I'm sure that's exactly what I need."

Her friends looked at her with varying expressions of disbelief and horror on their faces. They had heard Cathlean express her disdain for British Honduran men and often observed that while she mostly rejected them, she allowed them to buy her drinks at the club and would occasionally disappear for a sexual encounter with one of them. She considered them a means to an end, below her status in society, and definitely unworthy of her. She may be a prostitute—let's face it: that's what she and her friends at the Booty Bunker were—but she was picky. She felt she was special; her body was special, deserving of only the best men that society had to offer. She was undeterred in her goal.

CHAPTER 5

Cathlean, and others like her, targeted white soldiers and other foreign tourists visiting British Honduras. Some women they knew or had heard of had gotten lucky and had caught the eyes of these men, who fell in love with them, married them, and took them with them back to their country of origin. Young women especially targeted the British soldiers who lived in towns and cities all over British Honduras. Because British Honduras was still considered a British colony, but working hard to change its name to Belize. England maintained a strong military force there, intended to stave off the ever-impending invasion by Guatemala. To further complicate matters, Guatemala was a neighbor who had always claimed British Honduras as one of its *distritos*, or territories.

As far back as 1940, Guatemala has claimed ownership of British Honduras, voiding the Anglo-Guatemalan Treaty of 1859. If not for the British soldiers' presence at all times, it was a definite fact that Guatemala would have invaded British Honduras a long time ago. Guatemalans have always referred to British Hondurans as *paisas,* short for *paisanos* or countrymen. Guatemalan history and geography text books went so far as to include British Honduras in their maps as part of Guatemala. Cathlean remembered her mother Ernestina, saying that when Ernestina had lived in Guatemala as a child, buses, public transportation, and even some government buildings would have the Spanish phrase *'Belice es nuestra!'* (Belize—the name they already called British Honduras—is ours!) clearly displayed on them. Most likely because of this overhanging threat, previously, then, and for many decades to come, the practice had been for England to keep a sizeable regiment of military personnel in place for protection of the country of British Honduras.

Also, there was an inordinate number of *Guates* or *Guatemalans* in British Honduras, who crossed the border daily to find work there, then take their British Honduran pay back to their own country. Guatemalans didn't recognize a border between their country and British Honduras, believing it to be one country, and were highly offended if anyone mentioned the existence of such.

When Belize would later gain its independence from Great Britain on September 21, 1981, British Honduras had already become known as Belize in 1973. British soldiers began to leave Belize, staying only long enough to train the Belize Defense Force, Belize's own military force, developed and charged with the daunting task of keeping the country safe from Guatemala or any would-be invaders. The worry was that this military departure would cause Belize to be seen as a vulnerable and defenseless country, now that Britain had withdrawn its most formidable forces.

Another reason for the presence of British military in British Honduras could be a loose *quid pro quo* arrangement where Great Britain tried to show its gratitude to British Honduras, who had sent a large contingent of soldiers to fight on Britain's side in World War I. Many modern-day British Hondurans could boast a father, brother, or some male relative who had "gone off and done time in the war" as they would say proudly. All over the country, there were reminders of British gratitude toward British Honduras: forts, parks, plaques, and buildings all referred to the war and the help given by British Honduras to secure eventual victory. Even in a small town like Dangríga, there was an area north of town called "Scotsman Town," where a tall concrete wall had been erected. At one time, it had been a firing range that the RGBW—the Royal Gloucestershire, Berkshire, and Wiltshire Regiment—used to train local soldiers for combat but later was seen as a reminder of assistance given and lives lost by Dangrígans in the war. It was not much to look at today and had deteriorated over the years, but Dangrígans still considered the area holy ground.

CHAPTER 6

In 1963, when Cathlean returned to British Honduras, throughout the years prior to that time, and even in those years immediately following what would later become Belizean Independence Day in 1981, British soldiers were considered the ultimate prize, the "catch" with whom local women could get together, form a relationship, have children, and escape from their mundane lives. When British sailors received occasional shore leave, or when the soldiers were allowed leave, they visited clubs and other venues where Belizean women went crazy upon seeing them! Here was an opportunity to dress their best and strut in their finery so they could catch a white man's eye. Soldiers' and sailors' leave days were looked forward to; it was the time to watch and wait for. To some, it was almost on a level comparable to the second coming of Jesus Christ! Mothers would dress their daughters up, and those mothers young enough or attractive enough would themselves "do it up" so they could snag a rich white man. In their minds, "white" or "Caucasian" was synonymous with wealth and prestige.

British Hondurans, who scornfully deplored this behavior, many of them considered haters by the very women they criticized, called the women unkind, nasty, ugly names like "soldiers' taffy," "soldiers' sweets," "soldiers' whores," "harriers" (so called after the very fast fighter jet planes flown by the British soldiers), and other names that couldn't be mentioned in polite society. They considered these women prostitutes of the lowest level: not only were they selling their bodies, but they were also selling their souls by targeting the foreigners for a specific, calculated, and selfish purpose.

Somewhere in this convoluted process, the women were also selling their heritage, because their hope was that they could leave British

Honduras. Instead of staying to preserve and strengthen the country for future generations, they were willing to go start over and build families somewhere else. And where did most of these women and their "conquests" end up? Some went to Canada, Germany, Australia, and other countries, but the majority wound up in England, ironically considered the land of the oppressors, they who'd dared to colonialize the "savages", as English people called British Hondurans.

Yes, many British nationals saw British Honduras as an uncivilized country: many times, British sailors and soldiers assigned there believed they were being punished or abandoned to be forced to protect such a godforsaken country. The "sell-out" British Honduran women welcomed the dream of potential wealth, while at the same time, they looked forward to the "bonus" and self-validation of giving birth to mixed-race children. Mothers gambled, praying that their offspring would be light-skinned enough to pass—to be accepted—when they eventually moved to England with mixed parents.

This is somewhat reminiscent of the situation in the southern United States of America, specifically Louisiana, in the city of New Orleans, where *creoles* spent many moments of their lives in angst, calculating how much black blood they could have in their white French bloodline that would still allow them to pass and be accepted as white in the white man's world. Some had even gone as far as to separate groups by quarter dilutions, creating descriptive terms like quadroon (quarter African blood mix), octoroon (one-eighths African blood mix), etc., to separate the people with different levels of melanin appearing in their skin.

Thousands of miles away, the large Belizean ethnic group, *Kriols*, descendants of the West Indian-Caribbean French, believe similarly in the desire to be accepted if their skin color is light enough. Many *Bakra*, an unflattering term for white or light-skinned British slavemasters of African origin, residing throughout Belize, were automatically thought to be better than the natives because of their fairer complexion. However, these were not the men these "soldier taffy" women wanted. No, the hope of potential mothers of mixed-race children, was that their children be sired specifically by British soldiers and sailors, not by Bakra men, because they might produce black children! The mothers wanted their offspring would be able to pass, which was in direct contrast with the desire of some British Honduran nationals, "purists" concerned with maintaining pure

Belizean bloodlines. They felt that these sell-out women were committing the cardinal sin of diluting the rich blood of British Honduran generations: children of Baymen, Mestizos, Mayans, logwood cutters, and Garífuna existing in Belize since as far back as anyone remembered.

With this kind of dichotomy existing, these debased women were considered doomed, their haters taking delight in seeing the women and their half-breed children rejected and left behind in Belize when the soldiers and sailors returned to England. Often, the military men went back to their wives, girlfriends, fiancées, and families who were ignorant of, in denial of, or unwilling to accept the tangible results of their men's dalliance in that "damned barbaric colony" of British Honduras.

Cathlean knew all this, yet she decided that she would deliberately seek out a white man, someone who would, like in the soon-to-become-popular American soap Calgon commercial, "take her away." She needed an intervention, a new focus; "working" and taking care of her son were very difficult and not fun at all! Sure, she attracted men in her over-the-top sexy clothes and sensuous moves on the dance floor, but she feared that she was attracting the wrong men, namely Garífuna men whom she absolutely didn't want and couldn't stand. She believed they had no money, vision, or jobs but had way too many children. They were either useless like Sperm, or child predators like her "uncle"—Alex's dad. She knew she would have to step up her game and get with a white soldier soon; it was time to start doing that the very next time she went to the club—most likely tonight!

CHAPTER 7

That night, when she went to the club with her girls, she dressed even sexier than usual. She went right up to the door of the club, hugged the man at the door, rubbing her scantily clad bust all over him. He, of course, had no choice but to let them in; they were regulars, after all, and he knew Cathlean would be very "nice" to him later. She strutted into the room, her girls in tow, all of them dressed with the main objective of displaying their physical attributes to the maximum, like wares on sale at the market. After all, they were on sale and didn't care who knew it or had a problem with it.

Once they got settled at a table, drinks miraculously started appearing in front of them. They asked the waiter who their benefactor was, and he pointed to the corner by the bar where three or four men stood. One man stood out from the pack; Cathlean could see that he was white, but his features were indistinguishable from where she sat. He waved with a bottle in his hand, and she waved back hesitantly. She decided that she was going to be coy and play hard-to-get in true Cathlean style. She could do this, but in the meantime, she would make sure he noticed her to see what she was working with and what she could do with it.

She jumped up, grabbed her friend's arm, and rushed to the dance floor, where she danced in such a blatantly "come hither" way that all the men looked at her behind as she shook her sexy body in sensual invitation to any who cared to approach her. The thumping rhythm of Garífuna drums playing Punta music called to her; she danced with complete abandon, breasts swaying in her low-cut top, buttocks shaking and moving as if they had a life of their own. After dancing to three songs back-to-back, she and her friends stumbled back to their table and thirstily grabbed their drinks, greedily sucking them down, trying to cool off from their exertions on the floor. Her friend Betty looked up and kept looking behind Cathlean, as she noticed a man coming over. "Oh, girls, looks like we got company. Here comes the man who bought us drinks earlier. He's right behind you, Cath."

Cathy, fanning herself with her hand, half-turned. Looking over her left shoulder, she could see the white man from the bar as he walked over to their table. He wasn't as tall as he'd previously appeared, and, as she raised her eyes to his face, she observed that he was older, paunchy, slightly balding, and wearing glasses with thick lenses. He was really not that attractive, but he had a nice set of teeth when he smiled, as he was doing now. "Well, hullo, how are you?" He stuck his right hand out at Cathlean. "My name's John, and who might you ladies be?" He looked at the ladies, then turned back to Cathlean. His eyes lasered in on her, taking in her heaving cleavage and her sweating face.

"I'm Cathlean. This is Betty, Bridgette, and that's Alice. We're the 'ABCs,'" she said with a laugh.

"Well, when you make another friend, make sure her name starts with a *D*, then you'll be the 'ABCDs,'" he said jokingly. "Cathlean, I just loved your moves on the dance floor. If that's the way you dance all the time, I can see why you ladies are in such great shape. Oh, allow me to buy you another drink. What'll you have, the same?" He motioned the waiter to come over and take the drink orders.

"You're very smart to get the ABC reference, John. Pull up a chair, sit down," Cathlean said with charm and sweetness. She was thinking that John was not cute, but he seemed nice and mannerly. She'd just have to observe him to see how far this went. Just then, one of her "sometimes" men approached the table to ask her to dance. Taking one look at John, she stood up and went to the dance floor with her man-friend, where she proceeded to ramp up her sensual, sexy dance moves another notch or two.

Her body gyrated, grinding on Vince, her dance partner, but every so often, she would look back at her table to see if John was watching her. He was watching, all right, mesmerized, with a look of pure desire on his face. Cathlean laughed, twirling around and allowing Vince to bend her over, and he met her move for move, stroke for stroke. She could tell that he was getting hot and bothered; she could feel his erection rubbing against her. He looked like he was in lustful agony. At that moment, she walked off the floor, deciding that she had tortured him long enough. Cathlean knew exactly how far to go and when to leave a man wanting; besides, John was already baited and ready to be pulled in.

When they got back to the table, John stood and pulled her chair out for her. Vince tried to grab a chair so he could sit with them. He looked pointedly at John as if telling him to move, but John ignored him. Cathlean gave Vince a look that made him suck his teeth and stalk away in disgust. John was smitten; everyone else in the immediate vicinity could see that he was. Cathlean, rather pleased to see her effect on him, thought, *Tonight, I'll put the first step of "Operation Snag-a-Soldier" into effect. He's not my type, but I suppose he'll do. Let me work my magic. He won't even know what hit him!*

And with that realization firmly in place, she soon indicated to her friends that she was ready to leave the club so she could work on the next stage of the plan. John fell right into his place in the plan by asking Cathlean if he could take her home. She refused but coyly gave him her address. He was tagged, bagged, and ready for the plucking—he just didn't know it yet!

The next day, the ladies were gathered around at the Booty Bunker, rehashing their experiences from the night before. "Girl, did you see that cute guy that was pushing up on me on the dance floor? And Miss Cathlean, you nasty girl, looked like Vince was about to do you right there. I thought you didn't like Garífuna men. You changing your mind on us?" taunted Bridgette, never one for holding back.

Cathlean looked at them and smiled mysteriously. "No, can't you see that I was using him to make the white man jealous? I don't want a Garífuna, but I didn't say I wouldn't use him to get what I want. I gave John my address, and the way he was drooling, I know I got him like a yellowtail snapper on the end of a hook! He may not look exactly like my type, but you watch: he'll call on me soon, and I'll go out with him. See, he bought us drinks. I just know he has money!" Her eyes lit up at the thought. She was very confident in herself and was already calculating in her greedy mind how long it would take to get John to fall in love with her. For someone who'd always claimed that she needed a man of means to help her raise Alex, the thought of her son never once crossed her mind!

CHAPTER 8

Within a week, John had called on Cathlean, inviting her out to an evening of dinner, followed by dancing at the club where he'd met her. Cathlean was flirtatious toward other men even in John's presence; she craved male attention as much as she needed the very air she breathed. At one point, John got out on the dance floor with her, but he embarrassed himself and her with his uncoordinated efforts and moves. He sat down, contenting himself with watching Cathlean and her numerous male partners as they gyrated and danced on the floor. Every time she came back to the table fanning herself in an attempt to cool off, John had her favorite drink waiting for her; it was clear that he had appointed himself her benefactor and protector for the evening. When the club closed, he escorted her out to his car and, in gentlemanly fashion, made sure she got home safely.

To say that John was falling fast and head-over-heels for Cathlean would be an understatement. It was clear to everyone around that he was "whipped" though she had not yet been sexually intimate with him. Women whispered to each other, wondering how this would end. They didn't like Cathlean because she was beautiful and had everything they wanted; they wanted to see her fall hard and fast, so they mentally rubbed their hands together with glee, hoping to see her get her comeuppance. They wanted her to be one of those ruined women that soldiers romanced, impregnated, and abandoned in British Honduras. Sadly, they couldn't wait to see things go wrong for Cathlean.

Over the next few weeks, Cathlean and John were inseparable; the only time they were apart was when he had to check back into barracks in Belize City to fulfill his military duties since John was indeed one of the British soldiers stationed in Dangríga. Cathlean discovered from her conversations with him that he was a chaplain and counselor in the army, and his job was to talk to soldiers who were homesick, missing their families, and away from home for the first time in their lives. He was a quiet and caring, gentle-natured person who really loved and enjoyed helping everybody.

Cathlean introduced him to Alex about a month after meeting him, and when she saw how gentle and attentive the man was toward her son, she was relieved to continue to pursue her "Operation Snag-a-Soldier" campaign. She made sure that she kept John dangling like a puppet on a string, acting very seductively toward him but playing coy and innocent when it came to actually consummating their relationship. She didn't find John at all attractive; he was about twenty years her senior, balding, and paunchy, but as he continued bombarding her with expensive presents and spending lots of money on her and her son, she forced herself to continue to see him.

One day, she decided it was finally time to reward John with some sex, the only thing of value that she had to offer—what she'd sold to the highest bidder in her very recent past. That Sunday afternoon, Cathlean asked one of her friends to watch Alex while she arranged for a rendezvous with John. They drove to the beautiful little village of Hopkins and booked a villa for the day. John was so overjoyed that intimacy with Cathlean was finally going to happen; he did not know what to do with himself.

As soon as they entered the room, he turned to Cathlean, pulled her toward him, and awkwardly attempted to kiss her with sloppy wet lips. She pushed him away, trying to catch her breath, as she said, "Wait, John. Slow down, please. We have all day. What's the rush?" In her mind, she was thinking, *This man doesn't turn me on. I feel nothing for him, but I know that I can do this.*

She closed her eyes for a few seconds, imagining sexy Vince and how he'd made her feel when she danced with him. If she concentrated really hard, she could see John morph into Vince in her mind. Good, it was working. The illusion would make the distasteful liaison a lot more bearable for her, so, after a minute or so, she turned to John and pulled him toward the bed.

John willingly allowed himself to be dragged over. Cathlean quickly and expertly relieved him of his jeans and polo shirt until he was down to his underpants. John was panting loudly in her ear, sweating a little, as he reached for Cathlean's blouse with trembling fingers and pulled it carefully over her head. Having done this, he was still left with the daunting task of removing her red lacy brassiere. After allowing him to struggle with the bra clasp for a few minutes, Cathlean impatiently pushed his hands away. "Let me do that, John. My goodness, you act like you've never done this before." John blushed a bright red, looking away, but Cathlean was perceptive, if she was nothing else. She grabbed his chin, making him look her directly in the eye. "Wait, haven't you done this before? John, are you . . . are you a virgin?!"

John blushed again, hanging his head. "Yes, Cathy," he stuttered, "I'm a virgin. I was going to give my life to God and was training to be a priest, but then I decided that was not the life for me. I still serve as a chaplain, but I decided that I wanted to save myself for marriage. I love and care for you, Cathy, so I'm ready for you to be my first." He swallowed audibly, Adam's apple visibly bobbing up and down in his throat as he nervously awaited her response.

What the bloody hell? Was this guy for real? This had to be a joke, right?! Cathlean didn't want to have to be anyone's "first," but she remembered her goal, and figuring this was one more stumbling block in the way of getting what she wanted, she knew she could do this as long as she kept her eyes on the prize. Besides, seduction of johns was what she did for a living; she could definitely handle John. Silently, she finished undressing, leaving her lacy, matching bikini panties on, and dragged John by the waist of his briefs until he was standing directly in front of her, erect penis fiercely tenting the front of the briefs, and trying to poke through the fly but not quite making it.

Unhesitatingly, she reached into the fly, dug in, and pulled out his penis. He was fully erect, but his was one of the smallest penises she had ever seen on a grown man in her whole life! She found herself wanting to laugh at his size, but the look of pain on John's face made her stop herself. Feeling sorry for him, she decided that this was not the time to mock him because he was in a fragile place; her next moves could cause irreparable damage to his psyche. For once, in a very rare moment of unselfishness, she actually considered someone else's feelings before and other than her own.

Cathlean pushed John on the bed and yanked his briefs off completely. She started stroking and caressing him as she watched his reaction to see what he liked. She flicked her tongue over his flat brown nipples, blew on the whorls of fine blond hair surrounding them, and sucked on them. John drew in his breath at the contact, as if afraid to breathe. He closed his eyes very tightly, panting; every time Cathlean sucked on his nipples and stroked his penis, he would squirm, but he didn't grow any bigger. She looked at his reaction and could tell he was getting near the point of no return, so she quickly peeled off the rest of her clothes and placed his hand on her own nipples, pushing them toward his mouth. She figured she was going to help him with everything . . . oh, what a pain this was!

John tentatively licked at them, not knowing what to do next. Cathlean pulled his right hand down so he could touch her dampness, but the man had no imagination whatsoever, so she found herself whispering to him, "Go on, John. Stroke me, touch me. I'm not going to break. You won't hurt me." As he stroked and pawed ineffectively at her, he could feel moisture at the junction of her thighs, but he really didn't know what to do next. Cathlean, more disgusted than turned on, decided it was high time to end this fiasco, once and for all.

Taking pity on him, she grabbed a condom and rolled it on his penis, then straddled him as she pushed him into her. She started swirling her hips in slow motion and brought John's hands to her waist. He held on for dear life, frantically lifting his hips from the bed and pumping into her. Cathlean was just starting to get into the groove as she imagined herself with Vince, pretending that she was riding him; she remembered the size and feel of his erection on her buttocks while dancing with him.

Suddenly, John grabbed her painfully, thrusting up and groaning. "Cathlean, oh, I feel something, ohhh, oohh. What's happening?" All this in a strange guttural voice as he experienced his first-ever climax. He appeared to pass out, so Cathlean had to lightly slap his face to awaken him. She couldn't believe that he'd left her hanging and unsatisfied; not only was John unattractive to her, but he also had zero sex game! She would have to fix that. But . . . he was nice to her child and had money, though, so she would have to be satisfied with that and teach him how to please her.

After an hour, she got up and showered, then she woke John up so he could shower and take her back to town. John jumped up with a huge grin on his face and tried to pull Cathlean toward the bed, ready for an encore. It was clear that he was clueless about her dissatisfaction with him, but one dirty look from her made it clear that she was royally ticked off. He got up and went to the bathroom, where he showered, and got dressed. As soon as he walked back out, she grabbed her bag and stalked to the door, which she yanked open hard. They approached his car in uncomfortable silence, Cathlean angry and disappointed and John wary but happy. He was no longer a virgin; next time, he could speak with experience when others were discussing sex. He previously had not been able to relate, but now he felt like he was the man! He whistled and sang with the music on the radio, tapping on the steering wheel, pleased with himself and the world, more deeply in love with Cathlean than ever. She sat stiff and unmoving, leaning toward the passenger window, face turned away from John. She refused to speak to him and tell him what was wrong, preferring to sulk to herself like a spoiled child.

When they got back to Dangríga, John entered the Booty Bunker, stopping to talk to Alex, while Cathlean stomped off to her room without even saying good-bye. Alex, previously a quiet child, had started coming alive under the one-on-one attention he was getting from John; he looked forward to John's visits more than Cathlean ever did, and he was often sad when John left for home. He hadn't seen his cousins in a while, had made few new friends other than the other kids at the Booty Bunker, but John was his special grown-up friend, even if he talked funny.

Cathlean's friends were initially wary of John and still looked down on her for falling into the "soldiers' taffy" trap; they still didn't think that she should have picked John as her target. They knew that she was "settling" to get what she wanted from him, and, knowing her taste in men in the not-so-distant past, they could tell that John was absolutely not her type at all. They loved Cathlean and wanted the best for her, but since they could tell that John was a nice gentleman who loved their friend and little Alex, they decided to leave the situation alone and wait around to help her pick up the pieces if and when he left her . . .

Betty was at the Booty Bunker when John and Cathlean arrived. She saw and heard Cathlean slam her door without even speaking to Alex or anyone else. She figured she'd find out later what had occurred, so she said hello to John, making small talk with him, and tried to make up for her friend's lack of manners. Soon, after a few awkward moments, John hugged Alex and left. Betty knocked on Cathlean's door. "Hey, Catt, what's wrong with you, girl? Are you okay?" she asked.

"No, I'm not okay." She pulled her door open. "Alex, go play outside. Grown-ups are talking." After he ran off, she said, "Girl, can you believe it? He was a virgin, and even when I showed him what to do, he still couldn't take care of business. And his thing, it was so small! I'm going to have to teach this man about sex and how to please me." She was working herself up to her previous angry state. "Not only is he old and unattractive, but he can't even put it down in the bedroom!"

Betty chuckled. "Well, you just had to have a white soldier. You ready to give up on this now?"

"Hell, no, Betty. I just have to work harder. Maybe I'll have to get drunk to sleep with him, but I'm not giving him up. He loves me and Alex, so what's a little sex issue? Besides, I can get that from anyone else, anyway." She smirked as she said this, her brain working overtime to figure out how she'd overcome this latest hurdle. She'd continue to date John and would just have to teach him about sex; either he learned, or she would stay with him but get her sexual needs met on the side.

CHAPTER 9

Over the next couple of weeks, Cathlean rejected John, ignoring his little notes and all attempts by him to see her. Her friends took her to task for treating John so badly, but Cathlean knew what she was doing; she'd given John one taste of her sexy body, then made him sweat out the interim until the next time she allowed him in her presence again. Around the end of the second week of Cathlean's non-contact with John, she finally relented, allowing him to take her out of town to shop for herself and Alex. They checked into a hotel once more, and even though Cathlean was anxious about spending the weekend with John, she was also eager to try to teach him some sex moves so she could live down the disaster of their first encounter.

Unfortunately, the second encounter proved more disastrous than the first, if that was possible. John embarrassed himself by climaxing as soon as Cathlean had taken his and her own clothes off; he had not even penetrated her yet! If Cathlean really cared for John, she knew that she would be a lot more patient with him, but in her mind she resolved that she would give him sex anytime he wanted it, but that she would fake orgasms and not bother trying to teach him anything! She remembered that when she originally planned her campaign, she hadn't decided if she'd planned to fall in love with her white soldier, so she felt justified in her decision to change the rules as she went along.

What rich irony that she worked in the sex trade business, but she'd met someone who couldn't satisfy her sexually! When she really thought about it, she wondered if God was punishing her for the fraud she was perpetrating on John. She would work on being nice to him, dole out sexual favors when he gave her gifts and pleased her in a non-sexual manner, and hope that that was good enough so that he would marry her. She also found out that John had had a particular nasty bout with meningitis as a young man, which had rendered him sterile. This meant that even though Cathlean would not realize the mixed-race child part of "Snag-a-Soldier," she was willing to take a chance that everything else would come together very well.

She would really step up her game so that John would fall more deeply in love and would continue to remain enamored of her. Like a Black Widow, she would spin her silken web, slowly but surely trapping John in it while he was unaware. However, unlike the predatory spider, Cathlean was not planning to kill him; she just wanted to use him to get what she wanted for herself and her child. Cathlean cold-bloodedly, methodically, and unemotionally planned her deception of John.

Exactly one month after their weekend getaway, John knew that he wanted to marry Cathlean. He didn't know how she had crept into his heart and taken up residence there, but he felt like he absolutely couldn't live without her another day. He decided that it was time to make his next move.

One afternoon, John gave Cathlean money for a hair appointment, and after she left home, he appeared at the Booty Bunker to ask her friends for their blessing so he could propose marriage to her. They reluctantly did so, not because they didn't like John but because they were worried that he would find out that Cathlean didn't love him or that she didn't love him the way he deserved to be loved. He was a nice man, but they worried that they were condoning Cathlean's deception and manipulation of his feelings—that he loved and cared for Alex was what convinced them that it would be fine. They had heard around town that John had already been approached by people to whom he'd never spoken before. Supposedly, they expressed varying degrees of concern that John, not being a local, didn't know that prior to his arrival, Cathlean had been a tease who'd conceived her stepfather's baby as a teenager; was a well-known, high-priced prostitute; and a selfish person who considered herself too good for her own countrymen—thus, latching on to him only because he had money. They also told him that she planned for John to take her and Alex to England with him when he left British Honduras. John calmly reassured Cathlean's friends that nobody would stop him from marrying her if she would have him and that he didn't care what anyone said about the woman he loved. Convinced that he meant what he said and that their friend would be fine and well taken care of by John, they agreed that he should go ahead and propose marriage to her.

The next day, John went to see the local jeweler, Mr. Nick, who gave him a reasonable price on a beautiful 18-carat gold ring with an intricately designed emerald setting that reminded him of the lush, gently rolling green hills of Ireland, a place he had visited once on a high school nature trip. Emeralds were also Cathlean's birthstone, and he knew the color would glow nicely against her milk-chocolate brown skin. With everything in place for the big moment, John was ready to do his thing.

John invited Cathlean to dinner that same night. After their meal, he went down on one knee and proposed to her. She happily accepted, crying genuine tears of happiness to realize that the culmination of her dreams was actually at hand. Once she accepted his marriage proposal, they went to Cathlean's house and woke Alex up to tell him that they were getting married. Alex was very happy to hear this, indeed! Finally, he would have a daddy of his own and be like all his friends who had mummies and daddies. Maybe he would even get a baby brother like his best friend Rory.

Over the next few months, Cathlean and her friends were busy planning her wedding. John ordered a wedding dress to be made by his mother's dressmaker in England. Cathlean was over the moon with happiness; she was getting what she wanted, and whenever the nagging voice of her conscience whispered in her ear that she was wrong for marrying John without being in love with him, she pushed it aside and proceeded with reserving the church, securing the reception hall, and ordering a suit for Alex, who was thrilled to be giving her away to John during the upcoming nuptials.

CHAPTER 10

On Christmas Eve that year, just before midnight mass, Cathlean and John were united in holy matrimony. The wedding was the talk of the town, especially for the gatecrashers, who stood outside waiting to see Cathlean's dress that they'd heard so much about, and the bridesmaids, Cathlean's former roommates from the Booty Bunker, all prostitutes who forgot the last time they had darkened the doorway of a church. A few of these women had never ever seen the interior of a church in their entire lives, so some of the elders of the community stood by, expecting the wrath of God to descend on such undesirables by destroying the church during the ceremony. They even cursed the minister for agreeing to perform the ceremony, believing in their own small way that he should have refused to officiate a wedding for a "reformed" prostitute. But in spite of all the negativity from the haters, everything went very well, and the couple were wed in grand style, just as Cathlean had planned.

The gatecrashers—she was sure she saw Tooth and what appeared to be three of his children among them—trailed the wedding party to the reception, where they unashamedly enjoyed partaking of the food and drink provided. That was the problem with having a party to which folks she'd grown up with were not invited; they simply ignored the formality of RSVPs and showed up regardless of what anyone thought. Cathlean decided that this bad habit was fine this once, because everyone could then witness that she and John had legitimately married. In addition to this, they could also enjoy his wealth and largesse.

Some potential "soldiers' taffies" were already at work on John's colleagues from his regiment, who were also in attendance at the wedding.

These women hoped that they, too, like Cathlean, could be the next lucky one to snag themselves a soldier. They could also see themselves marrying in the near future, so they pulled out all the stops, resolving to themselves that nothing would stand in their way.

The festivities ended early the next day, after which John, Cathlean, and Alex left town to head for Belize City in John's military-issue Mini Moke, a small, square, camouflage-colored jeep, the predecessor to the Humvee that would come along and later become the popular choice for militaries in Great Britain and other countries worldwide. The plan was that the new family would spend the night in Cave Branch (Cathlean couldn't even pretend to want a honeymoon), then continue on to the city, where John had already secured living quarters off-base for his new family. She felt like she was on top of the world, giddy at the thought that she'd achieved the plan put into motion so many months ago. She was a little surprised at how quickly she'd gotten what she wanted.

All Cathlean's friends from the Booty Bunker, neighbors, acquaintances, her sister Salomie, and Salomie's children had come to see them off. Sperm, thankfully, had not been there to ruin the moment . . . Come to think of it, Cathlean realized, she was surprised that she hadn't seen him; he wasn't one of the revelers at the wedding reception, even though he loved his Heineken beer. He especially loved it when he could get it for free! She hoped his absence meant that Salomie was getting rid of him since she deserved much more than a leech masquerading as a man. Cathlean could only hope!

She looked at the lush, green countryside speeding by, thinking that even though she didn't love John, she would make an effort to make him happy. He'd already asked her permission to adopt Alex, and she'd willingly consented; Alex was John's son in every sense of the word but for the legal paperwork which she would sign now that they were married. Alex was overjoyed that he had a daddy; he and John had bonded irrevocably, a link that would serve them well in their future years together. Alex cried when he said good-bye to his cousins, but he was more excited to start a new life. John had told him about the other soldiers' children, and he couldn't wait to meet them.

By Boxing Day, John and his family arrived at their new home, where they gratefully fell into bed to get some much-deserved sleep. Within the next few weeks, Cathlean settled into her new life; Alex was on break from school, but she and John had already registered him in Wesley School, where he would begin his Standard One year on January 8 of the new year.

Alex was constantly underfoot; Cathlean hadn't had to deal with him on a one-on-one basis for any length of time over the last few months, so she was impatient with him and was often cold and uncaring. Alex wisely learned to stay out of her way, only coming alive when John arrived home at night after each workday. He would regale John with his adventures with his new friends, everything he'd done during that day, and John would patiently listen to him. John became increasingly skilled at equally sharing himself with a jealous, pouting Cathlean, who would glower at him because she felt that she should get all of John's attention when he got home. She experienced her usual problem of being rejected by other women; she claimed that the other soldiers' wives hated and were jealous of her, so she couldn't spend any time with them. Truthfully, she was becoming bored rather quickly.

One day toward the end of January, John came home with the news that he had been called home and was being redeployed back to England. He was scheduled to leave on Valentine's Day, so he had exactly two weeks to pack up and get ready to ship out. Cathlean's fear was that she and Alex wouldn't be able to accompany John when he left, but he reassured her that he was going to do his darndest, even use his military connections, to make absolutely sure he wouldn't leave without them!

For Cathlean, this was the final piece of her plan coming together; she had a momentary pang of guilt in which she wondered why everything was working out so well, but she quickly squashed the feeling, justifying in her mind that if God didn't want things to work out, they wouldn't have come together like they did. She refused to dwell on the fact that Satan, lover of chaos, was also powerful enough to make things appear like they were on-point, to lull the unsuspecting or unwary into a false sense of security. Cathlean happily wrote two letters: one to her girlfriends at the Booty Bunker, and the other to Salomie, telling them her good news. She strutted around with a light step, and a light heart, knowing that she was about to leave her uneventful life in British Honduras behind. She was starting her new life as Mrs. John Putnam, and she was not ever going to look back, at least not if she could help it!

PART II

February 1964
London, England

CHAPTER 1

The intercontinental jumbo jet landed with a slight bump and taxied into the hangar at London's Heathrow Airport on a gloomy, overcast day. Cathlean, John, and Alex Putnam deplaned with all the other weary travelers after their long twelve-hour flight from British Honduras. Alex looked around, eagerly taking in all the sights; Cathlean, grateful to be back on English soil after many long months, admired the Valentine's Day decorations which attempted to add some cheer to the damp, mist-covered day. John was relieved to be home and was just happy that they could clear customs so quickly due to his military travel status.

Within ten minutes, they were at the baggage carousel awaiting the few suitcases they'd brought with them. Having sold almost everything that they'd owned in British Honduras, John and his family traveled light, planning to purchase all new items and articles of clothing once they got settled in London. Besides, with the vast difference in weather and climate between British Honduras and England, most of the clothes they'd worn in British Honduras would no longer be considered appropriate.

Truthfully, and if John wanted to be honest with himself, he wanted a chance to spoil Cathlean by giving her everything; new clothes seemed like a great way to start. As the luggage came around, John grabbed it and loaded it onto a cart, then led Cathlean and Alex through the door and out to the curb, where they quickly prepared to board an available taxi. John strode quickly and purposefully, head held high, and chest stuck out. He wasn't a tall man, but right now he felt about ten feet tall, ready to take on the world and to carve a place in it for his woman and his new son.

Cathlean shivered in her long overcoat through which she could still feel the biting cold. Brrr! this was the one thing she hadn't missed about

England. For the short time she'd been back in British Honduras, which enjoyed a warm, tropical climate most of the year round, she'd truly forgotten about the cold English climate. She quickly pulled the hood on Alex's jacket over his head, but he was jumping up and down so much that it kept falling off. Exasperated, she shook her head, sucking her teeth and yelled at him, "Boy, would you please calm down? And keep that hood on. You'll catch your death of cold!"

For the moment, Alex subsided, while John, chuckling indulgently, hurriedly ushered Cathlean and Alex into the back seat, where Alex sat for about a minute, before immediately popping up and down like a jack-in-the-box. He was really excited and didn't want to miss a single thing; he also wanted to ask John how far they would be going, but one look at his mother's face warned him that he should hold his questions for later. John dusted his hands off and jumped into the front passenger seat; slamming the door shut, he gave the driver the address of the location to which they were headed.

Soon after they took off, Alex finally wore himself out and fell soundly asleep. The next thing he knew, he was being shaken awake by John, who excitedly exclaimed, "Wake up, Alex. We're here. Let's go see my mum and dad! Come on, now, come on." He jumped out the front seat, grabbed Alex, and raced toward the front door of a large, imposing red brick house. He fumbled through a bunch of keys, but as he picked through them, the door was flung open from inside.

A petite brunette and a tall, angular, white-haired gentleman stood in the doorway. John bent at the waist to envelop the woman in a big hug, while the man slapped him soundly on the back. "Oh, John, welcome home, son, and who is this young man? Come in, come in. I'm Grammie Beth. Close the door. You're letting the heat out!" She hugged John, grabbed Alex by the hand, and started to pull the door shut. She was beaming with excitement at the sight of her son. After all, it had been a couple of years since she'd last seen her boy.

Just then, another man, tall, sandy blonde, and movie-star handsome, came around the corner heading for the door. "Wait up, Mum. John, hey, welcome back. How are you? Heard you finally got married, old man. Where's the wife? Is she with you?" He looked around and went toward the cab, where he saw a beautiful black woman sitting in the back seat. "Hello, Miss, I'm looking for my sister-in-law. Where is she?" He looked toward the passenger seat and observed the cabdriver in his seat and the young lady in the back. He looked at her once more, then at John, puzzled.

Cathlean climbed out the taxi and stood in front of the man. "I'm John's wife, Cathlean. And who might you be?" She stuck her hand out, tilting her head backward to take in his full six-foot-three height. She wondered if this was John's brother but could see no resemblance to her husband at all.

"I'm John's brother Geoff. John told us he's married a foreigner, but he didn't tell us you were black. You know? Not all devils are white." He pointedly ignored Cathlean's outstretched hand, looking as if he'd rather spit on it than shake it. "I'm on to you, Cathlean. You'd better treat my brother right, or you'll hear from me!" With that he pivoted on his right heel, striding toward the front door, where John and his father stood staring, shocked at Geoff's rudeness. Pushing past them, he entered the door where he saw Alex leaning against the wall by the sitting room. "And she brought her black brat too? John, old man, hope you know what you're doing. Hullo, Mum." He bent to kiss her cheek.

"You need to apologize to your brother and his family right now, Geoff. I will not tolerate rudeness in my house." Beth was small but ferocious and firm; you could tell that she was a scrapper who had no problems keeping her boys in line and wouldn't back down from a fight. "Go on, say you're sorry, Geoff, right now!" She stood there tapping her left foot, waiting, a terror to behold.

By this time, Cathlean had walked to the door, where John took her hand and pulled her inside. "Mum, Dad, this is Cathlean, and you already met Alex, her son. Cathlean, my parents Beth and Elton. And this jerk is my brother Geoff, whom you already met and who yelled at you outside. Let me take your coat. Washroom's down the hall. Please feel free to use the facilities." He could tell that Cathlean was nearly in tears; he couldn't believe that this was his wife, who was normally self-possessed and confident. He turned on Geoff angrily. "Still a bully, I see. Please don't ever disrespect my wife again, or you will pay. She's my wife, and there's nothing more to discuss. Apologize to her at once."

"All right, all right. Can't anyone take a joke around here? I'm sorry, Cathlean. It won't happen again. Can we start over . . . friends?" He smirked, sticking out his hand, but she shook her head, ignored him, and stumbled down the hall to the bathroom, her vision blurred from her unshed tears. Alex could sense the tension between the adults in the room, but Grammie Beth took his hand and led him to a small washroom behind the kitchen. After he washed his hands thoroughly and wiped them on a thick, fluffy towel, he followed her into the spacious dining room. Geoff, John, and Elton went to the taxi to get the luggage. Elton tipped the driver, and they brought everything inside.

When it had all been taken upstairs to the spare bedroom under the attic, everyone washed up and joined Alex, Cathlean, and Beth in the dining room. Beth had laid out a sumptuous feast, and everyone, realizing that they were starving, quickly sat and began passing dishes around. Elton and John talked military strategy, with occasional input from Geoff. Beth tried to engage Cathlean in conversation, but Cathlean responded in monosyllables, clearly not comfortable with her surroundings.

Cathlean was worried that Beth would be astute, in a way that only a mother could be, and pick up on to the fact that Cathlean didn't love her son, so Cathlean kept her eyes lowered to her plate. Alex, normally reticent and shy, was a chatterbox, boasting about his exploits with his daddy John back in British Honduras. He talked about the really long airplane ride with his parents. Cathlean gave him a look of warning, and he immediately piped down, a tad less excited and animated than he'd been a few moments before.

At length, the excruciatingly long meal ended, so pleading fatigue and a headache, Cathlean took Alex's hand and went off to bed. John, Geoff, and their parents remained in the dining room, an awkward silence descending on the room. Beth, striving to ease the tension, said, "John, when do you have to report to base? Do you have your orders, and where will you be stationed? Cathlean and Alex are charming. Congratulations, I think you did well." All this was said in one breath, as if she had to express herself within a certain amount of time or expire from not being able to speak her thoughts.

John had never seen his mother so flustered. Taking pity on her, he grabbed her hand, looked directly into her eyes, and said, "I'll be posted at Nottingham, Mum, where Dad used to be stationed during his service. It's not very far from here. Yes, I hit the jackpot with Cathlean and Alex. I love them dearly. Dad?" He looked to Elton, awaiting his comment. As it had been when John was younger, Elton's approval meant a lot to John. Elton was always brutally honest about things as he saw them.

"Son, they seem like nice folks, and I apologize for Geoff's behavior earlier, but get used to that reaction. I hope you're ready for it. Ignorant people will make ignorant comments, but as long as you love Cathlean, you should be able to overcome anything. When do you have to report to Nottingham?"

"In another week, Dad. I'm not too worried about people's reaction to Alex and Cathlean. We'll deal with it. Is there anything I need to know about Nottingham? At least I don't have to go far to get to work every day. Can we stay here until we can get a flat of our own?" John looked at Geoff, who was scowling darkly, out of the corner of his eye. "What, Geoff, you got a problem? Spit it out, man!"

"I can't believe you're dumping your wife and her brat on Mum and Dad while you go off to work every day. Don't expect them to coddle and wait on her. She seems to be really spoiled."

"And how long did you live at home before you finally moved out?" John asked. "We'll only be here for a couple of weeks, not like it's any of your business. Why the attitude toward my wife?"

"I've got my eye on her. You can tell her that I said that. If she gives Mum any problems, I will deal with her." Geoff glared at John, jumped up, angrily pushing his chair back. "Mum, Dad, thanks for dinner, g'bye!" He grabbed his coat, stomped to the door, and stormed out the house in a huff.

"What is his problem?" John asked, bewildered. He loved Cathlean and thought everyone would fall for her the way he had. His parents shook their heads, gathered up the dinner dishes, and headed for the kitchen. John helped them clean up, then bounded up the stairs to go check on his wife and son. He knew Cathlean needed reassurance; he didn't think she had expected to be totally rejected or so immediately disliked by anyone. He wasn't worried about Alex; Grandma Beth and he would get along just fine—John could tell just from seeing them together earlier that evening.

When he entered their room, Alex was occupying the bottom of the bunk beds that John and Geoff had slept in when they were boys. He had finally wound down from so many adventures in one day and was snoring like a locomotive. Cathlean was sitting at the edge of the bed, and John could tell she had been crying; he gathered her into his arms, trying to soothe her. Cathlean stiffened in his embrace, still very upset. Raising her red eyes to his face, she declared, "John we cannot stay here. If Geoff

41

ever disrespects me again, I won't be responsible for my actions. You know how I was when you met me. I don't tolerate that stuff from anyone, even your family. I think Geoff's a jealous ass."

"I'm so sorry, Kit-Cat, but he's always been a jerk and a bully. He won't bother you again. We'll be gone within a few weeks, so I don't want you to worry. Can we please go to bed now?" He had hoped that he could get lucky tonight, but Cathlean was so distraught that he knew that that dream was not going to be a reality. "I almost forgot. Happy Valentine's Day, baby!" He handed her a red velvet box.

"Oh, what is it? I didn't get you anything." She greedily tore into the package and pulled out a stunning emerald choker necklace that exactly matched the stone setting in her engagement ring. "This is beautiful, John. Thank you." She allowed him to hold her just a little longer, then pushed him away. She knew he wanted sex, but she just couldn't deal with the disappointment of bad sex tonight, not after all she'd gone through. And besides, why did he always want sex? She was tired! Turning, she got into bed and tensed up when John climbed in beside her. He reached for her, but when she stiffened, he sighed, turned his back on her, pulled the covers up, and fell into a deep sleep.

CHAPTER 2

A week later, John, about to embark on the last few years of his stellar military career, checked into base at Nottingham, joining the very elite Worcestershire Sherwood Foresters Regiment. He was ranked a Sergeant Major and resident counselor, partially continuing in the role to which he'd been assigned while serving in British Honduras. Between fulfilling his duties and reacclimating himself to the pace of life in England, he actively sought off-base living accommodations for himself, Cathlean, and Alex.

He asked his dad to accompany Cathlean on searches and interviews with potential landlords, just to make sure that she wasn't being taken advantage of or asked to sign anything questionable. Near the end of the second week, Cathlean found a wonderful, mid-sized cottage within five miles of the base in a middle-class area known as Warminster Wilshire County. She couldn't wait to show it to John because she was certain that he would love it just as much as she did. Elton, Beth, and Alex liked it and also approved; John would be the last one who needed to agree.

When he arrived home that evening, he, Cathlean, and Alex went back to the house, where they met the landlord and signed the rental paperwork. What made the deal sweeter was that the terms were "rental with option to buy," with 25 percent of monthly rent applicable toward the future purchase price. Cathlean couldn't wait to move from her parents-in-law's home; they had been nothing but sweet and welcoming to John's new family, but she longed to get back to being mistress of her own home.

Cathlean still believed that Beth knew that Cathlean didn't love her son, but as long as Cathlean was not abusive toward John, and he appeared happy, Beth would not interfere. Alex flourished in the elder Putnams' home; he was the first grandchild, and they completely spoiled and doted upon him. "Geoff the jerk," as Cathlean dubbed him, continued to drop in a few times each week, and for Sunday dinner, but he refrained from making snide comments. It wasn't because he'd come to like Cathlean but because he knew his parents would make him leave if he misbehaved toward Cathlean or her son. Not to mention John would give him the stink-eye whenever he looked like he was about to say something inappropriate. If Cathlean was happy to move from her in-laws', Geoff would be ecstatic!

On a grey, drizzly day in March, John and his family moved into their new home. They didn't have much to pack, having kept their purchases to a minimum while waiting to move from the elder Putnams'. John spent quite a bit of money on a whirlwind shopping spree as they set out to acquire furnishings for their house, but he did so uncomplainingly. He was gratified to see Cathlean happy for the first time since their return to England. He'd expressed to his mother that he was a bit concerned that Cathlean had been pining for home, and he thought she'd been about to ask to be sent back to British Honduras. He was relieved that she was returning to her usual animated self, but little did he realize Cathlean had had no intentions of returning to British Honduras because that would have been an admission to her girlfriends that the plan that she'd so carefully schemed had failed!

CHAPTER 3

John and Cathlean enrolled Alex in a primary school they felt would comfortably meet their needs. Without a car of her own, it was important to Cathlean that Alex's school be within walking distance since she'd have to drop off and pick him up each day before and after work. Alex had also discovered that a few of his neighbors attended the same school, so he was happy to be with his new friends. After the first weeks of school, he begged Cathlean to allow him to join the local Boy Scouts troop. When she agreed, albeit reluctantly, he was very excited, and just like that, in the way that only children can do, he began adjusting very quickly to his new environment.

Cathlean was slower to adjust, being naturally reticent to avoid friendships with the mothers of Alex's friends. She was just not comfortable befriending women, either thinking that she wouldn't fit in to their neat little social circles or assuming that they'd be envious of her beauty and style. If not for these assumptions, Cathlean would've never had problems making friends—she was charming and charismatic but really lacked the social skills required to be comfortable with other women. Surprisingly, she did make one female friend, a very non-threatening Indian woman named Mayris, who adored Cathlean, and whose son, Kamal, was one of Alex's good friends.

Conversely, Cathlean got along very well with men, especially because she was beautiful and sexy, and they always competed for her attention. Maybe it was also because she often dressed provocatively and was flirtatious with them—after all, old habits were hard to break! This was probably what Geoff sensed about her demeanor when he had first met her; it probably explained why he felt it was his duty to protect John from her feminine charms, but John was too much in love to see any flaws in Cathlean. To that end, Geoff kept a close eye on Cathlean, which she found very irritating.

What made matters worse was that Geoff wouldn't fall for Cathlean's charm; men usually turned into blathering idiots in her presence. Even Mayris's husband, Kamaly, wanted a piece of Cathlean—he gave her the eye immediately upon being introduced to her by Mayris. Cathlean stayed clear of him, though, because he was a lowly cook in the army and couldn't do anything for her if she needed something from him. Geoff would be a very tough nut to crack, but Cathlean wasn't easily discouraged.

Cathlean was bored trying to find ways to fill the hours while John and Alex were gone, so she applied for and got a part-time job at a fuse manufacturing company in Warminster, which handled large military contracts for John's Sherwood Foresters' Regiment. She also took on light clerical duties to fill up her day and keep herself out of trouble. She could feel herself getting restless, terrified that she would fall into her old "work" habits; she wanted to stay busy. John was offended that she chose to work, and he was not very supportive of her job because he was paid well for his military duties. He argued that he could take care of his family very well without her assistance. To keep the peace though, he gave in, reluctantly allowing her to continue to work.

Things settled into a predictable routine: John would leave for work each morning, Cathlean would take Alex to school in time for the 8:45 a.m. bell, go to work, then she'd pick him up at 3:45 p.m. John would arrive home around 6:00 p.m., they'd eat dinner at 7:00 p.m., John would catch up on paperwork, Cathlean would help Alex with homework, then they'd watch television, and Alex would go off to bed a couple of hours before his parents. John and Cathlean continued to maintain an active sex life; Cathlean continued to fake it, but John, due to his inexperience, was unaware he was being short-changed. In fact, he was blissfully innocent to the fact that anything was lacking from their sex life.

Six months after Alex started his new school, he joined the boys' soccer team. Cathlean would go to his weekday games, and John would join her for weekend games. Turns out that Alex was quite the little star, and his parents could not be more proud of him. Through his athletic prowess, Cathlean found herself in the not-unpleasant position of "mother of the star," and she was happy to bask in the reflection from Alex's glory.

John was equally proud, his pride stemming from seeing his son blossom not from being in Cathlean's or John's reflected limelight, while Cathlean whole-heartedly embraced her new position in Alex's limelight.

After Alex had been playing soccer for a year, his coach approached Cathlean with the idea of starting a women's soccer team. He wanted her on the team, and Cathlean, having attended all of Alex's games, and gaining some knowledge of the finer points of the game, was flattered to be asked to join. She was terrified that she wouldn't be able to measure up, but she asked Alex to teach her the specifics of the game. She tried out and couldn't believe she actually made the team. Some of the other boys' mothers joined too, so she started befriending them, not so much as friends, per se, but as teammates, united with the common goal of competing successfully against other teams in the newly formed Women's Soccer League of England. Although Cathlean begged Mayris to try out for the team, Mayris wasn't at all interested; she was content to be a great cheerleader from the sidelines.

Cathlean played Striker; she was a very fast runner and ferocious kicker, who often found herself working out frustrations with her life on the soccer field. In so doing, she became quite proficient at the game— seeing her in action explained why Alex was a star in his own right. Vaguely, Cathlean could remember her mother boasting that Cathlean's father had been a semi-professional soccer star, actually a very popular celebrity and player, both on and off the field, a ladies' man back in his day. Cathlean supposed she and Alex had inherited their soccer skills from him, but she couldn't confirm that this was the case since she'd never lived around the step-father himself, after he'd left Cathlean's mom.

Cathlean's world became all about soccer. She lived and breathed the game, either supporting and attending Alex's matches or participating in her own games, which Alex and John would attend on Saturdays. She also whole-heartedly embraced league activities and unwittingly became domesticated, fitting right into the role of mother to her son Alex, a role with which she was still not entirely comfortable. To the world outside, and to those in their immediate circle, Cathlean always appeared to be the ideal wife and support for her husband, but looks could often be deceiving.

In the midst of soccer playing, and mummy role-playing, Cathlean was still able to fit in some military wives' activities that made John look good. She volunteered to lead quarterly rummage sales and bake sales, where she proved herself an instant hit with her Belizean desserts and delicacies. Cathlean saw that John was well-respected and regarded in the British Army, having come from a long line of distinguished military men, so for the moment she was content to bask in his reflected glory.

CHAPTER 4

Geoff, in his insecurity at being the only male family member with no military career to speak of, continued to belittle John and snipe at Cathlean and/or Alex, but he always backed off when John threatened him with bodily harm or mocked him for being jealous because he was the handsome one, yet had no steady girlfriend or wife. At times, Geoff seemed genuinely puzzled at John's good fortune. He secretly admitted to himself that John was lucky, but he'd never say so out loud. John was the plainer, older, balding one. How had he been able to find himself such a beautiful woman?

Through Cathlean's attendance at some military functions with John, she met a few Belizean women, other "soldiers' taffies" who admitted in their own little social circle that they were a little disappointed because their "Snag-a-Soldier" or "Snag-a-Sailor" dreams and schemes had not quite worked out the way they had anticipated. For many of them, the sting of rejection by their husbands' families was hard to take; in some cases, they were forced to live with in-laws who treated them like domestic help and not at all like family. Some pathetically held their final trump card, their mixed-race child, very closely to them, as it was the very last bargaining chip that was available to them.

A few of them pitied Cathlean because she had no mixed-race child to tie John to her, but Cathlean laughed at them, secure in the fact that she had nothing to worry about because her soldier was completely and utterly head-over-heels in love with her. He needed no mixed-race child, often stating that Alex was his real child, the only one he needed. Cathlean actually felt superior to these women: she was a proud mistress of her own home, her in-laws treated her like family (well, all except Geoff), and she was a star in her own right. She had never considered herself a "soldiers' taffy" anyway and actually loathed that demeaning name more than she'd ever acknowledge!

She learned to avoid these pathetic women, never wanting them to think for one moment that she desired their friendship. She considered herself a class or two above these grasping, greedy bitches and thought it served them right to be experiencing problems like culture shock and loss of their husbands' affection, now that said husbands had returned to the loving bosom of their families in England.

Cathlean conveniently forgot that her own lying, deceitfulness, and scheming to get John is what allowed her to be in the position she was in today. She considered herself justified in doing what she had to in order to snag John, but she didn't think about the fact that she still disliked having sexual relations with him and still found him unattractive, in spite of the fact that John loved her and her son.

CHAPTER 5

Cathlean was steadily growing tired of the rainy and cold climate in England. She'd kept in touch with her Belizean girlfriends, and on this particular day, she received a postcard depicting a beautiful sunny day in British Honduras. She could see the aquamarine Caribbean Sea glistening in the beautiful, sleepy-looking village of Plascencia, and smell the salty air and fresh flowers, and she suddenly began to cry uncontrollably. Sobbing, she realized that she really missed her friends and her home country and didn't want to be in England anymore. She just desperately wanted to return home.

She knew, because of the huge retirement gala that the military had thrown for John last month to commemorate his many years of service, that he would be at home every day now. But he was always underfoot! In addition to giving in to his demands that she quit her job, she literally chafed at the forced "lovey-dovey togetherness" of having to spend so much with him; it didn't matter at all that he was her husband! Her marriage had been much easier to fake when John was working, leaving the house each day, but now that he had no job, she thought he was at home too much. In addition, after all the years in England, Cathlean still felt displaced and powerless and unable to figure out what to do about John. This did not sit well with her; all she knew was that this was not a situation she particularly liked. It was time to get back to her home turf or go stir-crazy!

Cathlean thought fleetingly of the beautiful, specially customized mother-of-pearl inlaid musket that John had received for all his years of illustrious service. Engraved with his initials, rank, the dates of his service, John was so damn proud of that thing, and Cathlean once remarked, jokingly (but seriously), that she thought that he should sleep with the musket. Or better yet, she could see herself using it to kill him and end his miserable existence, which in her mind was also causing her misery. Of course, if Cathlean really loved John, she knew she wouldn't mind having him at home all the time, but even she couldn't fool herself into thinking that she was happy about the fact that he was retired. Only when he was available to jump up in the middle of the day to take her on expensive shopping trips, or accompany her to some event where she could show him off like a trained pet, or if he was able to comply with something else that she demanded of him, could Cathlean appreciate John's retirement and presence.

Alex, a tall, strapping sixteen-year-old, was an honor student in his second year of high school. He continued to play varsity soccer, was on the debate and chess teams, and was in so many activities that he was never home anymore. Cathlean and John would visit the elder Putnams from time to time, but Cathlean felt like Beth mostly tolerated her, while Beth and Elton really loved Alex and looked forward to his visits. Geoff was always at his parents' home, and many times Cathlean begged off from visiting so she wouldn't have to run into him; they still didn't get along, but both cared about John, so they faked it for his sake. Geoff brought a steady parade of his little waiflike, child-women to dinner, but apparently they weren't "keepers" because none of them ever seemed to wish to return a second time. Geoff's parents despaired of him ever getting married and giving them grandchildren.

Cathlean heard a car door slam and heard John trudging wearily up the stairs. The minute he entered, he could see that she'd been crying, so he quickly put his arm around her, concern in his eyes. "Hey, what's wrong? Are you in pain? Why are you crying?" He pulled her toward the couch.

"Nothing's wrong. I'm not hurt, John. Why don't you let me go?" She turned away from him.

"Please don't lie Kit-Cat!!!!!!! What's wrong? Tell me, maybe I can fix it," he coaxed, bending toward her.

"John, I said nothing's wrong, but if you really must know what the problem is, I'm sick and tired of the cold! I'm tired of all this rain. I want to return to Belize where it's nice and sunny. You're retired now, so we can go. I don't want to live here anymore. Can we go?" she begged, stroking his arm and running a hand over his bald spot. She tried to look as pitiful as possible.

"What, leave England? Alex has two more years of high school. Why can't we wait?" he asked.

"Because I want to go now." She pouted. "I miss my friends, the weather. I'm tired of England!"

John stroked his chin, thinking about his parents who were getting older each day. He wanted to be here for them as they aged, but, as usual, he couldn't deny Cathlean anything her heart desired. He was already trying to figure out how to make this happen for her without slighting his parents. Cathlean was right, it was bloody cold in England, and he too, longed for a warmer climate. He fondly remembered sun-soaked days in British Honduras and thought that it would not be a bad idea to go back there.

"All right, Cathlean, let me look into some things. I want to see how I can continue to receive my pension in British Honduras. We need to ask Alex if he wants to go, or stay with Mum and Dad. There are many other things to consider . . ." He stopped his thought, catching Cathlean as she launched herself at him.

"Do you mean it, we can really go? Oh, John, thanks, I love you, I love you!" She was getting her way, so she was willing to say anything she thought he wanted to hear. "When can we leave?"

"I'll call the disbursement office and see how to arrange for my monthly pensions to be transferred to British Honduras. We'll talk to Alex tonight when he gets home and see what he thinks. I should call my parents too." He turned and picked up the telephone and dialed Beth and Elton right away.

Cathlean hugged herself with glee; they were really going to leave! She wasn't worried about Alex; he would do what she wanted, period. He always did, just like John. Cathlean tried to eavesdrop on John's conversation with his parents, but she couldn't follow the one-sided responses. She felt a slight twinge of guilt that she was taking John away from them, but she consoled herself with the thought that "Geoff the Jerk" would take care of them. He practically lived with them anyway! She knew that he, most of all, would be very happy to see her leave; he'd never warmed up to her. She had no friends to whom she had to say goodbye; they were acquaintances, nobody she would miss too much.

When John finished with his telephone calls, he took a pen and paper to map out a plan in his usual orderly style. He, like Cathlean, believed that Geoff would take care of Beth and Elton; John's retirement checks would be accessible from any Belizean bank; Alex would probably not have issues with completing his last two years of high school in British Honduras and everything else should work out. His only regret was that he wouldn't be around to see his parents as they aged, but he could always visit, right?

"Cathlean, Alex has two more weeks until the end of the term. Finals begin this week. Let me contact a real estate agent about putting the house on the market (they had bought it after two years of renting). If we start packing now, we should be ready to go after Alex's term is over. We can leave in two or three weeks, tops!" He twirled her around excitedly—very un-John-like, Cathlean thought.

"Thank you, John. I really appreciate this." she smacked him loudly on the lips. He grabbed her, happy to see her happy; this was his Cathlean that he loved, the one to whom he could deny nothing.

Cathlean turned away, a bounce in her step, as she went to the kitchen to fix John's favorite meal. She couldn't believe it was so easy; she'd always been able to get him to give her whatever she wanted, but this time, she was especially grateful. She didn't realize that she missed British Honduras so much; until now, when she was planning on returning, it really hit her, and she wanted this so bad. It was time to go home.

When Alex scampered up the stairs two hours later, he could smell the mouthwatering aroma of his favorite meal before he even opened the door. "Hullo, Mum, Dad, where are you? Something smells good . . . mashed potatoes, mmm!" He threw his bag down and headed straight for the kitchen where indeed his mother was cooking his and his dad's favorite. They both loved potatoes in any form, especially paired with fried chicken, like it was today. Dad was sitting at the table jotting something down on paper; Mum was standing at the stove. She turned the flame off and set the last piece of chicken to drain on a paper towel. "What is going on? Is something wrong?" asked Alex.

"Why does something have to be wrong?" She asked, swatting at him with a dishtowel. "Go wash up, now, let's eat!" Alex skipped off to the bathroom and was back in one minute flat. He grabbed his plate, piled fluffy mashed potatoes, green peas, and three giant pieces of chicken on it.

"Mum, what's going on? Dad's and my favorite on a Tuesday?" He asked, chewing rapidly.

At a nod from John, Cathlean said, "Alex, we're moving back to British Honduras when your term's over."

"What? When did you make this decision? Dad, are you okay with this? . . . What about Grammie and Grampa? What's going to happen to them?" Alex questioned in a panic.

"We just decided today, son," John said. "Your grandparents are staying here with Uncle Geoff. You'll finish high school in British Honduras. How do you feel about that?" He and Cathlean looked closely at Alex. They were concerned that he was not going to want to leave England, but he'd come with them regardless of his objections. It would be easier to get his buy-in, though, so John prayed silently that Alex would agree to leave without having to be coerced.

"What about soccer and my chess club? Can I think about this? I also need to go study for my killer Chem and Biology finals tomorrow." He took his half-empty plate and a drink and went to his bedroom. Cathlean and John were encouraged that Alex seemed concerned but not particularly upset at the news. They knew he had a lot to think about, but if he decided to stay in England, his grandparents would be happy to have him. Uncle Geoff? Maybe not so much. They would have to wait and see; either way; they knew that they would have to be prepared for the outcome.

The next day, when John drove Alex to school, they were both silent, but Alex asked suddenly, "Dad, do you want to leave Grammie and Grampa again? I know you did before, which is how you met Mum, but do you want to go? If they get sick, Uncle Geoff will be mean to them. Maybe I need to stay and take care of them." He seemed about to say more, but John held up a hand to stop him.

"Your mother wants to go, and I want her to be happy, so we're going. We'd like you to go, but if you want to stay, we'll support your decision. We know you want to go to Oxford after graduation."

"I'll think about it, Dad, but I have to go. See you later. Wish me luck on my finals!" Alex said, opening the passenger door and jumping out quickly. "Hey, Ralph, Kamal, wait up!" he called out, spying his best friends. John shook his head, marveling at the energy and athleticism of Alex, who was tall, lanky, and just fulfilling the promise of what he'd look like as a grown man. John smiled indulgently, thinking about how he'd much he'd grown to love Alex these last eleven years. He wondered how a move back to British Honduras would affect Alex, but he was sure it would all work out.

The next two weeks flew by. The younger Putnams were referred by a military contact to a very professional and caring realtor, Mrs. Lincoln, who knew a couple with two children who were interested in buying the house. Mrs. Lincoln managed to secure an escrow that would close in two weeks, but if there was any delay, Elton had agreed to conclude the transaction on John's behalf.

Everything went exactly according to plan. Alex aced all his examinations with flying colors, and to make matters better, he reluctantly agreed to move back to British Honduras with them, with the caveat that he could come visit his grandparents during breaks, if he felt so inclined. If he wanted to, he'd also be able to return if he wished to attend university at Oxford, his grampa's and dad's alma mater. He also made vague plans to return to join the British Army after college, following the Putnam tradition, but right now, he just wanted to get going so he could start enjoying the summer in British Honduras!

Cathlean and John sold everything, including their clothes, since they wouldn't be needing those heavy winter items where they were going. The couple who bought their home purchased it fully furnished, which saved Cathlean and John having to deal with disposing of the furniture. They packed light, planning to buy lighter, tropical weather clothes upon their arrival in British Honduras.

On an unusually warm day in June, Elton and Beth drove John and his family to Heathrow, but Geoff did not accompany them. As a matter of fact, he'd made himself scarce the last few days before John's departure. He'd put up a token resistance at having to stay and care for his parents, but he couldn't hide his glee at the fact that the competition for his parents' affection was leaving.

Cathlean surprised herself by discovering that she'd actually grown to care for the elder Putnams . . . they were the closest thing to parents to her, especially Elton, and she suddenly found herself teary-eyed at the thought of leaving. She hoped to see them at least once more before they died—after all, they were in reasonably good health—but nobody could predict the future. At the airport, she hugged Beth hard, thanking her for the kindness that she'd shown to Cathlean and Alex.

When Cathlean remembered the horror stories told by "soldiers' taffy" wives, which she was *not,* she realized that she had been truly blessed. She resolved right then and there that she would make a new concerted effort to love John, realizing that he was giving up everything for her and her child. If she'd had any doubt about John's love for her and/or her child, this was the ultimate proof that he really loved them. She, in return, loved him, but in a non-sexual, chaste way.

PART III

June 1974
Belize City, Belize

CHAPTER 1

It was a hot, sweltering day at Phillip Goldson Airport. The Putnam family welcomed the heat after the cold climate in London. A young dreadlocked gentleman pulled up in a cab that had seen better days but definitely was in better shape than the death-trap Cathlean had ridden in when she'd arrived in Belize in 1963. She smiled fondly, remembering Tooth and his antics and missing his chatter. This cabdriver was all business, speaking in a lilting accent. "Hello, hello. My name's Anthony. Where to, sir, miss? Hi, young man. Welcome to Belize!" He smiled at them.

Cathlean had to think for a moment, then remembered that British Honduras had officially been renamed "Belize" a year before her return. Some sources indicated that the name "Belize" was derived from Sir Peter Wallace, a Scottish pirate credited with being one of the first settlers at the mouth of the Belize River. Another said that the Dominican priest, Delgado, recorded that Rio Balis (*or beliz,* a Mayan word meaning "muddy watered") was one of three major rivers to be crossed while traveling north along the Caribbean Coast to the Bay of Honduras. Either way, the name had been changed; this was just something that Cathlean would have to get used to in her grand return to the country of her birth. Looking around at the bustling airport, she felt primed, ready for the challenge.

"Please take us to the Ramada Inn, sir," John responded, mopping his sweating red face with a handkerchief. "We're the Putnams. I'm John, she's Cathlean, and this is my son, Alex. Whew, I'd forgotten this heat!" He was drained already, and they had only just arrived.

"Just in from jolly old England, I see," said Clive, glancing at their luggage tags. "The Ramada's a great hotel, you know? It's owned by

Americans. You'll like it." He stowed their luggage, then opened the doors, ushering his passengers into the car. Again, Cathlean couldn't help but chuckle as she thought about Tooth's twist-tie contraption used for "locking" his taxicab's passenger doors.

With a jerky start, Clive maneuvered the car out the gate. To Cathlean, the airport appeared seedy, desperately in need of a good coat of paint; vendors lined the walkway selling all types of fruit, nuts, and fresh vegetables. *Ah, capitalism and Belizean dollars at work,* she thought to herself.

She looked out on both sides of the cab, noting the long line of people snaking out from the customs area. She shuddered, sympathizing with the sweaty, disgruntled passengers queuing up. She thanked God that John had his military pass, which allowed him to bypass the long lines and be processed through very quickly. The fact that he was an authoritative-looking man didn't hurt either!

Clive skillfully drove onto the newly constructed freeway connecting the highway with the path leading from the airport. Co-existing alongside the shabbiness, his passengers could observe small gratifying signs of progress and improvement. John knew, and had often discussed with Cathlean, that although Great Britain and the United States poured lots of money into developing Belize's infrastructure, as with many Third World countries, much of that money didn't get to where it was intended. Dishonest politicians often controlled such donations, uncaring if they were accused by Belizeans of dishonesty or lining their pockets and filling their own personal coffers with the funds.

Alex hunched down in the backseat next to his dad. He was thrilled to be in Belize, but he was a little resentful toward his parents for making him leave England, when he could've enjoyed his summer with Ralph and a few more of his school chums. Once the plan to leave had been put in motion, Alex felt like he'd been swept in the tide, any objections brushed aside like cobwebs. He knew from experience that once his mum made her mind up about doing something, he and John had to go along or suffer the consequences. Alex pitied John for being weak where Cathlean was concerned; he thought that John just didn't seem to have a backbone, letting her run over him like the proverbial tidal wave. Alex knew his mum was nothing to play with; he'd personally experienced the full force of her wrath whenever she was denied her desire.

CHAPTER 2

Alex and his family stayed at the hotel for two months before Cathlean started getting that itch about not seeing her Booty Bunker friends in Dangríga. She'd no intention of going back to her old job with the girls, but she definitely wanted to show them how much her status in life had improved. After all, what was the use of having achieved her desires and "coming up" without being able to rub her success in the haters' faces? She wanted to strut her stuff all over her hometown, and by God she would do so at every opportunity she got; she didn't care that the price was her soul.

The whining and cajoling began in earnest that night when John came home. "Hey, John," she purred, running her forefingers up and down his arm in the way she knew he loved. "I was thinking . . . it's costing us too much to stay in this hotel, besides I really hate living out of a suitcase. What do you say to us heading home to Dangríga? I know of a wonderful house that's up for sale, one you'll really love. Also, Alex has been invited to spend a month in Water Caye, which is closer to Dangríga than to Belize City. We can enroll him in Dangríga Ecumenical High, he can go off and enjoy the rest of his summer, and he'll be ready for school when it opens in September. Can we, please? Please, please, John?" She pouted in that sexy, irresistible way that got him every time.

Alex walked in, catching Cathlean at the end of her plea. He stopped, turning to leave the room. He knew his mum would get her way, as usual. Darn, he thought, why can't Dad man up and stand up to her? *Here I am, just trying to get settled in, and she wants to leave again. What is her problem, and is this how it's going to be forever? I just can't wait to leave home!* These thoughts whirled through his mind as he waited for John to give in and agree to Cathlean's newest demand. The only thing in Alex's favor was that she was agreeing to his vacation on Water Caye; he couldn't believe she was going to let him spend time away from her with his new friend Ainsworth and his family. She'd already said no when he'd first asked, but it seemed like now he would get a lucky break!

"Oh, baby, of course we can move," John said. I was thinking to myself yesterday that we need more permanent living arrangements. Alex, son, what do you think? Want to move to Dangríga?"

"Doesn't matter what I think, Dad. If you don't mind, I don't mind. Can I really spend a month at the Cayes? Let me run tell my friend what's up!" He bounded out the room, worried that Cathlean might change her mind, as she had been known to do when she wished to be mean. Alex knew her brand of love often involved infliction of pain; love/hate was but one of the hues in his color palette of pain. He guessed he didn't need to understand it; he just had to accept his mum the way she was.

Within a week, John, Cathlean, and Alex were packed up once more and found themselves on the Hummingbird Highway traveling to Dangríga. Multiple fruit trees were in bloom at this time of year; summer painted a nice picturesque view that kept the family engaged and enchanted even when the trip tended to became long and tedious. Alex watched his mum come alive as she animatedly discussed with John some of the funnier escapades that had taken place in England. Alex had already heard some of the stories, but he listened anyway, and for the first time, in spite of himself, he found himself entertained by her tales. He was mesmerized by her storytelling style and her funny British-Belizean accent; he could see why John was hooked on her. Even he, Alex, knowing Cathlean's tricks, was still swayed by her charms, though he'd sternly promised himself that he would not succumb. He silently applauded her, reluctantly acknowledging her devious skills—point and match to her!

PART IV

Alex's Story

CHAPTER 1

Once Alex and his family arrived in Dangríga, he was reconnected
with his cousins, his aunt Salomie's children. Manny, "Sperm,"
so called by Alex's mum, was still very much in Salomie and their children's
lives, so even if Cathlean thought him worthless, he was still around. Alex
shunned the drama between the adults as he feverishly prepared for his
trip to the Cayes; he was looking forward to enjoying his summer before
having to register for and start in a new high school.

Exactly one week after arriving in town, Alex was down at the local
dock boarding a speedboat with his pal Ainsworth and family. He threw
his knapsack into the rear of the boat and excitedly jumped in next to
Ainsworth. Alex couldn't stop staring and looking around, full of awe at
the blueness of the water, the soft lapping of the waves against the side
of the boat, and the salty spray drenching him and the other passengers.
Ainsworth's older brother Robb, sister Layla, parents Millie and Dennis,
and their able "skipper" Anthony settled in for the ninety-minute run to
Water Caye.

Alex felt a healing peace settle over him as they skimmed over the
water. He would forever after seek to be on or near the water whenever
he was troubled, needed to think, or wanted to reconnect with nature
and calm his spirit. For the first time, he felt he was truly in his element:
in this moment of self-discovery, he found water a natural balm to his
psyche. He flashed back to his life in England, remembered doing very
well on the swim team there, but he didn't think he'd ever felt this feeling
of wholeness and contentment before. He inhaled deeply, filling his
lungs with the salty air as he looked forward to a month of sun-drenched
experiences on the Cayes.

The passengers must've all dozed off a bit because next thing Alex knew, he was being woken up as Anthony expertly cut the engine and nosed the boat onto the whitest beach Alex had ever seen in his life. He, Ainsworth, Robb, and Dennis all jumped out to help tie the boat off. He puffed up with pride to be doing "men's work," while Layla and Millie sat back and let them take care of business. The water was warm and slick as it caressed their legs and calves; they quickly waded through it, pulling the tow rope and securing it to one of the posts near a makeshift jetty. The men pulled everything out the boat as Anthony helped Millie and Layla climb out onto the shell-strewn beach. Ainsworth and Alex ran up the narrow walkway and up the two steps that took them directly to the stout, secure-looking front door of the quaint, weathered cottage. Dennis unlocked the door with a flair, ushering the boys inside. Robb and Ainsworth immediately threw their gear into the first bedroom they came to, a roomy one with a bunk bed on one side and a cot on the other. They quickly opened the windows to let fresh air in, chattering excitedly. "Hey, Alex," said Ainsworth, "go ahead and choose which bed you want. Robb and I will take the other two. Put your bag in here." He opened a narrow closet door behind the cot.

"Oh, Ains, this is so cool and very nice. I'll take the cot, if you really don't mind. Thanks!" Alex said, stowing his bag in the closet, then sitting on the cot as he bounced up and down in it. He just couldn't keep still; he wanted to see and do everything right away. "Come on, let's go swimming."

"Wait, let's see what Mum and Dad are doing before we go anywhere," Ainsworth responded.

So they ran to the front room where everyone was gathered. Miss Millie and Layla were putting groceries away, and Dennis and Anthony were each drinking a cold Belikin beer. After the boys got permission to go swimming, they dashed out the door, promising they would be back in time for lunch. Robb, the eldest, had been coming to this Caye long enough, so he knew the favorite spots. He proudly led them down to his "cool-out," a sandy little cove where there was a sizeable body of water, naturally formed by the sand dunes to create a private swimming pool.

The water was warm, and because it was separated from the main body of the Caribbean Sea, there were only tiny ripples, not large enough to be called waves, running through every so often. Even the brisk wind hardly disturbed the surface of the aquamarine water as Alex jumped in and stuck his face under to look at the many multi-colored fish as they swam by. Alex tried to grab some of them with his bare hands, but he was not able to. Maybe that was a good thing because they would've cut his fingers up if he'd caught them by their fins. Robb and Ainsworth tried to challenge Alex to see who could hold their breath under water the longest, but Alex won that contest; he hadn't been swim and dive team captain all those years in England for nothing!

When they got tired of swimming, Ainsworth dragged Alex off to a wooded area so they could pick red, juicy sea grapes, golden mangoes, and ripe bananas. They ate a few, then stashed the rest in a shirt they'd knotted and turned into a bag so they could transport the goodies back to the house. Alex wanted to eat more now, but Miss Millie was like his mum Cathlean when it came to him ruining his appetite before eating a meal she'd prepared; she would go ballistic. He would wait until after lunch to eat more fruit—besides, the trees were loaded, and it wasn't like they were in danger of eating all the fruit during this visit. They turned, heading toward the house before anyone had to come find them.

The boys rinsed off at a shower in the backyard of the house, then came in, got dressed, and joined the family as they sat down to a meal of sandwiches, juice, and crisps, or *chips* as Alex had to force himself to remember they were called in Belize. In the short time he'd been in Belize, he found himself mentally reviewing his speech before uttering a word because he was already being ridiculed for "speaking British," called "limey," or other derogatory terms. Even Ainsworth, his best friend, often teased Alex about his speech, mocking him mercilessly about his intonation and diction.

Belizeans spoke broken English, a dialect more commonly called *Kriol* and were often intolerant of others who didn't speak the "language." In schools, governmental posts, and official places, the Queen's English was the official language; Belize was, after all, British Honduras, the only English-speaking country in Central America, but most unofficial business and communication was done in Kriol. Uninformed foreigners often identified the dialect as patois, like that spoken in the West Indies, but it wasn't, since patois is broken French while Kriol is typically broken English.

Alex had been through this before. He remembered how traumatic it was for him when he'd first arrived in England at five or six years old and spoke only Kriol. His new friends would laugh and make fun of him, his teachers would chastise him for not speaking proper English, and when he came home crying to Cathlean, she's told him to "buck up and deal with it." John, on the other hand, had taken Alex's transformation from "uncivilized foreigner," or "coconut" as Alex was called by some of his classmates, to be his personal mission. John had done as much as he could to smooth Alex's transition into British society, one into which the vulnerable boy had then been thrust against his will.

In the short time that Alex had been back in Belize, he had been mocked and teased for speaking "too proper," so he'd started making an effort to speak Kriol but with somewhat disastrous results—he was constantly ridiculed for speaking with a British accent. Now, he'd come full circle: the language thing was one more dark hue in the color of his pain; he often wondered to himself why he had always had to suffer so much. However, Alex considered himself a resilient person; he believed, blindly optimistic, that he would be fine, that everything would all work out. If language was one more hurdle to climb in his life, then so be it; he would tackle it and master it—no problem!

The days on Water Caye seemed to fly by. Alex didn't know if it was because he, Ains, and Robb often planned activities that took them from the house early in the morning to late in the evenings, but no doubt about it, the month was quickly coming to an end. The friends hiked, biked, fished, learned to set basket traps to catch the pretty blue crabs, and even went deep-sea diving with Dennis and Anthony to collect some conch. They thoroughly enjoyed dinners Millie prepared with the fresh catch each night; they felt adult, happy that they could make a meaningful contribution to the meals.

The nearest neighbors on both sides were about half-a-mile away, so often the families would get together in the evenings for bonfires, barbecues, crab/lobster/conch "boil-ups," and other social gatherings. They even had Friday night "jump-ups" where everyone shook off their inhibitions and threw themselves into the revelry. On Sunday mornings, most folks attended the one non-denominal church in town. The Caye community was strong and flourishing; families prided themselves on being able to do on the Cayes what they did at home but at a more relaxed pace.

CHAPTER 2

Alex called his parents once a week, speaking to Cathlean as he was required to do but really conversing animatedly with John as he told John about everything he was doing on his vacation. Alex really missed John; it was the first time they'd been separated for a long period of time in the eleven years since John and Cathlean had married. Alex was ambivalent toward Cathlean, finding, to his surprise, that he really didn't miss her at all even though he assured John that he missed them both.

On the last Saturday night that Alex and his friends spent on Water Caye, there was a huge bash since most people would be returning home to spend the last few weeks of summer preparing their kids to return to school in September. This affair was going to be grand indeed; everyone was expected to wear their Sunday best or whatever Sunday best was in a casual, island environment.

Miss Millie and the women cooked mountains of food and local favorites: rice and beans, tamales, potato salad, stewed chicken, fried ripe plantains, fresh vegetables, coleslaw, and stewed fish. And desserts, oh my! There was bread pudding, tarts, cassava cake (also called "plastic" because of its transparent appearance), jam rolls, home-made mango and soursop ice cream, potato pudding, coconut crust . . . the works. The men brewed rum punch and checked their fermenting homemade wines for readiness. Alex, Robb, Ainsworth, Layla (she was allowed to tag along sometimes, especially today), and others ran back and forth doing errands, picking up ice, shopping for last-minute ingredients, and helping the women as they prepared the food. Mouthwatering odors permeated the entire Caye air, and there was an excited atmosphere of anticipation everywhere. People could hardly wait until it would be time to sample the goodies; six o'clock couldn't come fast enough. Alex stared at the clock on the wall in the Community Center every time he got a chance to, but it seemed like it was broken. He knew that it was indeed working, just working extremely slow.

At about 5:30 p.m., Miss Millie and the other mothers sent their children home to get ready, reminding them to wear the nice clothes that they'd picked out that morning. Millie and the other adults would get dressed at the Community Center, but Alex and his friends raced home to change into their finery. They then hurried back to the hall so they wouldn't miss anything; they wanted to see everyone as they arrived at the party, especially the cute young ladies in their beautiful dresses, representing all the bright colors of the rainbow. They also checked out the other young men, all decked out in their best clothes, sizing them up as potential rivals for the young ladies' attention.

Alex was standing near the door helping to escort some of the older ladies to their tables. The other young men had been ordered to perform the same service, much to their dismay, but they realized that they need to cooperate and help out now to get their freedom later. As he turned aside to whisper something to Ainsworth, he saw Ains's eyes grow round and glaze over as he looked at something behind Alex. Alex became nervous, wondering what was behind him.

"Hey, Ains, what's the matter, man? Hey, snap out of it!" he urged, waving his hands in front of Ains's face. "What's up, man?" But Ainsworth just kept staring, not bothering to answer Alex at all. Alex slowly pivoted, turning around to see what his friend was staring at. Then, he too stopped, staring, mouth hanging open at the vision of the most beautiful girl he'd ever seen in his young life.

She was tall, blossoming curves all in the right places, long brown hair in braided cornrows flowing down her back. Her reddened, lush lips parted in a provocative smile to show small, glistening pearly white teeth as she looked around the room. She wore a simple rose-pink chiffon dress trimmed in white lace, innocent-looking yet sexy at the same time. White gloves went from elbows to her fingertips, her right arm held protectively by a dark Indian-looking woman with long hair flowing down her own back. This appeared to be the young lady's mother because the resemblance was strikingly obvious. The mother narrowed her eyes at the young men, tossing her head as she swept into the room, daughter in tow. Ainsworth eventually found his voice as he croaked, "Man, did you see her? Who is she? Congratulate me, Al. I think I've just seen my future wife, and she's wearing gloves. I've absolutely got to meet her. Help me out, friend, please help me!"

He started toward the table where the young lady and her mum had seated themselves, but his mother, seeing what was happening, came over, grabbed his and Alex's arms, and pulled them toward the kitchen. "Now don't you boys embarrass me. Leave that girl alone. Her mum won't let you near her, so forget about it." With that, she shook both of them hard so they had to look at her.

Alex asked in a hoarse voice, "But who is she, Miss Millie? Where does she live?"

"In Dangríga, her name's Sherrette, but didn't you hear me? Her mother Miss Ida will not let you get anywhere near her child. They say she's saving Sherrette for someone white or special, not some little black boys like you two. Now stop staring, and go help those ladies find their tables. Go on!" She gave them a push; Alex almost fell over his feet as he walked to the door but kept looking back at Sherrette. He felt like his brain had turned to mush, and he could see Ains was also having problems walking. *Sherrette,* he thought, trying the name out in his head, a *lovely name for a lovely girl.*

The rest of the evening passed in a blur. Alex was sure the food was the most scrumptious he'd ever eaten, but it could've been cardboard for all the attention he paid to it. He couldn't believe how a few hours ago, he couldn't wait to enjoy the food, but now, he was full from staring at Sherrette all night long. Ains noticed because he was also doing the same thing. At one point, he even reminded Alex that he, Ainsworth, had seen her first and that she would be Ains's future "babies' momma."

Alex ignored Ainsworth, figuring that he, Alex, would have many opportunities to meet with and speak with Miss Sherrette once they got back to Dangríga. He hoped she lived nearby and that they would possibly even go to the same school. He vowed to himself that he would be nice to Miss Ida, knowing instinctively that this was the best way to get to her daughter. With that thought in mind, he approached their table and introduced himself to mother and daughter. Miss Ida was pleasant but not overly friendly. Alex kept his eyes lowered respectfully, trying hard not to look at Sherrette, who was even more devastatingly beautiful

71

up close, if that was possible. Alex felt his mouth go dry.

"Hello, my name is Alex. Can I get you ladies some punch?" he croaked, looking at Miss Ida.

"That would be lovely, young man. I'm Miss Ida, this is Sherrette. Are you here with Millie and her family?" she asked, letting Alex know that she'd seen the little interaction earlier between Miss Millie, Ainsworth, and himself. She tilted her head to the side, curious, awaiting a response.

"Yes, I am," he stated. "Can I get your daughter a drink too?" he said, peeking at Sherrette.

"Yes, please," she answered in a clear voice, looking at her mother who frowned angrily at her.

"Young lady, he asked me. Don't be so forward! Yes, get us both some punch," she ordered.

Alex gave them a little smile and hurried off on what seemed like two left feet to get their drinks. He didn't know how he didn't spill the drinks, but in a few minutes, he'd brought them and placed them carefully in the center of the table. Sherrette smiled at him then sneaked a look at her mother.

"You talk funny, Alex. Mother and I were wondering where you're from. We've never seen you in Dangríga before, and that town is too small to hide in. What is your story?" She sipped her drink.

Clearing his throat, which was now extremely dry, he said, "Well, I just arrived from England last month and was living in Belize City, but I'm originally from Dangríga. I'll be starting my third year at Ecumenical High School in September. I've already done my first two years in England."

"Oh, I'm starting at Ecumenical High too," she said clapping her hands. "Maybe I'll see you on campus." Miss Ida gave her a look, pursing her lips in disapproval. "Mama said I can't have friends."

"That will be quite enough, young lady. Finish your drink so we can leave. Say good-night."

"Good night Alex. Good-bye!" she said, making a face at her mother carefully so she couldn't see.

"Good night ladies. Good-bye!" Alex said, smart enough to know when to retreat. He and Miss Sherrette were definitely not saying good-bye forever; he would see her in Dangríga, he thought . . . yes!

CHAPTER 3

A short while later, Alex and the family left the party and headed back to their house. They were already packed for an early departure the next day, so all that was left to add was the clothes they'd worn to the party, plus the pajamas they would wear to bed. Ainsworth pouted, whining that he hadn't spent time with Sherrette, while Robb boasted loudly about the girl that he'd met and how they planned to hook up once they got home. Alex, wanting them both to be quiet so he could think about Sherrette, pretended to be very sleepy, faking yawns until they finally shut up and fell asleep. He didn't get much sleep that night, and when he did doze off, he dreamed about Sherrette.

The next morning, they all got up early, had a hearty breakfast, cleaned the cottage up, then helped Anthony to cast off as they headed back to Dangríga. Everyone was talking about the great time they had had at the party: Layla, normally a quiet girl, excitedly discussed the different dress styles and which ones she wanted her mother, Miss Millie, to make her once they got home. Dennis seemed a little hung-over from all the homebrew he'd consumed last night, Anthony was his usual cheery self as he took the wheel and turned the boat toward home. Ainsworth and Robb talked nonstop about the girls they met at the party. Again, Alex wished they would just shut up so he could think about Sherrette.

He realized he was the only one being quiet; he stretched out with his eyes closed, thinking he'd probably fallen in love for the first time in his life. He thought he finally understood his dad, how John would do anything for Cathlean because he loved her so much. Alex daydreamed the entire way back, not as anxious at being reunited with his mother as he thought he would be. Somehow, he felt calm, in control, ready for his life. He'd get through the next few weeks; if he didn't see Sherrette in town, he knew he would once school started—now that was something for him to look forward to!

The sea was a little choppy on the return trip, so it took almost two hours for the vacationers to get home, but they did so without mishap. John was waiting at the dock for them, and Alex was very happy to see him; Alex couldn't wait to unburden himself and talk to John about what was in his heart. Alex felt the familiar glow of love for his dad, but at the same time, he felt the ache at his mum's absence. He'd been gone a month—what was so important to keep her away on the day her son returned home? John shrugged, reading the unspoken question in Alex's eyes.

"Welcome home, son," he said, hugging Alex close and patting his back. "Mum's gone to a baby shower for one of her friends," he said, explaining Cathlean's absence as he was always used to doing.

That's interesting, Alex thought. *She's the least maternal person I know, yet she's at a baby shower celebrating impending motherhood. She couldn't even come welcome me home!* He felt the usual ache in his heart as he thought of Cathlean and the color of pain that came with her love. Turning, he hugged his dad back and said, "Dad, I'm so happy you're here. I have so much to tell you!" So they walked off the pier together—Alex, a head taller, muscular, and dark; John shorter, paunchy, and white. They made quite a contrast as Alex shortened his stride so John could keep pace with him. John skipped along like an excited kid; he was so happy his boy was back home where he belonged.

As John came around to unlock Alex's door, Alex stopped abruptly. "Dad, I smell liquor on you. Have you been drinking?" He sniffed the air as he leaned toward John.

"Well, I had a little nip earlier today. Don't tell your mum, please?" John looked earnestly at Alex.

"It's still early, Dad. And you drove over here to pick me up. You know that's dangerous."

"Please, son, leave it alone. I'm not drunk. I can drive a few miles to the house. Hush, now!"

Alex gnawed on his bottom lip, frustrated and not entirely happy with his dad's response. He knew Cathlean was difficult as a mother; he also saw many times how difficult a wife she could be, so he shrugged his shoulder, climbed into the car, deciding not to say any more. The situation would bear watching, though: he wanted to make sure John's drinking was a one-time thing, not a Cathlean casualty.

CHAPTER 4

Alex and John walked into their new two-story house located near the beach in front of downtown Dangríga. The family had moved in upon their arrival in Dangríga; the house had been found by one of John's former contacts from the time when he'd previously served in Belize as a soldier. John had trusted him completely, having wired the funds to his friend's bank so he could purchase the house for John's family. Upon seeing the house, Cathlean had burst into tears, declaring it "the perfect dream home." John was very happy that Cathlean was pleased; he knew how hard it could be to satisfy his wife. Alex was just happy to be able to live near the water, but he hadn't had a chance to get used to his new home because he's gone off to the Cayes the day after they moved in.

Now Alex stood back shading his eyes with his hand and stared up at the house. His room was at the top, actually a former attic converted to a bedroom. There was a laundry room and two bedrooms on the first floor: a master bedroom that his parents shared and a second guest room. The Great Room was a nice size, and the kitchen was furnished with the newest and latest-model appliances, all in stainless steel. There was one large bathroom on the first floor, while Alex had a half-bathroom with a shower and commode next to his room. He was extremely happy with the set-up; he was far enough away to guarantee his personal privacy yet close enough for when he needed to hang out with his parents or to run to the kitchen to grab a snack.

Alex entered the front door behind John, and although he'd had a large breakfast before leaving Water Caye two hours ago, his appetite perked up at the scent of John's special crumpets and bangers (sausage). John was often the cook in the Putnam household, his specialty definitely being breakfast. Grammie Putnam had tried to teach John how to cook; her instructions had been around traditional English food. John had learned to cook Belizean foods from his military buddies. Even Cathlean, when in a good mood, would take time to teach him to cook some of the more complicated Belizean dishes, especially desserts, which John enjoyed way more than he should. Alex ran upstairs to drop off his gear, then came back to the kitchen where John was sliding plates out of the oven.

"Wow, Dad, crumpets? Haven't had those since we left London. Mmm, thanks!" Alex said all this between bites and with his mouth full of food. He hastily wiped the corners of his mouth as John gave him a look but didn't say anything. If Cathlean had been home, Alex knew he would've been royally scolded.

"Hey, slow down. The food's not going anywhere," John said with a laugh. "I swear you've grown in one month. Just taller, though. You never seem to get any bigger. I don't know where your food goes."

"I don't know either, but great breakfast, Dad. I ate so much at the party last night. Oh, I want to let you know . . . Dad, I-I met a girl. She's beautiful. I know you and Mum will love her. She lives here in town and will be going to Ecumenical High like me. Did I say she's beautiful?" He stopped.

"Slow down, son. Start at the beginning. When did this happen? Tell me everything . . . slowly!"

"Oh, sorry. It was last night at the party. She's about fifteen. She came to the party with her mum, and Ainsworth says he's in love and wants to marry her so she can have his future babies. But Dad, we connected, I know we did! She made fun of the way I talked, but I still want to be her friend. She's sweet and smelled good, and she's funny and, guess what? We'll be going to the same high school."

It was one of the longest speeches Alex had ever made, and John shook his head smiling. So his son had caught the love bug, eh? Alex was in for it now. John responded, choosing his words with care, "Well, that's nice, son, but take things slow. You don't want to get too serious at such a young age. You have your whole life ahead of you. Just be careful and don't get trapped into a relationship where you're not getting the love you need. Go slowly. Don't just look at this girl's beauty. Check out her heart, and see where it leads you." With that said, he turned away, a look of pain on his face.

For the first time in many years, Alex realized that John knew that Cathlean didn't really love him. Maybe due to the more adult relationship developing between father and son, John was finally able to let his son see a little of the father's vulnerability. It also sounded like John was trying to warn Alex against being fooled into marrying a pretty face incapable of deep, genuine love. Alex both pitied and admired his dad for sticking it out in a marriage to a selfish, unloving woman, but he, Alex, vowed that he would not allow this particular color of pain. *Nope,* Alex thought to himself in the manner of the young pitying their elders, *that's not going to happen to me. Not to me at all.*

His stomach full, he got up, scraped off his plate, washed his dishes, then went up to his room to empty his knapsack and wash his dirty laundry. Once he settled in, he would try to find out more about Sherrette—he wanted to know where she lived, what her home situation was, what she liked to do. He was ready to pursue the courtship full-on and knew that information was what he needed to begin. He also knew that he had Miss Ida to contend with, but what about Sherrette's dad? What was the story there? There hadn't been a man with them, but that didn't mean he didn't exist. He could've stayed in Dangríga working or doing something else while his family visited the Cayes.

Alex decided he would talk to Miss Millie, who seemed to know something about Sherrette's family, but how could he do so without making Ainsworth angry? Ains was the first real friend Alex had made since returning to Belize, his best friend who Alex wasn't prepared to lose over a female. But the million-dollar question remained: was Ains really serious about pursuing Sherrette, or was he just talking crazy? Ains sometimes had the attention span of a flea. Alex would see what Miss Millie had to say before saying anything about his feelings to Ainsworth. Yes, that's what he would do.

CHAPTER 5

Alex, ever the strategist, had created a plan, so he set out to execute it as soon as possible by going to visit Ainsworth and family the next day. He figured they'd all want to rest up today after their month-long Caye trip. Alex also had some things to do right now, like calling his friend Ralph in London to tell him about his new life in Belize, his recent Caye trip, and his first girlfriend.

The next few weeks passed in a whirlwind of summer activities and proved somewhat frustrating for Alex, because even though he hung out with Ainsworth and Robb a few times, he never got a chance to actually visit their home to talk to Miss Millie about Sherrette. John teased Alex about his girl, asking what was going on, to which Alex admitted that he had not seen her at all since returning to the mainland. Alex noticed that Cathlean never asked how his trip to the Cayes had been, but he believed she could tell that he'd had a great time because he couldn't stop talking about how much fun it had been. He learned to tone his excitement down in her presence after she'd said to him once, "Boy, can you please shut up about your trip? I'm glad it was nice, but I don't want to hear any more . . . Please!" He was hurt by her attitude, but, in typical Alex fashion, he held his peace.

John's reaction was the total opposite. He realized how important the trip had been for Alex, an experience that was about to launch him into manhood and manly interest in the opposite sex and a new reason for enjoying life. Whenever Alex would start with "Dad, Sherrette is . . ." or "Sherrette said . . .," John would indulge him, listening intently, drawing Alex out so he could express what he was feeling. John even shared with Alex the benefit of his own very limited experience, which was funny, considering that he also had to admit that he'd had no prior experience until he met Cathlean.

A day or so later, Alex had ridden his bicycle up to the market to purchase some fish for Cathlean when he happened to see Layla standing to the side of a fish stall. After Alex parked his bike and looked around, he saw Miss Millie, so he quickly thought, *Oh, good, I can talk to her to ask how I can meet Sherrette or get her contact information!* Out loud he shouted in a high-pitched, excited voice, "Hey, Layla, Miss Millie, how are you both?" He swallowed nervously, continuing in a lower and what he hoped was a more manly voice, "Haven't seen you in a few weeks, Miss Millie. Can I ask . . ." His mouth snapped shut as he looked over to Mr. Peter's beef stall, approximately two stalls away.

His eyes grew round, and he could feel his face flush, for who should be standing there, a lovely vision in white cutoff shorts, colorful T-shirt, and red strappy sandals, but his girl, his fantasy, Sherrette. He blinked twice in rapid succession, hoping she wouldn't disappear; when he looked again, she was still there, so he approached her cautiously, looking around for her mother, unable to believe his good fortune. "Hi, Sherrette, how are you?" he croaked. "How have you been? I haven't seen you since Water Caye . . ." He licked his suddenly dry lips, realizing he was babbling. By now he was standing directly in front of her; he could smell her light, subtle perfume.

She smiled, showing the beautiful white teeth he remembered so well. "Well, if it isn't the Englishman. Alex, is it?" She chuckled slyly, putting her hand out to shake his. Alex quickly wiped his suddenly moist hand on the leg of his jeans, and he and Sherrette shook awkwardly. He drank in the sight of her, noting that the real thing was so much better than his memories of her. If anything, he thought, she'd become even more striking, her tan deep and golden all over. He even noticed something he'd missed at their first meeting: she had a cute little sprinkle of freckles across her nose, the only "imperfection" in an otherwise perfect face.

"Let me try again," said Alex. "Hello, Sherrette, how are you? How's your summer going?"

"Just fine, Alex. I haven't seen you around town, not like I'd been looking," she responded, recognizing and enjoying his discomfort just a little. "Are you registered for school yet?"

"No, registration starts next week. Maybe we can go together. Can I have your address? I'll come pick you up." He'd barely finished speaking when Miss Ida furiously descended upon them, a Mama Bear protecting her cub. He could almost see smoke popping out of her ears—she was that annoyed.

"Sherrette, what have I told you? No talking to young men, and no, you will *not* give him your number! Go away, you!" She turned to Alex. "Oh, it's you, the young man from the Cayes. I told you Sherrette is not to talk to boys. No offense, but please don't ever try to talk to her." She grabbed Sherrette's arm, dragging her away. Sherrette looked over her shoulder at him, a regretful expression on her face—at least Alex decided he'd interpret her expression as regretful. He waved.

"Bye, Sherrette," he mouthed at her. "See you at registration!" And just like that, she was gone.

Layla was laughing at him mockingly; Miss Millie looked at him sadly, shaking her head, saying, "Boy, I told you not to try to talk to that girl. Her mama has big plans for her. Leave her alone!"

Alex, previously an obedient child, resolved in his mind that this time, he wouldn't do as ordered; he would not go away but would continue to pursue Sherrette—he figured she was worth it. He turned to buy the fish he'd been sent to get, distracted the whole time, thinking about how to get Sherrette's address or information. He didn't know where she lived, either, but this was not London; Dangríga was very small—how hard would it be to get her information? He approached Miss Millie, undeterred by her frown. "Miss Millie, can you please tell me where Sherrette and Miss Ida live?"

"No, I will not! I'll tell your mum on you, Alex. I don't want to see you get into trouble." With that, she turned to Layla. "Girl, stop your grinning, and let's go. There's nothing funny about this." They turned and walked away, leaving Alex standing there, disappointed and irritated at Miss Millie.

As he walked over and pulled his bike up, he observed a tall man standing next to a beat-up "taxi," if one could call the multi-colored contraption that. The man shook his head at Alex, nodding pityingly, and said, "No, boy, you don't want to do that. Leave that gial alone if you know what's good for you. Miss Ida don't play!" Alex glared at him, jumped on his bike, and headed home.

"Dad, Dad, I saw her, I saw her!" He called out, jumping off his bike and running up the steps. "She was at the market." He stopped short as Cathlean came out the kitchen. "Mum, where's Dad?"

He's not here. What? Did somebody die?" she asked, alarmed. "Slow down, Alex. Tell me!"

Alex stopped abruptly, sorry that his dad wasn't home. "Nobody died, Mum. I saw Sherrette, the girl I met at the Cayes. We'll be going to the same school and everything!" He couldn't control his excitement even when Cathlean appeared to be less than excited at his revelation. She, ever the spoiled one always demanding and expecting Alex's love, could already pick up on the fact that she was about to have some female competition for her son's affection. She, for the first time, would not automatically come second in Alex's life. She'd already abdicated the number one position to her husband John, whom she totally dominated, so she'd never felt threatened by being number two. She vowed to herself, *I'll be darned if I'm going to share my spot with that forward little hussy!*

Cathlean resolved there and then that she was going to find out all she could about this Sherrette person as soon as she could; she had her ear to the ground and had her sources. Her girls at the Booty Bunker would help, or they had friends who knew stuff. She would get to the bottom of this. In the meantime, she said sweetly, "Ooh, that's nice. My son is in love. Hey, my son's in love," she teased. Alex, happy that she seemed openly supportive, told her what had happened at the market. He ended on the sad note that Miss Ida had warned him away from Sherrette. Cathlean was immediately offended that someone thought that their daughter was too good for her boy. She didn't want to see Alex with anyone, either, but that was not the point. Her son would be with whomever he wanted.

CHAPTER 6

Try as he might, Alex couldn't get information on Sherrette, didn't know where she lived, nor could he get any information about her! On the first day of school registration, he dressed in pressed jean shorts, a green polo shirt, high-top shoes, and had John drop him off at school. He didn't want to ride his bike since he knew he would perspire; he wanted to smell good for Sherrette because he was sure he would see her at school. When John dropped Alex off, he asked if Alex needed him to come to registration with him, but Alex said no, only asking if John could return to pick him up later.

Alex jumped out the car, making sure he had all his school transfer papers and other documents required for registration. He looked around for Sherrette or her mum but didn't see either of them anywhere, so he took his place in a long, ever-growing line of excited students and parents. The noise was overwhelming, and as the line continued to grow, Alex saw Ainsworth and Robb get in line behind him while Layla and Miss Millie headed to freshman registration. Suddenly, it dawned on Alex that this would be the line that Sherrette and Miss Ida would be in when they arrived, Sherrette being a freshman in the new year. Just as he thought this, they arrived with much fanfare: Miss Ida with her nose in the air, walking like she meant business, stomping across the floor, neither looking right nor left. Sherrette, fresh and lovely in a yellow sundress and white sandals, followed reluctantly behind her, eyes downcast and looking at her own feet as she walked.

Alex, drawn like a magnet, left his place in line and walked behind Sherrette, trying to catch her attention. When she saw him out the corner of her eye, she looked at Miss Ida's back, then at Alex, then back at her mum once more. With a quick twist of her body, she reached into her back pocket, pulled out a piece of paper, and threw it at Alex. He quickly put his foot on the paper, just in time too, because Miss Ida turned around, perpetual frown in place, trying to see where Sherrette was. She glowered when she saw Alex and pulled her daughter by her arm, turning toward the registration desk. Sherrette glanced at Alex once more, happy to see him picking up the paper she'd tossed him.

Alex, acting as if he'd found the Holy Grail, swooped down and picked up the piece of paper. When he unfolded it, he saw that she'd written, in clear cursive, her full name, Sherrette Gales, her telephone number, and a cartoon face drawn at the bottom of the note. Alex wanted to jump up and kick his heels together. Hallelujah, he finally had the information he needed! He felt like he was walking on air throughout the rest of the boring registration process, but he was not complaining—today was a very good day! Alex felt like he was king of the world, and Sherrette would be his future queen. He skipped out, nearly dancing as he headed curbside where his dad awaited him.

John was standing near his car, arms folded, talking to the tall man that Alex had seen near the market the other day. Something seemed vaguely familiar about him, so Alex racked his brain trying to place the man. John pulled Alex to him and asked, "Did everything go well, son? What am I asking—of course it did. Hey," he continued, pointing at the man leaning against his ugly old taxicab, "Alex, say hello to Tooth. You knew him before you moved to England. Tooth, my boy, Alex."

Tooth took Alex's hand. "My, you're almost a grown man now. When I first met you, you were only five or six. Cathlean's boy, right? I would'na recognized you myself, but now I do remember you." He pumped Alex's hand vigorously, gold tooth gleaming in the sunlight as he grinned happily. "You're a proper English gent now, but maybe I can introduce you to some of my children. I have twenty-two of them, you know? When you lived here, I had eighteen of them, but I had four more while you were gone!" All that was left was for Tooth to pound his chest Tarzan-style; he was so proud of himself.

"Hello, Mr. Tooth. Nice to meet you again. I may be going to school with some of your kids." Alex said, finally getting a chance to speak. He was thinking, *This guy's a character. Twenty-two children? Who has twenty-two children? How could he make money driving that beat-up taxicab?* Alex turned to John, remembering his exciting news. "Dad, I saw her. I saw Sherrette, and guess what? I got her telephone number, so I can visit her!" He almost jumped up and clicked his heels together.

"Just Tooth, no 'mister' necessary, boy. I gotta say, be careful, that girl's mum won't want anyone to come courting. I know how excited you are to know her, but slow down. A few months ago, one of my boys tried to step to her, and I swear Miss Ida put a hex on him. He's never been the same since." He drew closer to Alex rolling his ever-present toothpick between his tongue and gold tooth. "Some even say she's a witch!" He ended on a dramatic note, almost in a whisper. Alex felt a chill crawl down his spine, but he ignored it. What did this old man know about Sherrette? Alex vowed that he would succeed where Tooth's son or any others had failed; he was that confident in himself.

Soon after their little chat, Alex and John left Tooth, heading for home. They'd traveled along in silence for most of the way, when suddenly John said, "Alex, what d'you think about what that man said? Don't know anything about hexes, but we're in Belize now, son. These people are very serious about hexes, or Obeah, as they call it. You know they say it can be buried in your yard, under your stairs, or take the form of some herb or root that can be mixed in with your food. I've seen some things that I can't explain, especially living here in Belize. All I want to say is go slowly, and be careful. I don't mess with things I don't understand. From what I hear, best way to combat Obeah is to buy a bodyguard at some outrageous price. You'd need to wear it on your person at all times."

Alex stared at John, shocked; he couldn't believe his levelheaded dad was talking about Obeah. John always existed firmly in the real world, never had flights of fancy nor had ever expressed an opinion regarding otherworldly matters. Alex had heard things about black magic and such back in England, and when he'd announced to his chums that he was moving back to Belize, they'd warned him to be especially careful of evil spirits and the undead, which they claimed existed and lived openly among the living there. Alex had scoffed at the thought, but now, he felt a little uneasy, especially since John seemed to be open to the idea of the existence of such things. He shrugged, saying, "Dad, please don't worry. I think Sherrette is worth whatever I have to go through. I'll be careful, and I'll be sure to watch out for Miss Ida's Obeah. Maybe I'll have to go get one of those bodyguards that the local witch doctor makes so I'll be safe." He chuckled. "Believe me, Sherrette and I will be together. You'll see."

John just looked at Alex, not saying anything more, and soon, they pulled into their driveway and went into the house. "Hullo, Cathlean," John called out. "We're home, dear. Alex is all set for school."

Cathlean came out the kitchen wiping her hands on a towel. Appetizing smells filled the house; Alex thought he smelled beans and curry spice. His stomach rumbled as he realized that because he'd been anticipating meeting with Sherrette so much earlier that day that he hadn't had much breakfast. He was starving, so he quickly rushed to the bathroom to wash up, while his parents greeted each other. He could hear Cathlean asking how things had gone, while she put the finishing touches on the food. When Alex returned to the kitchen, he saw rice, red beans, curry chicken, fried ripe plantains, and coleslaw set out on the table. His mouth watered; everything looked wonderful—he knew it would be because even though she didn't do it as often as she could, Cathlean was a great cook.

"Please say grace, Alex," Cathlean said, and Alex quickly complied, saying a very short prayer before digging in. He piled his plate with a lot of everything, as his parents looked on with disbelief. "Don't pile your plate up like that. You can always go back for seconds," Cathlean protested, shaking her head.

"Mmm, Mum, this is really good. I knew it would be—you know curry's my favorite seasoning," he said between huge bites of food. "I'm very hungry. I didn't have much breakfast, remember?"

"Dear, he's a growing boy, leave him alone," John said to Cathlean, smiling indulgently. His boy could really eat! Alex was quite an avid athlete who excelled at all sports, so he never gained an ounce. He was all gangly arms and sinewy muscles, but he was deceptively strong and physically fit.

Cathlean watched as John looked at Alex; she was a little irritated that John indulged Alex in what she thought was bad habits and improper etiquette. She didn't want Alex embarrassing her with the way he ate, especially in front of her old friends whom she still continuously tried to impress with whatever "class" they'd learned in England. She believed in her own mind that her girlfriends would be looking to her for guidance on how to eat, behave, and conduct themselves since she and her family had just returned home. "Queen Cathlean" had come back to live among the uncivilized heathen.

Even though he never did, she forever worried that Alex would mis-step and do something to ruin her "lady of the manor" persona that she used to impress her former Booty Bunker pals. Cathlean's arrogance knew no limit; as usual, everything was about her. She would be mortified to know that those she tried to impress just laughed at her behind her back, shaking their heads at what they considered her antics. They'd learned to expect anything from Cathlean because one thing was for sure: she never disappointed!

CHAPTER 7

After Alex had gorged himself on food, he excused himself from the kitchen, ignoring his mum when she mentioned something about the dishes. He knew John would take care of that chore, so Alex went to his room to telephone Sherrette to say hello and make sure that he was dialing the correct number. He was so happy that she and her mum, like his parents, were one of the few families who owned a telephone; they were still considered a luxury, but John qualified for one through his military connections. As Alex listened to the line ring, he tapped his fingertips impatiently on the bureau, hoping Miss Ida wouldn't pick up. It was definitely his lucky day: not only had he called the right number, but Sherrette's sweet voice, not Ida's, filled his ear as she answered.

"Hello," she said hesitantly, "who would you like to speak to?" Her sensuous voice calmed Alex.

He closed his eyes, breathing a short prayer of thanks. "Uh, hullo, Sherrette. This is Alex. I just wanted to say that I'm glad we had a chance to talk earlier. I hope you didn't get into too much trouble with your mother. I'm so happy we'll be going to the same school." There was so much he wanted to say, that he could feel himself babbling. "Sorry, let me hush up so you can say something."

Sherrette's laugh tinkled through the line. "Yes, Alex, slow down so I can say something too. Let me have your telephone number before my mum catches me talking." She quickly jotted down the number he gave to her. "I can't talk long, but I'll call tonight after she goes to bed. Oh, she's coming right now." Her voice dropped an octave or two. "G'bye, English. We'll talk tonight!"

He could hear Miss Ida's voice coming into the room, causing

Sherrette to hang up rather abruptly. Hearing the dial tone, Alex looked the receiver, shaking his head as he slowly hung it up. Then he grinned from ear to ear as he leapt onto his bed; he lay faceup on top of the covers thinking about Sherrette. "Yessss," he shouted, right fist punching the air. "She'll be mine, Miss Ida, just watch!" And with the absolute trust and innocent confidence of youth, he punched his pillow and lay down for a nap, unconcerned about any pitfalls his vow to have Sherrette may lead him to encounter. He slept soundly, waking up two hours later, refreshed and ready to take on the world.

CHAPTER 8

When Alex came downstairs after his nap, he found Cathlean doing laundry. She was happy to make use of the manly muscles available to her, so she loaded him and John down with wet, colored clothes to be hung on the line outside. She spread the white clothes out to bleach on a patch of grass set aside in the backyard for that purpose. She would gather them up after about an hour, rinse them in a bluing agent to make them sparkling white, then hang them up to dry on the clothesline.

Cathlean didn't like drying clothes on clotheslines as she'd grown up doing because she thought it was uncivilized; she felt she'd come too far for that! She much preferred the use of her heavy duty, frontload chrome-and-white dryer that matched her family-size washer, both of which she had begged and cajoled John to purchase for her across the border in Chetumal, Mexico, since items like that were not readily available in Belize or were way too expensive to purchase from the few stores that carried them. Today, even she could see that it was better to take advantage of the beautiful tropical sun, which dried clothes within a matter of hours, leaving them smelling fresh and clean. On rainy or overcast days, she happily traded the clotheslines for her dryer, making no apology for the fact that she liked that drying method better anyway.

Traditionally, in Belizean society, laundry washing was considered women's work, but Alex and John both enjoyed helping with the task of hanging clothes on the line since they'd never had the opportunity to do so back in rainy England. Alex found that doing this with his dad was somewhat therapeutic, and it also gave them an opportunity to talk about manly issues outside of Cathlean's earshot. Alex really wanted to talk with John about Sherrette, over whom he worried that he was already starting to obsess. He wanted to talk about new love, what to do about it, and how it was possible to know when one was in love. He looked around for his mum, but she was inside the laundry room, which gave him the perfect opportunity to approach John for a man-to-man talk.

"Uh, Dad, I just talked to Sherrette, the girl from my new school, and from the Cayes, the one we talked about earlier. I really like her, Dad, and even though Miss Millie, Mr. Tooth, and Miss Ida already warned me off, I want to ask her out. Don't say anything to Mum, but I want to take Sherrette to the movies. What do you think? Can I, please? Can I?" He waited with bated breath.

John locked eyes with his son. He had to look up a little since Alex now towered over him. "As we discussed before, you need to slow down and be careful. You heard what Tooth said: these people are serious when you don't listen and stay out of their way. Besides, you're young, and you have two years of school to finish. Why don't you see if she's still available after you graduate? By then, she can decide for herself if she wants to date you." He eyes were serious behind thick-lensed glasses.

"But, Dad, I've never been interested in girls before . . . she's my first. I promise my grades won't suffer, and if they do slip, I give you permission now to stop me from seeing her then. You taught me to do the right thing. I'll be respectful toward her. On second thought, maybe you should say something to Mum, then she can talk to Miss Ida . . ."

"Boy, stop. I can't think with you going on like this! Let me check into things and I'll get back with you after I see what happens. In the meantime, promise me you'll leave what's her name, ah, Sherrette, alone. We haven't been back here long, and I don't want to make people angry, so hold on."

"But, Dad, please, I . . ." Alex started, then abruptly shut up as he saw the look on his dad's face.

"I've said all I'll say on the matter for now," John stated sternly. "Wait till I get some answers, and Alex, leave her alone until then, you hear? I'm serious!" He wagged his right forefinger at Alex.

Alex was not stupid; he knew when to retreat, so he wisely remained silent. He hoped Sherrette would still call him that night but didn't say anything at all to John about the planned conversation. Just then, Cathlean called to them to come get more clothes to hang out to dry, so they stopped speaking and turned toward the house. Alex's heart was a little heavy because he'd have to wait to get permission to pursue Sherrette, but he wasn't really worried because love would conquer all.

CHAPTER 9

One month later, school reopened, and no other student was ready for school more than Alex. Try as he might over that last month of the summer, he couldn't find out where Sherrette lived! He supposed that the town was too small for her to not be found, but he didn't really push, as his dad, John, had not yet given his blessing for Alex to date Sherrette. Seemed like there was a serious conspiracy among the townsfolk in Dangríga to keep them apart. Alex accepted this only because he knew that once school started he would see her every day, and there would be nothing that anyone could do about it. Even though he and his friend Ainsworth attended several summer-end activities together like barbecues, picnics, etc., where he'd expected to see Sherrette, she never showed up. Someone even mentioned that she had probably gone to Orange Walk, a town north of Belize City, to visit her grandfather. Miss Ida definitely kept her lovely daughter on a short rein, but in a way, Alex was happy that if he couldn't see Sherrette, then neither could any other guys that may be interested in her. He was absolutely sure that once school reopened, she would be all his.

He and Ainsworth rode their bikes into the entrance to the school yard, parked, and rushed over to hang out with some of Ains's friends whom Alex had met during his short time in town. Alex anxiously scanned the crowds of students but couldn't locate Sherrette on that first hectic morning. He finally got lucky at lunchtime, though, when he saw her in the midst of a crowd of freshmen. She appeared calm, standing out from the crowd of insecure, stressed-out newbies. Alex couldn't help it; he rushed over to her. He felt like a drowning man finally being thrown a lifeline, or like a moth to a flame, or like any one of those other corny clichés. He wasn't ashamed to show his attraction to her.

"Sherrette, hullo, how have you been? I've missed you. How was the rest of your summer?" He realized he was babbling when a couple of her friends started chuckling over his too-eager greeting.

"Hello, English, I mean Alex. My summer was fine, yours? Tanzie, Myrtle, this is my friend, Alex." She introduced a short, dark, Afro-hairstyle-wearing girl, and a taller, brown-skinned girl wearing a long ponytail. Alex wasn't really interested in meeting her friends, but realizing they could be potential allies in his courtship of Sherrette, he graciously stuck out his hand and shook with each of them. Tanzie gave him an inappropriate "come hither" look under her eyelashes, while Myrtle looked at him, nose in the air, acting like he was a bug she'd like to squash with her shoe. Alex wondered what her problem was, but he proceeded, undeterred. He was in Sherrette's presence once more, and all was finally right with his world; he felt like the summer drought was over.

He drank in her lovely face, her scent, her presence, as his spirit quieted and settled. If he had had any doubt that he was attracted to her, one moment in her presence was all it took to reaffirm that what he felt was not just in his imagination. If the dazed look in her eyes was anything to go by, Sherrette appeared to be equally smitten with Alex. Alex sincerely hoped that John would allow them to date soon, or he would be royally screwed if he was forbidden to do so. He vowed to himself right there and then that Sherrette would be worth anything he had to do to be with her. He hoped that they would be able to date because he knew he'd have a problem staying away from her.

As he murmured, "Nice to meet you," to Sherrette's friends, the bell rang, signaling the end of lunch. *Darn it, just my luck,* he thought to himself, but he said aloud, "I'll see you after class, all right? I'll wait for you by the volleyball court. Can you meet me?" She nodded quickly, tucked her blouse more securely in her skirt, grabbed her lunch tray, knapsack, and ran to catch up with her friends. Alex could tell that she was flustered, and he smiled, pleased with the effect he had on her.

Whistling, he looked at Ains as they both rushed off to their next class. Ains shook his head, laughing because he saw that Alex was a goner. Ains realized he needed to move on from wanting Sherrette himself, so he said, ducking to avoid a smack from Alex, "Man, I hope I never have it bad like you, bro. That girl got you, and you haven't even had anything from her yet!" Alex glared at Ainsworth but didn't get a chance to respond as they quickly took their seats in trigonometry class.

The rest of the afternoon passed in a fog for Alex; he figured he must've responded correctly to questions asked of him in class because none of the teachers commented on his distracted demeanor. Since he was new to the school, they didn't know that he was normally more focused and attentive in class, but in many cases, they called on him to expound on points in class just so they could listen to his clipped British accent. Though they were appreciative of his accent, his classmates mocked him and made fun of the way he spoke. Alex couldn't help but reflect upon the fact that when he'd first moved to England, he was mocked for his Belizean/Caribbean accent. He remembered as a child newly arrived in London how John had had to intervene and soothe him on occasions when playmates or their parents called him "uncivilized," "Caribbean coconut," or worst of all, "jungle bunny," names that hurt badly as he'd struggled desperately to fit into his new home.

He sighed; he was older now and understood how things worked, that he would never quite fit completely in either of his two worlds: England or Belize. The only difference was that this time, his accent was something to celebrate and be proud of rather than hide. Truth is, Belizeans are Anglophiles at heart, loving everything English. Most Belizeans celebrated the British side of their culture and secretly envied and worshipped anyone who actually had had an opportunity to visit or live in England. A lot of Belizeans often looked for similarities between themselves and their British counterparts, gladly celebrating those commonalities. This desire was more of a "national heritage" kind of pride, not to be confused with the "soldier taffy" mentality, where Belizean women wanted to have children by British soldiers or sailors to legitimize themselves in England and in British society.

Alex impatiently kept checking the wall clock, so when classes ended at 3:30 p.m., he quickly grabbed his books and ran off to the volleyball courts at the back of the school. Sherrette wasn't there as yet, not that he'd expected her to be; he figured it would take her a few minutes. He sat on a bleacher, stacking his books on his left side, planning for Sherrette to sit on his right, if and when she showed up. He waited nervously, tapping his foot on the bleacher, rubbing a hand over his face.

After about five minutes, he spied Sherrette's best friend, Myrtle, leading Sherrette and Tanzie toward the bleacher where he sat. They paused dramatically in front of him, handing Sherrette off to him, like the precious package she was. She remained, while her two cohorts took themselves off to another set of bleachers—not too close, but still within earshot and eyesight, just in case they had to check Alex if he went too far with their friend. Alex stood, taking Sherrette's hand in his as he helped her sit next to him. He was so very happy that she'd shown up, that he just sat there grinning like an idiot. She smiled cheekily, secure in the knowledge of the effect she had on him.

"So, English, I'm here. What did you want to see me about?" she spoke first since he was being quiet. He just stared at her, so she snapped her fingers in front of his face. "Hey, Alex, I'm here!"

"Uh, hullo, Sherrette," he said slowly, as if coming out of a deep trance. "Sorry, how was your first day? I wasn't sure if you were coming, but I'm happy you did." He waved at Tanzie and Myrtle.

"My day was good. I'm going to really enjoy my drama class. The teacher is very nice. How was your day?" She started pulling her hand from Alex's but thought better of it, so she left it there.

"Biochem's going to kick my arse, but I'm looking forward to this year. Sorry I didn't get a chance to see you this last month, but I don't know where you live. So, how about it, can I get your address please, Sherrette?" He squeezed her hand, stroking and threading her fingers through his.

"My mother doesn't want me to see you or any boys, so I can't give you my address. One day I will, but not today," she said, finally pulling her trembling hand away from his and looking down at her feet. Her short uniform skirt rode high above her knees, showing an expanse of butterscotch-colored skin. She pulled it down self-consciously and sat primly at the edge of the bleacher seat.

Alex was afraid she was going to jump up and run away from him, so he spoke quickly. "Okay, I can wait to get your address. I know somebody else can give it to me, but I want to get it directly from you when you're ready. I have a lot of homework and have to meet a friend at the library, but I'm happy we had a chance to talk. Can you please call me tonight?"

She nodded, and they both stood up, awkwardly brushing against each other. Alex grabbed his things, and gave Sherrette a quick hug. He ran down a few steps to the ground, then rushed off in the direction of the library. Sherrette's friends came over, looking inquiringly at her, but she said nothing. Smiling, she hooked arms with them, and they all headed for the exit gate to get on the bus that would take them home.

CHAPTER 10

When Sherrette arrived, her mother met her at the door, hugging her and asking her how the first day of school had gone. She gave Miss Ida a brief synopsis of her day, careful not to mention the encounter with Alex. She hugged her secret to herself, savoring and thinking about it the entire time while doing homework. She'd never been interested in boys before, but there was something about Alex; she didn't know if it was the fact that he appeared and acted more mature than his age or that she loved to hear him speak with his funny British accent. She just knew she enjoyed talking to him and could hardly wait for her mother to go to bed that night so she could call him as promised.

Alex left school after spending some hours in the library; he had other homework to do when he got home too, so he made sure he'd made it there by six-thirty or seven that evening. He wanted to be ready for Sherrette's call if and when it came; he wasn't going to give her any excuse not to call.

Cathlean met him at the door when he arrived, asking about his day, and how it had gone. Alex looked past her but didn't see John. He responded to Cathlean's questions but finally just asked, "Mum, where's Dad?" He didn't want to be rude, but he wanted to see and talk to his dad.

"He went to a meeting and should be back soon. If you want to eat dinner before he gets here, go wash up. I think he'll be here in about a half-hour, but you don't need to wait if you're hungry."

"Oh, I'll eat now because I have loads of homework that I need to get to. What's for dinner?"

"Stewed fish, rice and beans, green salad, and fried ripe plantains. I even made grape Kool-Aid."

"My favorites! Yes, I'll eat now, then talk to Dad for a bit between homework assignments."

He went to wash his hands in the downstairs bathroom, while Cathlean placed his food on the table. Alex said grace and dug in: the codfish was tender and flaky, the rice and beans perfect, the green salad crisp and cool, the fried plantains hot, and the grape Kool-Aid ice-cold. Cathlean had done a great job on the meal, so Alex complimented her with every bite that he took. She sat across from him, smiling to see him enjoying the food so much. She seemed to be in one of her rare good moods, so Alex relaxed and told her about a few things that had happened at school on his first day. He, like Sherrette did while talking to Miss Ida, deliberately avoided mentioning Sherrette in any of his conversation with Cathlean about his day. He would save that part to share with John.

Just as Alex finished dinner, John came home. He too, asked Alex questions about school, so Alex excitedly repeated some of what had happened at school. If Cathlean wasn't present, he would have been tempted to tell his dad that Sherrette would be calling later, but instead he held his secret, and after catching up with John, he went off to his room, where he tackled his homework with gusto. He was a good, conscientious student, and most of the work that first week was review for him, so he had no problems completing the assignments. As he'd indicated earlier, Bio-Chemistry was new to him that year, so it would present the most issues. If he ever got stuck, he wasn't too worried because John could help since he held two master's degrees, one of which was in chemistry. Alex completed his work in short order, rushed through his shower, and was scrubbed and in pajamas by ten o'clock, staring at the telephone, willing it to ring as he impatiently awaited Sherrette's call.

He must've dozed off because suddenly the telephone rang, and upon looking at the clock, he saw that the dial showed 10:30 p.m. When he blindly snatched up the telephone, he even accidently popped himself in the face with the receiver in his eagerness to get to the call.

"Hi, Alex," a whispering voice said. "This is Sherrette. I can't talk too long because my mum may wake up and hear us, but I wanted to talk to you before I go to sleep." She sounded drowsy herself.

"Silly girl, I know it's you. Who else would be calling me at this hour?" he said, laughing. "So tell me what's going on. Did you get homework today? How are you?" His tongue tripped over the words because she made him so nervous every time he spoke to her. He forced himself to relax and regulate his breathing.

"Well, which question do you want me to answer first?" she asked, giggling flirtatiously.

"You're laughing at me, and I'm trying to be serious," he complained. "So, how are you? I suppose we can start there."

"I'm doing just as well as I was when you asked me earlier today. I finished all my homework, which was a whole lot! I expected that my first year of high school will involve a lot of work, so I'm not too surprised. What about you, English? Oh, do you mind that I call you that?" she teased.

"I did all my homework too. I had a lot of it, but I guess these last two years of high school will be serious preparation for sitting for my general certificate of education (GCE) examinations. I would have had to do the same in England, anyway, so no problem there. And, yes, I think it's cute that you call me 'English.' I don't mind at all." He didn't add that he would always associate that nickname with her and that he thought it was special and intimate. "So, Miss Sherrette, what nickname should I call you? Wait, I know, I'll call you 'Sherr.' What do you think of that, hmmm?"

She giggled. "I think 'Sherr' will be just fine, reminds me of the American singer Cher, but English, I have to go. I believe I hear my mother in the bathroom. See you at school tomorrow."

"For sure, Sherr," he said, her name a caress on his tongue.

"Got to go now, bye!" she said, quickly hanging up.

Alex slowly hung up the receiver, a huge smile on his face. He jumped up, used the bathroom, and returned to bed, falling into a deep sleep until he was awakened by his alarm clock at 6:30 the next morning. He sprang up, got ready, ate breakfast, then rushed off to school to see his "Sherr."

As usual, he'd met up with Ainsworth and a couple friends by the time he arrived at school. He didn't see Sherrette until lunch time, when he and his boys joined her and her friends so they could all eat together. He and Sherrette again agreed to meet after school, establishing a routine that would define their association and relationship for the next few months: lunch together, meeting after school, and telephone calls right after homework, and after Miss Ida had retired to her bedroom at night. Alex no longer bothered John about dating Sherrette since he was already able to see and talk to her every day anyway.

Being the natural athlete that he was, he tried out for and of course made the soccer, volleyball, and basketball teams. In addition, he ran track, the 800 meters being his event of choice. How he managed to balance these activities and keep up his academic grades was a miracle, but he seemed to have no problems doing so. He discovered that the second term curriculum at Ecumenical High was comprised entirely of sports; all the students would be divided and placed into five main groups named after past benefactors of the town. Alex wanted his reputation to be in place before he really had to prove himself. Sherrette was even able to attend a few of his events whenever she could convince her mum that it was necessary for her to stay late at school to support the athletic program.

Alex was falling more and more in love with Sherrette each day. She was as necessary to him as the air he breathed, and from where he could see, she reciprocated. He found himself trying to devise ways to sneak around and see her away from school and her chaperones: Miss Ida, Myrtle, or Tanzie.

CHAPTER 11

One weekend near the end of the first term, Alex got his wish when the Third-Formers had a chance to go on a nature trip to visit a Mayan ruin in the Punta Gorda District. There were numerous ruins scattered all over Central America, especially in Guatemala and Belize—both mutually claimed and shared some Mayan ruins, such as Chichen Itza, because it straddled both countries. One of the highlights during the year was for schools to be granted the privilege of visiting such historical, residential sites of communities, history, and artifacts left behind by the proud, modern-thinking Mayan civilization, a very ancient civilization of people rumored to have a direct lineage to the gods.

A few select First- and Second-Form students were also invited to go along on the adventure based on their excellent grades; Sherrette was one of the few chosen. Miss Ida was reluctant to allow Sherrette out of town, away from her supervision, but she was eventually pacified when the history teacher, Mr. Brooks, made a special trip to her home to sit down and convince her that the trip would be well-supervised and was very well earned by her daughter and the other few invitees.

Alex was over the moon with joy! He couldn't believe that he would have Sherrette to himself for a whole three-day weekend. In his mind, this could count as their first official/unofficial date. He figured he would finally get a chance to work on their relationship, for that's what it was to him—not puppy love, but a relationship. The bus would leave on Friday morning, so John made sure he dropped Alex off at the pickup point on time. He had a brief moment of worry when Alex pointed out Sherrette sitting there at the bus stop waiting too. He looked from her to Alex with a puzzled frown on his face as he tried to figure out what he was missing.

The way Alex's eyes lit up, John knew his son was more in love than the last time they'd talked about Sherrette.

"You didn't tell me your little girlfriend would be on this trip, son. What's going on?" he asked.

"Nothing, Dad. She makes good grades, so she was picked to go on the trip. I had nothing to do with it." He tried to look innocent, shuffling his feet awkwardly, not quite meeting John's eyes.

"You'd better not do anything I wouldn't do, but I think I should say something to Mr. Brooks."

"No, Dad, please, you can trust me? Don't embarrass me by saying anything to Mr. Brooks. Nothing's going to happen, I promise!" He clutched at John's arm, trying to stop him in his steps.

John hesitated, staring into Alex's eyes. "You'd better be on your best behavior, you hear me?"

"Yes, Dad, yes, I promise." Alex's sincerity must've convinced John, who just hugged his son and waited until he got on the bus, which had just pulled up. John nodded at Sherrette, waving at both of them as the bus took off. John walked back to his car, head bowed thinking hard, wondering if he should tell Cathlean that Alex's "girlfriend" was also on the trip going far away, way out of town. Then he remembered that Alex had always been levelheaded, had never been in trouble, and usually exercised good judgment. Maybe this time was different, if the gleam in both their eyes meant anything. John was going to try not to worry too much; after all, he too had a three-day weekend to spend with Cathlean, which he hoped would work in his favor—especially if he had anything to do with it.

When John got home, Cathlean was still asleep, so he quickly undressed, climbed into bed next to her, and pulled her into his arms. She stiffened, turning her back to him, mumbling that she was sleepy and requesting that he just please leave her alone. He still tried holding her, figuring she'd at least let him "spoon" her, but she cruelly and rudely pushed at him, causing him to almost fall off the bed.

He became sad at the thought that she still didn't like to sleep with him or engage in any sexual activity with him. He'd hoped that as the years went by and Alex grew older and pursued interests outside the home, Cathlean would warm up to him sexually and they would "go at it like bunnies"! Alas, it wasn't to be . . . instead she seemed colder than ever and had resumed occasional visits to the Booty Bunker to hang out with the girls. John just had to accept the fact that she would never truly be happy with him even though they'd been together a while; he also didn't know what to do about it.

Alex, in the meantime, was having a wonderful time. He sat next to Sherrette and happily joined in the songs that everyone was singing. Folk music had arrived in Belize with a vengeance, and everyone lustily sang along to Simon and Garfunkel's "Bridge Over Troubled Water," accompanied on the guitar by one of the white Peace Corps teachers who taught at the school. Everyone loved the Beatles, so they joined in on a few of those songs, too. Between the songs the kids learned from church, from school, and from listening to the one local radio station choice, Radio Belize, they also sang some local and traditional songs—the dirtier, the better. Mr. Brooks and Ms. Bucknor half-heartedly protested some of the song lyrics but decided to ignore songs like "Barge Turnover":

> Barge turn over, barge turn over, big fat Jerry made the barge turn over.
> Barge turn over, barge turn over, big fat Jerry made the barge turn over.
> Where was Jerry when the barge turned over? Under the bow peeling his banana!

This song seemed pretty harmless on the surface, but it was the stressed words like "banana" that caused you notice the innuendo contained in the lyrics. After singing this one several times, the kids launched into serious songs like the new release by George Baker, "Una Paloma Blanca" ("A White Dove"); these songs were a salute to their Hispanic heritage, even through the lyrics were English:

> When the sun shines, on the mountain, and the night is on the run,
> It's a new day, it's a new way, and I fly up to the sun.
> Una paloma blanca, I'm just a bird in the sky; una paloma blanca,
> over the mountains I fly,
> Yes, no one can take my freedom away (oh no one can take my freedom away)!

Next they lapsed into "Jesus Loves Me, This I Know" and "Michael Rows the Boat Ashore," gospel numbers that most had learned in church or in Bible summer camp, when American evangelists came to minister to the Belizean people. They sang "Michael Rows the Boat" in the "rounds" format: different groups making their entrance at different points in the song. Everyone laughed as they sometimes got confused; the trick was to stay in place in the song with the group with which you entered at the start, but some people just couldn't keep up!

Finally, they closed the song session with a funny Garífuna song called "Fadiri" ("Father/Priest"), which tells the story of an old woman who goes to church to ask the Father for bread. The priest doesn't give the woman any bread but instead gives her the *misericordia* blessing in Latin.

Alex didn't know all the songs, but he hung in there, singing with gusto. Sherrette sang high and clear in her beautiful, angelic voice, charming all who listened. Everyone sang until they were hoarse, and because the trip was going to take about four hours, some quickly settled down and went to sleep. Sherrette also started nodding off, and Alex swelled with love as she turned and lay her head on his shoulder. He reached his arm out in a sneaky time-worn move, laying it on the back of her seat.

Teachers had already warned students about fraternizing with one another on this trip, and they glaringly frowned on public displays of affection. Alex was their favorite because he was smart, and they all loved Sherrette because she was pretty, so they pretended not to see them cuddling in the seat. Besides, Alex and Sherrette, there were other couples on the bus, including some of the teachers. The folks in charge decided they'd ignore what they were seeing for the moment, figuring they would remind students of the rules later when they arrived at their destination and got settled in.

The bus chugged along at a good pace on the narrow, winding roads commonly found in Belize and many Third World countries, where money for infrastructure and road construction was scarce. Several times the driver had to pull over to let other vehicles go by, and eventually the bus stopped at a small town at about the halfway point so the travelers could stretch their legs, buy food and snacks, or take a bathroom break. Once everyone was corralled back together after about twenty minutes, the driver took off again, for an uneventful second leg of the trip. The coastal highway they traveled on ran parallel to the Caribbean Sea, azure blue and glistening brightly in the morning sun. To those who stayed awake and cared to appreciate it, the sea appeared calm and placid, like clear turquoise jewels. Such scenery could not have been man-made but God-created; it was truly a sight to behold!

CHAPTER 12

When the bus finally pulled into a large clearing in Punta Gorda, also known as PG, everyone disembarked and were assigned to the four lodges: two for males and two for females. Mr. Meggs read and checked off names from his trusty clipboard, assigning some lucky students rooms with their friends. Some weren't so lucky but had to accept where they were placed because, as Mr. Meggs stated, "There's no special housing, folks. This is non-negotiable!" He stared everyone down when he said this, expecting protests, but nobody said a word, knowing it would be pointless to do so. They also knew Mr. Meggs didn't play; he was considered over-the-top and just a tad crazy.

After he introduced the travelers to the staff of six, he warned everyone to "buddy up" to use the showers and bathrooms, which were a little ways off and separated from the main residence area by beautiful, trimmed yellow and red hibiscus flower hedges about six feet tall. He sternly admonished them that under no circumstances could they wander off, or they could have an unpleasant encounter with tarantulas, snakes, or scorpions. Everyone listened attentively, antsy and eager to go get settled into what would be their home for the next few days. Alex went off with Ainsworth to find their place, while Sherrette took off with her friends. Everyone wanted to freshen up before lunch, which had already been prepared for them by the lodge managers, Mr. and Mrs. Jenkins. There was a groundskeeper, a nurse, and a couple of cleaning women who also doubled as food servers.

In thirty minutes, everyone gathered in the large hall of the reception area, set in the center of the four lodges. Belizean favorites like johnnycakes, powder buns, tamales, potato salad, etc., were served; the agenda was pretty open that first afternoon, so students could go exploring after they ate, hang out in their lodge, or take siesta in the many hammocks strung up between trees and available all over. The trek to the Mayan ruin was scheduled for eight o'clock the next morning, so everyone needed to get to bed early to prepare for that, but otherwise, the afternoon was wide open.

After lunch, Alex and Sherrette found themselves in a boisterous group of ten students, comprised equally of males and females, heading off to visit the Mayan Ketchi village they'd passed about a mile back from the lodge. The students, feeling as if they had stepped back in time, were shocked to see little naked brown children, with straight black hair flowing down their backs, as they ran around and played in the red claylike sand. The children stopped playing, gathering curiously around the strangers, reaching out to touch their arms or clothes. Some of them were fat and cuddly, some thin and serious, but they were all adorable, and all appeared healthy and happy.

Old, toothless men sat at their doorsteps whittling spears, wooden fishhooks, jewelry, and other such items from wood they got from their own backyards. The students would find out later that the Jenkins couple from the lodge helped out their neighbors by taking the handmade items to market for the villagers once a month, making it possible for them to earn just enough money to get by. Women were bent over open fires, stirring pots of beans and meat, and testing and tending their *comals*, flat metal round surfaces on which they made corn and flour tortillas, and cooked vegetables for their meal. Some were scraping, cleaning, and roasting *piccari*, wild pigs found in the forest nearby.

Alex, ever the bold one, walked up to some of the women and asked them what they were doing. They seemed to understand him, and though he couldn't understand what they were saying, by pantomiming and drawing in the air with their fingers, they were able to communicate. The men seemed less friendly, but Alex approached the oldest-appearing one, probably the Village Elder, who had long, gray hair, was shirtless, and wore a white, diaper-looking wrap around his lower body. The man appeared wary and somewhat frail, but Alex charmed him into showing Alex how to pick bamboo stalks to cut and make whistles, how to whittle, and how to shape and sand the fishhooks he was making from the durable, multi-hued *siricote* wood growing abundantly in the area.

The friends couldn't wait to get back to their lodge, having learned a small lesson in humility that afternoon, because they could see that even though these people were not wealthy, they seemed to make do and appeared to be satisfied with their simple lives. After about an hour-and -a-half of walking, they arrived at the lodge, loaded down with freshly picked fruit and little gifts given to them by the friendly villagers, who gave of the little they had. The friends sincerely hoped they would get another opportunity to revisit the village before they left the area on Sunday. They'd have to wait and see.

Early the next morning, everyone was up and enjoying a scrumptious breakfast which they had to finish by 7:00 a.m. Fresh, ripe papayas, mangoes, bananas, guavas, watermelons, and honeydews was served in abundance, along with fresh, baked bread slathered in butter and jam and scrambled eggs provided by the numerous chickens, ducks, and turkeys scratching around in the soil at the lodge.

Mr. Meggs handed each student a schedule, which included an itinerary of the trip to the Mayan ruin, a list of ten items they were assigned to observe, analyze, and report on, and a brief history of the ruin itself. Everyone was in great spirits as they piled on to the bus, stomachs full, a sack lunch in hand, and properly dressed in shorts and stout walking boots. They all either carried or wore a jacket or cardigan to wear if it got too cold on the way back to the lodge later that evening.

Some with delicate skins, or those not used to or allergic to sandfly and mosquito bites, like Alex, liberally applied insect repellent to exposed skin on their arms, legs, and faces. Even though he'd been in Dangríga for several months, he had not become used to mosquito bites—his skin would break out in ugly red rashes, and the bites would swell, turning into large blisters. As a matter of fact, if asked, he would say that it was the one thing he hated about being in Belize. But he was not a complainer, having learned how to suffer silently by observing his father's interaction with his mother. Alex prided himself on being a trooper, one who always went along with the program.

They rolled out at precisely 7:30 a.m., some falling asleep right away, some students again singing camp songs and songs they'd learned in school. They sang some of the same songs they'd sung on their original trip from Dangríga to Punta Gorda (PG) and added a few other favorites. The trip would take two hours, so Alex and Sherrette again sat comfortably together, while other couples also paired off in spite of warnings against it by Mr. Brooks the night before. Teachers pretended that they didn't see what was happening; they said nothing. Everyone was excited, yet mellow and cooperative; nobody wanted to change the mood at that moment. They settled in for a relatively quick ride to the Mayan ruin.

After one hour and forty-five minutes, the driver turned off the main highway onto a bumpy path, somewhat overgrown with grass and strewn with dried branches. He pulled over, and Mr. Meggs gathered everyone around, waking the ones who were asleep and herding them all off the bus. "Listen up, everybody," he bellowed in the still morning air. "We have to walk about a quarter of a mile to the actual ruin site. As you all know, this one is called N'im Li Punit, or the 'Ruin of the Big Hat.' You'll see why when we get there. Observe everything, even minor details, please."

He paused, looking over the tops of his glasses. "We'll meet our guide when we arrive. Remember to stay together in buddy groups, and always keep your buddies in sight. We don't want anyone getting lost or snake- or tarantula-bitten, or stung by scorpions. Most of the time, if you leave those creatures alone, they'll leave you alone too. Anybody misbehaving and not following the rules will be brought back to the bus and will not get their opportunity to see the ruin. We'll go directly to the ruin with our guide. Make sure that you take notes to answer your questions because that assignment will be due by Friday. Any questions?" Nobody spoke. "No? Okay, let's go!"

They turned, trudging along at an energetic pace along the rock-and-grass pathway. Within a half-hour, they came upon a clearing in the midst of the forest. A wizened old gentleman came forward from a little shack constructed and perched upon six-foot high posts of blackened, tarred knotty pine. He looked like a throwback to another era and reminded the students who'd gone to the Mayan village yesterday of the old man who had taught them how to whittle. Alex blinked, thinking it must be the same toothless man they'd met before, but this one greeted them in a high, quivering voice: "Welcome to N'im Li Punit, everyone! I hope you enjoy your tour." He shook hands with Mr. Meggs and Mr. Brooks. "Now, don't touch anything unless I give you permission to. Don't wander away. Rest a few minutes and drink some water—but not too much! Then let us begin."

He pointed the visitors to a well, where a galvanized bucket and dipper sat on the edge. One of the boys threw the bucket in, and two of them hauled it up together. The water was sweet, cool, and clear; it tasted really good after their sweaty half-hour trek. After everyone had had a few sips, they regrouped and took off behind the old man. They'd only gone a few paces when they saw a huge pile of stained, dirty-appearing, weathered rocks. The largest piece was most of a Mexican-style hat, with smaller pieces of what used to be the brim, scattered on the side of it. Here and there, splashes of brilliant colors—red, pink, blue, green, and turquoise— could be observed in the bands around the adobe-clay-colored crown of the hat. "Now, what do you see, students?" asked Mr. Meggs expectantly.

"A hat!" they all shouted, disappointed by the old pile of stone. Some kicked at stray rocks on the outer edge of the ruin. Bugs and ants quickly skittered out of the humans' way.

"Yes, this, students, is the 'Ruin of the Big Hat'! It's one of the oldest ruins in Belize but one of the smallest, so it often gets overlooked. Tourists and students often visit Xunantunich, the 'Maiden of the Rocks,' in the Cayo District, or Altun Ha in the Belize District, but we have this one in our southern part of the country, so we don't have to travel so far. Some of you who speak the Garífuna language will understand the word *punit*, which means 'hat', because it's close to the Garífuna word for 'hat,' which is *bunidi*. Belize is famous for its mingling of cultures, languages, lifestyles, and architecture. Look at the way the Mayans mixed mud, clay, and sand to make building materials. We don't know what they used for mortar or to hold the material together, how they measured to such perfect scale without our modern-day equipment, or even how they created paint, but we know they were very skilled and creative."

The students slowly walked around the crumbling ruin, and the old guide warned them again not to touch anything because snakes and scorpions had made their home in parts of the hat. In contrast, beautiful multi-hued birds flew above, loudly scolding and calling to each other in the still, late morning air. At the far end, directly behind the most intact part of the hat, Mr. Meggs pointed out a *stella*, a tall concrete slab planted vertically in the soil; it was green, morass-stained, and weathered with age, the stella appeared to be propping up the hat. Thought to be loosely coined from the word *stalagmite*, this stella had hieroglyphic drawings of topless Mayan women carrying buckets on their heads, and men playing a game with large balls, which many archaeologists claimed was proof that Mayans had created the game that would later became known as baseball. They could see drawings of naked children with bowls of fruit on their heads and something that appeared to be toy spears in their hands. There was also a market square scene where fruit was piled up and spread out on what looked like mats or blankets, most likely for sale. Unlike the hat, there was no color or paint on the stella, making it appear as just a plain cement slab sticking out of the ground. In many places, the drawings were faint, almost obliterated, but this stella had held up in a most excellent condition.

Mr. Meggs reminded the students about the questions they needed to answer after viewing the ruin, so everyone got busy with that task. Some of the questions were fact-based, but many of them were subjective, based on personal opinion and reflection. The teachers and the guide walked around helping the students with the answers or clarifying what was needed in response to some of the questions asked. Everyone got involved with that part of the tour, but some grumbled loudly, disappointed because all the ruin was to them was a pile of dirty rocks! Appalled at the condition of N'im Li Punit, Mr. Brooks secretly agreed, having visited it as a boy when it was in much better shape.

He turned to the guide and asked, "What is being done to try to preserve the ruins in better condition?" The old gentleman shrugged his shoulders, stating that it was really too bad that nobody in government cared about ruins, especially not N'im Li Punit since it's small and not very well-known.

CHAPTER 13

A number of students who finished their assignment early walked away in a group to explore the other side of the clearing where the ruin was, looking closely at the ground in hopes of maybe discovering their own ruin, perhaps missed by other eyes in the past. It was a well-known fact that where one ruin was discovered, there were, most likely, many undiscovered ones. Unfortunately, the jungles eagerly reclaimed these abandoned ruins, making them undiscoverable, especially as time marched on. The would-be archaeologists walked around for almost thirty minutes, careful not to stray too far or to separate from each other, but alas, they did not discover any new ruins that day.

Soon, they headed back to the main area to join their teachers, the guide, and the others as they prepared themselves for the trek back to the bus. By now, high noon, the sun was at its zenith; it had gotten very hot and steamy in the tropical jungle air, so everyone was panting and sweating profusely. Even the big hat appeared to glisten in the noontime sun, its vivid colors almost blinding to the naked eye. Everyone gathered once more by the well and had some cool water, which had remained cold and refreshing in spite of the warm day. After they'd all drunk their fill, they thanked their guide and started walking back to the bus. The guide accompanied them part of the way, and, with a sad wave of his hand, he returned to his lonely home atop little N'im Li Punit.

The group was quiet as they hiked back to where they'd left the bus; some felt they were on hallowed ground as they became overwhelmed by the almost-tangible spirit of the Mayans. Mostly, they were contemplating the fact this area that had once been inhabited by a great, powerful people, now almost completely forgotten—a lost civilization disrespectfully relegated to grudgingly occupy a few pages in history books about Central America, an empire which had now degenerated into ruins.

Alex and some of the stronger hikers arrived back at the bus, where they sat around and cooled off as they awaited their colleagues. Soon after everybody had arrived at the bus, the teachers advised everyone to sit and eat their lunches. They each had a pack of cold fruit, a sandwich, chips, and soft drinks. In a cooler, there were also frozen popsicles known as Ideal and the sweeter, richer version made with condensed milk, called Milky Way. Everyone ate their fill, including their driver, who had remained behind, sleeping in the bus while his passengers were gone. A few students, still in a contemplative mood, talked among themselves about their visit to the Mayan ruin, and some even noticed that a few of the rocks in the bus stop area resembled those at the ruin site.

That again started some of the more adventurous students on the path of searching for ruins around the immediate area where they were sitting. Sherrette's friend, Alicia, found one promising piece of pottery that everyone agreed looked ancient and could potentially be a piece of Mayan civilization. Soon, it was time to head back; Mr. Meggs promised that he would get the shard of pottery to the experts and that if it was indeed authentic, maybe he and a small group could return in a few months with an archaeologist to check the viability of the area as one where Mayans may have formerly lived. The students, overjoyed that they could maybe make a contribution to their country's history in such a significant way, could hardly contain themselves as they headed back to the lodge. All was not lost: the tour of the ruin that many had decided was a waste of time was ending on a really good and promising note.

When the bus arrived at the lodge around 4:00 p.m., everyone piled out, tired but happy for having gone to the outing. They had two free hours before dinner at six, so people went off in groups to pursue their own activities. Alex, Sherrette, and their friends who had gone to the Mayan village were trying to decide if they wanted to return but eventually decided they had had enough of the Mayan cultural experience for one day, so they would pass. Mr. Jenkins, the manager of the lodge, told them that there was a small river a little ways down and that maybe some of the visitors would like to go fishing. A few jumped at the opportunity, and after getting some bait and fishing lines from the cook, they skipped down to the river.

It was a very beautiful day; the water sparkled like diamonds off the surface of the river, which was so clear that the wannabe fishermen and fisherwomen were able to see all the way to the bottom where large, fat fish rested or flitted through the water. Tilapia and a local favorite called *buttersii,* so named because of its buttery, melt-in-the-mouth texture, were plentiful. Even the dark, multi-limbed, menacing Black Mangrove trees standing tall above the water here and there, and as far as the eye could see, could not deter from the beauty of the river. The students, having been warned not to go into the water itself, due to its deceptively calm surface but deadly undercurrents, sat on the pier, legs dangling safely above the water, and cast their lines in with gusto.

They lowered their voices as they sat there because the would-be fishermen knew that to be noisy during a fishing trip would guarantee that they would not catch any fish. Sherrette sat next to Alex, of course, helping to bait the hooks, but scrunching up her face at the raw scent of chicken innards that they were using for bait. She didn't complain even though she could get away with being a prima donna with her looks. Sherrette was definitely not a bratty or spoiled girl; she was down-to-earth, natural, and unpretentious, which is one reason why Alex found himself falling for her.

The afternoon lazily crawled by. Alex found himself listening to his friends as they told the old often-repeated lore about sirenlike women called *suruciu* (meaning "naked" in Garífuna) or *sucias* (meaning "dirty" in Spanish). Somehow, the two terms were interchangeable, though, paradoxically, it was said that the women were not at all dirty but outrageously beautiful with long, wavy, dark hair covering their breasts and hanging to their curvaceous naked hips.

George, musing about *surucius,* suddenly blurted out, "Hey, so I heard they go around topless, walk on water, and lived in the mangrove branches in and near rivers." The others looked at him. Nobody needed to ask what he was talking about; the creatures were occupying everyone's mind.

Albert joined in. "And they're so irresistible that they often lure fishermen away! My uncle, who's a fisherman, says he was told that if he ever saw one of these ladies, he should just try to run away."

Somebody else piped up. "But if they can't run, they should never look directly into the woman's face. One or two men who'd survived a *suruciu* encounter claimed that they'd become paralyzed in her presence and had only escaped because they'd seen her but she hadn't been able to see them."

Miriam shuddered dramatically. "Yeah, if a fisherman makes eye contact, he will jump off a pier or leave his boat to follow the stunningly beautiful women, never to be seen or heard from ever again!" She pantomimed a fast walk away from them, swaying her hips, and clowning as she did so.

Cliff boasted, "Hey, my own grampa, Baba Ben, had been one of the *surucia's* victims, and my mother, Baba's daughter, would be horrified if she knew I was here fishing near mangrove swamps. Oh, but what about Tata Duende? I heard he's a frightful and deadly one. Maybe he's nearby too!"

This mythical creature had roots in the Spanish influence on Garífuna-Belizean folklore. The word *tata* meant "daddy," and *duende* meant "goblin" or "imp." Mention of this "daddy goblin" struck fear in the hearts of children and adults alike. He was said to be a very ancient dwarflike creature, with a long, flowing white beard, a top-hat, and evil eyes that glowed red, especially when he focused on a child before snatching it away, never to be seen by its parents again. Children were cautioned never to be alone at night or wander far away from home. When parents needed or wanted to curb their would-be-wayward children, they just had to invoke the name Tata Duende, which was exactly how *their* parents had kept *them* in line. This was generational scare tactics at work.

Alex, horrified but trying to appear brave and nonchalant, scoffed at Cliff. "You people sure are crazy to be making up all this stuff. Stop, I don't want to hear any more!" To him, the *surucius* his friends described sounded like mermaids, which everyone knew didn't exist, right? Tata Duende—what? Please! But he shivered a little, pulling Sherrette closer to his side in a protective stance.

CHAPTER 14

About an hour into the fishing trip, Ainsworth grumbled, "man, Al, this is crazy. We didn't get a single bite in a whole hour? George caught ten tilapia, Albert snagged five buttersii, but you and me, we caught nothing? We should pack up now and head ba—" Before he could finish his sentence, there was a mighty tug on his line; if he hadn't been firmly planted on the pier, he would've been dragged into the water. "Hey, help me here, help!" he shouted, struggling to hold on to his line. Alex reached over to help, but whatever was at the end of the line was huge and ready for a fight.

"George, Albert, please come over here and help us!" he said as he and Ainsworth wrapped the line around their fists and prepared for battle. The guys came running over, and they all pulled on the line, letting it out and tightening it over and over so that whatever was there would begin to tire. Soon, the line slackened, and they pulled on it halfheartedly, thinking whatever had been there was gone by now. However, they still felt the weight on the line, so pooling their strength and putting their shoulders together, they gave a mighty heave, pulling up what was at least a thirty-five-pound fish.

"A tarpon," Ainsworth shouted excitedly. "Guys, we caught a tarpon!" They pulled with all their might, and when the big fish flopped on to the pier, one of the boys hit it on the snout with the heavy wooden fishing box. It jumped around some more, still fighting, angry at being captured, but Alex quickly threw a burlap sack over it, drawing the mouth of the sack closed and tying it up with some rope they had. The girls excitedly gathered up all the fishing gear as Alex and friends fought to carry their fine catch; they couldn't wait to get back to the lodge so they could have fish for dinner.

When they got back, Mr. Jenkins couldn't believe it. "My," he said, raising an eyebrow, "didn't know we still had big suckers like this one 'round here. Looks like a tarpon, which can be a freshwater fish. Must've lost his way at the bar's mouth where fresh and saltwater meet, trying to get back out to sea. You boys did good . . . which of you actually caught it?" He looked at them in wonder.

"Ainsworth did, sir," Alex said, pointing to Ainsworth and proudly slapping his buddy on the back.

"N-no, we all did," Ainsworth stammered. He hated attention and wished Alex had taken credit.

"Come on, stand around let me get a picture, then we can gut and fry this monster!" Mr. Jenkins said. "Doesn't really matter who caught it. You all get to boast that you caught the biggest fish around here in over twenty years! Smile big for the camera. Say cheese!" And he snapped the picture, promising to get each one of their home addresses so he could mail them a copy of it. Mr. Meggs also asked for a copy to enlarge and mount over the door of the history classroom; he was so proud that his class had done well. He wanted to be able to have bragging rights, too!

Then, Mrs. Jenkins and one of the other kitchen helpers got busy scaling, gutting, and frying the tarpon, along with the tilapia and buttersii that had been caught earlier. There was enough fish for everyone to get a decent-sized portion; it was served with coleslaw and plantain chips made by slicing and frying up green plantains (large bananas) found all around the lodge. Everyone washed the food down with Kool-Aid, and that delicious dinner was followed by generous helpings of creamy rice pudding, coconut or jam tarts, and homemade ice cream made from soursop fruit.

By the time dinner was over, everyone was full but not yet sleepy, even though this would be the last night of their trip away from home. One of the teachers, Mrs. Bucknor, decided that she needed to create a distraction for the students so they wouldn't try to go off and hook up with each other and get into trouble. She'd seen the look in some of her young charges' eyes. "Not on my watch!" she vowed, so she proposed that they have an impromptu talent show, giving everybody about fifteen minutes to prepare something they did well. Everyone was not expected to perform, but those who wouldn't couldn't wander off and were required to stay and watch the acts. Besides, everyone's presence was needed to vote a winner at the end of this "Evening of Talent."

Mrs. Bucknor asked all students interested in participating to give their names to her so she could work on the format of the program. Some people wanted to sing, some to act, and some wanted to do poetry. Alex decided he would do a Martin Luther King Jr. speech. Dr. King was his hero, so there was no decision that needed to be made regarding what Alex's performance would be. He tried to talk Ainsworth into singing a song, but Ainsworth declined despite having a lovely tenor voice. Sherrette agreed to sing even though she didn't like being the center of attention. By the time the show was ready to go, there were ten acts on the lineup: four songs, two poems, one speech, one juggling act, two comedy acts. The program would start at 8:30 p.m. so it could end at a decent hour because everyone had to get up early to pack and get ready so they could arrive in Dangríga by early Sunday afternoon.

The first item on the program was Rudyard Kipling's poem "If," recited passionately by Rupert Blanco. He was good, but the two songs that followed—one sung by Laura Lyle, the other by Joshua Jefferson—were great. Thomas Paul's juggling act was next and would've been perfect if he didn't lose one of the breadfruit as he was tossing it up. The breadfruit was green, hard enough to cause serious damage if one of the students in its path hadn't had quick reflexes to jump out of the way at the right moment.

Alex delivered Dr. King's "I Have a Dream" speech in his clear, British-accented diction, moving everyone in the audience to tears. At times, Alex sounded so much like the great orator that everyone could hear the passion and weariness in Dr. King's voice, as if he was right there in their presence and not dead for six years. Next came a comedy moment by Rick Campbell, exactly timed to lighten the mood at the very moment when it was most needed it. Lizzette Locario sang a quick, irreverent dirty ditty that almost had Mrs. Bucknor throwing her off the stage. Sherrette sang the "Lord's Prayer" by Malotte, her voice soaring and wrapping around the pure notes required for singing that hymn. With this boisterous crowd, a hymn should have been a downer, but it wasn't.

The last two acts were a Garífuna song entitled "*Abanh Uma,*" or "One Road," a crowd favorite performed by Larry Lyle, Laura's twin brother, who was just as talented as she. Gilly Gilchrist ended the round of performances with his comedy act but was barely allowed to finish it because it was a little dirty and contained a few choice curse words.

Everyone knew that Gilly aspired to be a comedian in real life; talk was that after graduation, he'd be going to California to live with an uncle while honing his skill as he appeared at comedy clubs in Hollywood and Los Angeles.

All ten acts had been presented. The audience now had the difficult task of picking the best one. They had all been surprisingly wonderfully presented, more professional in content and delivery than amateur. Mrs. Bucknor held up a hand to quiet everyone, then instructed, "All right, now everyone, you'll need to decide who has won tonight. Perhaps you can start by eliminating the non-winners. I don't want to call them losers because there are no losers here! Next, we can vote on potential winners, until we decide which act was the best. Who should we eliminate first, hmmm?" She peered over the tops of her glasses as the audience shouted. There were several Gillys, Larrys, Ricks, Lauras, Lizzettes, Toms, Joshuas, and Ruperts. Nobody called either Sherrette's or Alex's names, but it was so loud and chaotic nothing was getting done at all.

"Hold on!" Mrs. Bucknor yelled. "We'll have to do this a different way. Contestants, please come to the stage right away. I'll stand behind each person. Audience, please express your approval by applauding for your choice. Whoever gets the most applause will be the winner!" The contestants eagerly went back onstage, looking at their own friends and willing them telepathically to vote in their favor. Alex stood next to Sherrette, holding her trembling hand. She was shaking as she stood there, but he was very proud of her in that moment. He felt she deserved to be the winner because she was truly talented; it seemed like many in the audience felt the same way about her.

Mrs. Bucknor stood behind the first contestant; the applause and noise level from the audience were ear-splitting. As she moved along behind each contestant, it got louder and louder until the whole hall was shaking and vibrating. Soon, it became obvious that Alex, Sherrette, and Larry Lyle were getting the most and loudest applause, so Mrs. Bucknor asked everyone else to leave the stage. When only the last three contestants were left onstage, she slowly walked behind them, stopping at each one's back and holding her hand over his or her head so the audience could applaud for them.

The crowd couldn't decide between the three, but Sherrette seemed to get just a bit more boisterous applause than the other two, so she was eventually declared the winner. There was no prize, *per se,* since the contest was impromptu in nature, but the winner earned bragging rights to take back home with them. Everyone was happy for Sherrette, who blushingly accepted a bouquet of freshly picked hibiscus. Alex was especially proud of her; he really didn't mind losing to her at all. He even became bold and sneaked a kiss directly on her lips—their first kiss ever—while everyone looked on and applauded. Mrs. Bucknor frowned, but by the time she could protest, the brief kiss was over.

CHAPTER 15

Soon afterward, the festivities ended, and everyone wearily made their way to bed, sorry that their adventure and trip were about to come to an end. The travelers packed everything except for the clothes they were planning to wear on Sunday; it took them a while to settle down, but eventually everybody fell asleep after all the excitement of the day, afternoon, and especially that Saturday night.

The alarm went off at six o'clock Sunday morning so that everyone could get dressed and bring their luggage out to the front of the lodge. Next, they prepared to attend the mandatory 6:30 a.m. ecumenical worship service in the same room that the talent show had been held in last night. The service was a blend of catholic and methodist rituals since these two groups were the primary makeup of about 90 percent of the students. The other 10 percent was comprised of Seventh-Day Adventists, Anglicans, and Jehovah's Witnesses, who were allowed to be excused from the worship service all the others were expected to attend. Services were conducted by Mrs. Jenkins, co-manager of the lodge and also a deaconess and missionary of her multi-denominational church.

Directly after worship, everyone trooped into the dining room to partake of breakfast before they headed back home to Dangriga. As usual, breakfast did not disappoint. The students ate fried jacks, bread, flour tortillas, refried red kidney beans, fluffy eggs, sausage, and fried Spam. They drank copious amounts of Ovaltine, Brooke Bond black tea, Milo chocolate milk, freshly squeezed orange juice, mango juice, papaya juice, or a combination of all three. Everybody was handed a sack lunch for the trip back, and after hugging the lodge staff and grabbing their luggage, it was time for the students to pile onto the bus. After much confusion and noise, the bus took off at eight o'clock sharp, heading back in the opposite direction on the long, winding highway to Dangríga.

Some students halfheartedly started singing as they had done on the trip on Friday, but this time, it seemed lackluster and forced, so eventually they quieted down and fell asleep. They were tired and really just needed to rest because it would be time to go back to school the next day. The teachers, feeling good, breathed a sigh of relief, happy they had accomplished what they'd hoped to when they brought the students on this trip. There'd been no broken bones or emergencies, just a few mosquito bites, as expected, but nothing worse than that. None of the students had hooked up with each other sexually, at least not that the teachers were aware of, so they were reasonably sure there would not be any pregnancy scandals in nine months as had happened on at least two class-trip occasions in the past. There would be no stammering explanations needing to be offered to irate parents upon finding out that their little darling was a mother- or father-to-be.

Alex, again allowing Sherrette to lay her head on his shoulder, smiled as he thought about the little kiss they had shared the night before. He wondered how his parents had fared; now that he had a moment to think about them, he hoped that they had enjoyed their time together, but he was doubtful. He was smart and could feel the growing distance between John and Cathlean, a distance that he could see Cathlean encouraging. He worried that she was becoming bored because his dad had shared that she was starting to frequent the Booty Bunker again. Alex shook the negative thoughts away; he would enjoy the last hours with his girl and let his parents worry about their own issues.

In two hours, the bus arrived at the halfway point between PG and Dangríga; Alex shook Sherrette awake, and they joined the other groggy travelers getting off the bus for their bathroom break. Everyone walked around to stretch their legs, and upon returning to the bus, they began eating their lunches. The sandwiches, fruit, and chips were very much appreciated and enjoyed, and in half an hour, the bus was rolling out for the last leg of the trip.

CHAPTER 16

The countryside appeared quiet and sleepy in the afternoon sunlight; many villagers and inhabitants of the small towns they passed were attending church, as Belize was primarily a Christian country. A large percent of the population was Roman Catholic, the second largest group Methodist, third Anglicans, and fourth Seventh-Day Adventist. The last group was comprised of somewhat equal parts of Nazarenes, Jehovah's Witnesses, Assemblies of God, Mormons, Baptists, and Muslims; there was even a small group of Rastafarians, "Lions of Judah" who followed the teachings of the late great emperor and prophet, Haile Selassie of Ethiopia—these were mostly of Jamaican descent who had arrived in droves and had settled in Belize over the preceding years.

To round out the group, and to prove that even in a small country like Belize there were wildly varying versions of religious beliefs, there was a small contingent of Mennonites, about 10 percent of all the religions in the country. Mennonites were similar to American Amish in appearance and belief, simple farm people who lived off the land, grew fruit and vegetables, and brought them to town on Saturdays and Thursdays in their horse-drawn carts to sell at markets. They also sold eggs, pork, beef, and chickens which they slaughtered and dressed right there at the time of purchase by their clients. They got a lot of business because they were all white in a country of mostly black and brown people who waited curiously to see and buy from the "special" folks as they drove into town.

Mennonites didn't believe in driving cars, so they brought their wares to sell and their families to town in buggies hitched to strong, beautiful horses or mules. The poorer Mennonites who couldn't afford a buggy had their female family members ride in the driver seat of their horse-drawn cart, while the men and boys walked alongside the plodding horses, holding onto the reins. The men, stern-faced, unsmiling, usually wore the "uniform" of plain black shoes, long-sleeved shirts, dark pants held up by thin suspenders, and felt hats on their heads. The women, a little friendlier but no less aloof, wore laced-up shoes or boots and print ankle-length dresses or jumpers over plain white or pastel blouses, and they always wore lacy kerchief scarves tied on their heads. They wore no jewelry except for plain wedding bands. Interestingly, and perhaps even stranger, it appeared that rings were worn only by the married women, never by the men. One couldn't really tell if this was purely an indication of property ownership or if the marrying couples were too poor to purchase rings for both partners.

Curiosity aside, Mennonites, Amish-like folks, were hard-working, plain-appearing, dependable, no-nonsense group. Their children, dressed similarly to their parents, seemed to be the only ones to ever have fun: they ran around the stalls at the market on chubby little legs, their older siblings struggling to watch them as charged to do by their parents. Upon arrival at the market square, Mennonite youth, twelve to about twenty years old, helped with setting up and selling the wares brought to town. They worked hard, barely stopping for a short fifteen-minute lunch break, before resuming their place at their parents' sides. They did business briskly and were fair with their pricing, so they usually sold out within a few hours. They were popular with the locals because their produce seemed fresher, their eggs were larger, and their homemade cheeses and breads more appetizing and appealing to the eye, much to the chagrin of the local merchants.

At the end of the day, they packed everything up, cleaned the stalls until they were spotless, washed and flushed everything down the drains designed to transport the waste to the river flowing through town, then took off back to the mountains from whence they came. They were ghostlike, never buying anything, didn't mix with others, barely nodded at folks they passed, or spoke only to customers who'd purchased fruit, vegetable, eggs, peppers, spices, and meat from them. They were a mysterious, religious group, though no one was ever clear about who or what they worshipped.

Alex and his fellow travelers finally arrived in Dangríga at about one-thirty in the afternoon. Parents were there, anxiously awaiting their weary children. Alex quickly kissed Sherrette on the cheek and let her hand go. He'd seen her mother, and he was not going to let her go at Sherrette for being seen with him. Sherrette jumped off the bus and ran to Miss Ida, while Alex waited until four or five of the other students got off the bus before he stepped down.

A beaming John waited near the bus. He grabbed Alex, enveloping him in a huge bear hug before grabbing Alex's suitcase and leading him to the car. Alex thought he smelled liquor on his dad's breath, but he shook his head and looked back. He saw Mr. Brooks and Mr. Meggs unloading luggage and other items, so he looked questioningly at John. Before he could say anything, however, John said, "Yes, yes, go ahead and help, but hurry up. We need to get home!" He smiled proudly at his son, thinking that Alex was a nice boy. John was proud that he and Cathlean had raised Alex well.

Alex ran off to help unload the bus. With his help, that of the two male teachers, and a few other people, everything was offloaded in record time. Alex shook hands with his teachers as they thanked him for his help and said they'd see him at school the next day, then he ran back to the car.

CHAPTER 17

"So, Dad, how was your weekend?" Alex asked, buckling himself into his seat belt.

"I missed you, Alex, but you're back now." John refused to be sad because Cathlean had treated him coldly all weekend long. "Your mum missed you too. She's fixed dinner. Bet you're hungry, eh?"

"We ate lunch on the way back, but I can definitely eat some of Mum's good food. What'd she cook, something special for her baby boy?" He grinned as he said this, bouncing up and down. He sobered up, saying, "Dad, I smell alcohol. What's going on, you drinking again? You know it's not safe for you to pick me up while you're drunk. Mum do something to you? Tell me the truth, please."

"Boy, I'm not drunk, so I just had a little sip because I was excited to be seeing my boy after he was gone so long. I'm fine, so I'd appreciate it if you leave it alone. Mum made you some potato salad and fried chicken, some butter rolls, and creamed spinach. Special enough for you?" He glanced over at Alex as he changed the subject. He added, "Oh, she made you bread pudding too!"

"Mmmm, bread pudding? I may skip dinner and go straight to dessert. But Dad, I'm really concerned that you're drinking. Do you have a problem you want to talk about? I won't judge you."

"You need to ask your mum if you can just have dessert when we get home. Hey, I just saw your girlfriend, did you have fun with her? And, no, I repeat, I don't have a drinking problem, Alex."

"Daaad!" Alex wailed. "Please don't make fun of me, and don't change the subject. Sherrette and I are really in love. She is very special, but I'm worried about you."

123

John pursed his lips and completely ignored the question about drinking. "Just go slow as I've said before. You have your whole life ahead of you. I know you're sixteen, but you're still not full-grown. And you still have two years of school to finish, then you'll go on to college. Don't make any moves to jeopardize your future. She may be sweet and beautiful, but be careful." He put the car in gear, and they drove off.

John shut up after delivering his speech. Alex felt some of his euphoria from the trip dissipate as he contemplated his dad's situation, but then, he decided he'd better let it go for now. Within a few minutes, John was turning into the driveway of their home. Alex looked at John's profile and was surprised to see that John appeared to have aged while Alex hadn't noticed—or was it just over the weekend? Alex chose not to ask any questions about what had occurred; he figured he'd do so later. Right now, he braced himself for his first sight of Cathlean, but she didn't come to the car to greet him. It hurt a little that he'd been gone three days, yet she didn't seem anxious to see him at all. He climbed out the car, slamming the door with unnecessary force, as he grabbed his knapsack and trudged the few steps to the door.

As he shifted his gear and raised his arm to knock, Cathlean yanked the door open. "Welcome home, Alex. How was your trip? Go wash up for dinner, please." She stepped back.

"Hullo, Mum, I had a smashing time." He leaned over to hug her, but she sidestepped him.

"Go wash up, boy. Food's getting cold. John, you go wash up too. Come on now, both of you!"

And just like that, the peace that Alex had gained during the trip disappeared. Tension was suddenly very thick between him and Cathlean, so he turned and headed to his room. He threw his pack on the floor of his room and headed for the bathroom to wash up. *Some things never change,* he sadly thought to himself. He looked up at John standing outside the kitchen doorway. The silent communication with their eyes was enough for Alex to feel reassured of his father's love. Alex satisfied himself with the steady, warm color of John's love, which was what really mattered at the moment.

Father and son pulled their chairs out and sat at the table. Alex said grace, picked up the bowl of potato salad, and scooped a big helping onto his plate. He didn't think he was that hungry, but his mum's potato salad garnished with slices of hard-boiled eggs was the best. Her fried chicken, of which he grabbed a large breast, a golden brown, generously covered with spicy, crispy breading, was cooked just the way he liked it. The butter rolls melted in his mouth. Cathlean was a great cook as John's slightly sagging paunch could attest to. While John was active in the military, he'd been able to exercise each day, but now that he was retired, Cathlean's cooking was starting to settle around his mid-section. Alex, the athletic jock, made a mental note to talk to his dad about starting a workout routine next week, but for now he chowed down on the deliciously mouthwatering food.

Between bites, he regaled his parents with highlights of his trip, raving over the Mayan ruins, and his and other students' discovery of bits of pottery that they were waiting to find out if they were Mayan in origin. He saved the biggest story of all for last: the thirty-five-pound catch. After Alex finished telling the fish story, John immediately jumped up and came over to give Alex a congratulatory slap on the back, but Cathlean didn't move. She did seem interested in what Alex had to say, though, laughing out loud at some of the funnier moments that he mentioned. Alex was a natural-born storyteller, so he was sure to paint a picture for his parents to experience exactly what he had.

After eating, Alex hugged Cathlean tightly, for he'd truly missed her. She stood motionless, letting him hug her, but didn't reciprocate. Undaunted, Alex said, "Thank you for the food, Mum. It was wonderful. I'll have dessert later—can't eat another bite right now." He rubbed his stomach, pushed his chair back, and left the kitchen, heading for his room. He had homework to catch up on before school resumed the next day and he needed to get to it right away. If he finished early enough, he would try to call Sherrette too. He missed her already, after having been around her nonstop for the last three days. Alex smiled to himself, shaking his head; he just couldn't stop thinking about his girlfriend, main squeeze, or whatever he called her in his head!

CHAPTER 18

Life settled back into a predictable routine with Alex juggling classes, homework, and multiple student club memberships with sports and games, along with everything else. With the inexhaustible energy of the young, Alex seemed to have no problems keeping up. Third Form was typically hard anyway, since it was the first of two years where content and intensity of classes were ramped up to prepare students to sit for college entrance exams and focus on the general certificate of education, or GCE testing, in which England had directed that British territories like Belize needed to participate. Add a new girlfriend to the mix and the pressure was on, as they say.

At home, things seemed colder than ever between Cathlean and John, and Alex worried about them constantly. He had no problems staying out of the house, and out of their way, because of all his school and extracurricular activities, plus the few occasions where he could sneak off to meet Sherrette and spend a little time with her away from the watchful eyes of Miss Ida.

Late one evening, Alex was riding his bicycle down Ecumenical Way, heading for home, but the bicycle was wobbly and not working right. Alex safely pulled off to the side but was alarmed to see that he had a flat rear tire. No slouch when it came to fixing anything of a mechanical nature, he quickly pulled out his little tool box, got a spanner, and pried off the tire, only to discover that the inner tube was shredded. To his disgust, the damage was not something that could be easily patched, so Alex had to try to get a ride home get so he could his bike repaired. At that hour, there would not be many cars coming along, so Alex decided he'd better start walking. Undaunted, he rearranged his book bag, balancing it so its weight was more evenly distributed, and started on his long trek home.

He had gone about a half-mile or so when he heard a vehicle coming. When he looked over his shoulder, he saw a beat-up automobile, and as it approached, he saw his mum's old friend, Tooth. Alex was never so happy to see another person in his whole life! As Tooth pulled over, Alex could see him grinning, that gold tooth glistening as usual, even in the darkening evening.

"Bwai, Alex, English Man, whatchu doin' out here? Somet'ing wrong with yo' bike?"

"Yes, Mr. Tooth. I'm very happy to see you! My tire needs repairing. Can you give me a ride, please? I need to get to the store to buy a new inner tube."

"Ah done tell you, just 'Tooth', not 'Mr. Tooth'. No problem, man. Throw your books in the back. Let's tie your bike up. Maybe we can get to Lopez's before they close. Come on, come on!" He jumped out of the car, which to Alex seemed to be the very same one from eleven years before. The backdoor seemed to still be held closed with twine. Alex shook his head, thinking that some things never changed. Together they loaded the bike into the dilapidated trunk and tied the door closed.

While they drove the five miles to the bicycle store, Alex and Tooth caught up; Tooth was a nice fellow, if a little quirky, and he just loved to talk about his children. Alex held his breath, wondering if Tooth would say anything about a new baby in addition to the twenty-two he'd talked about months before, but Tooth must've read his mind because he said, "Well, Mr. Alex, I bin busy raising my kids, trying to take care of them because Belize trying to start mandatory child support collection. I don't need nobody to tell me anything or force me to take care of my children, you know? Nosiree, don't need that. And you, mistah, still sniffin' 'round behind Miss Ida's little gial? You betta not start having babies now, you hear me? Yo' way too young!" He eyeballed Alex fiercely.

"Stop it, mister—uh, please stop it, Tooth. It's not like that at all. You sound like my dad!"

"Oh no? Better keep it that way, young man, dem little gials are devious. Watch yo'self now!"

Thankfully, they pulled into the yard of Lopez's store at that very moment, so Alex didn't have to answer. They walked into the store, and when Alex found out how much the repair kit would cost, he panicked because he didn't have enough money on him. Fortunately, Tooth pulled out some loose bills and handed them over to Mr. Lopez, who quickly rang up the sale. It was getting late, and Mr. Lopez wanted to close up so he could go to his home at the top of the store and eat his dinner, the aroma of which had been wafting through the store all day. It was his favorite night tonight—pork chop night. He was already tasting the special seasonings Mrs. Lopez used in her cooking.

Tooth and Alex got back into the car, and within fifteen minutes, they got to Alex's house. John was pacing up and down in the driveway, clearly concerned because Alex was late. When John saw Tooth pulling up, he ran to the car and grabbed Alex in a bone-crushing bear hug as Alex climbed out. "What happened, Alex? I was so worried. Tooth, how're you, sir?" He shook Tooth's hand.

"Dad, I got a flat tire on my bike, and Mr. Tooth came along and helped me. Oh, please give him back his $20. He paid for the repair kit because I didn't have enough money." They unloaded the bike and book bag from the car.

"Thanks for taking care of my boy, Tooth. You're becoming our personal taxi service. First, you pick me up from the bar when I drink too much, now you're picking Alex up. How much do I owe you besides the $20?" He pulled out a wad of money and started thumbing through it.

"You don't owe me nuttin' but $20, and I was very happy to help your young man. Nice boy!"

"Come on, Tooth, I have to talk you into taking money when you drive me home from the bar. I owe you at least for gas for bringing Alex home," John protested, peeling several bills off the stack.

Tooth stepped forward and carefully took only one $20 bill from John, shaking his head. "This is enough. One day when I need it, I'll get money from you, but for now, thank you and good night!" He winked at Alex, turned, and walked away, whistling, then climbed into his car and left.

"That man's a lifesaver in more ways than one. Let's get your bike repaired, Alex. If we can't fix it tonight, I'll drop you off and pick you up tomorrow. We'll fix it by the weekend, don't worry."

"Dad, what do you mean about Tooth picking you up from the bar? Are you a drunk? What's going on? I've smelled liquor on you, but you haven't addressed my previous questions about this."

"Well, sometimes I drink, and he's been at the bar when I leave, so he gives me a ride home. Alex, leave it alone. I'm not a drunk. I just need a little every once in a while to take the edge off." He opened up the garage door, effectively ending the conversation and turning his back on Alex— and the problem.

"Dad, is it Mum? Has she done something? I'm worried about you," Alex pleaded.

"Nothing to worry about. Drop it, please. Now, let's fix this tire. Your inner tube is destroyed."

Alex knew that once John clammed up, Alex would not be getting anything more out of him, so they stepped into the garage and grabbed items they would need to start repairing the bike, but Alex was scared and worried for John. Alex clearly recalled the times when John had picked him up smelling of alcohol, but Alex had assumed that John had been depressed when Alex was out of town and had had a couple of drinks. As Cathlean became less and less available to spend time with John, he apparently turned to the local saloon for drinks, which provided needed solace and companionship.

Alex promised himself there and then that he would watch John and the situation more closely; Alex loved and adored his dad and worried about him constantly. Having decided this, Alex shrugged his shoulders and began handing John the tools as they were asked for. Thankfully, the bike was repaired in a short time; when they were finished, they washed up in the garage sink then trudged wearily into the house together. Cathlean wasn't at home, but she had left dinner warming in the oven, so they ate. After that, Alex went off to go tackle his long list of homework assignments.

CHAPTER 19

One Saturday afternoon, a few weeks later, Alex and his friend Ainsworth went out riding their bicycles. John had gone out to train a contingent of soldiers in weekend maneuvers, and Cathlean had gone with her girlfriends on a day trip to the border town of Chetumal to do some shopping for Easter, which was coming up in two weeks. Ainsworth, ever the adventurous one, challenged Alex to a fifteen-mile ride south to a deep-water quay known to the locals as "The Jetty." This was thought to have been one of the points of entry that ships used to offload or pick up goods and produce during the thriving days of trade between Dangríga and other parts of Belize. It had started falling into disuse and disrepair over the decades, but it had been revitalized in the mid-1960s and early 1970s.

For most of the trip, the ride was a comfortable one since the road was flat, with only one or two small hills that Alex and his friend traversed with ease. They were a little nervous about visiting this place because it was supposed to be a spot where disreputable folks committed disreputable acts like meeting up and getting together for illegitimate reasons: married men cheating on their wives, large drug deals, dumping of dead bodies, and other such types of activities were said to take place there because the law hardly ever patrolled the area. It was left mostly undisturbed; a lone watchman, occupying a small wooden kiosk mounted on elevated posts in the shallow water near the left side of the entrance, was the only inhabitant. It was rumored that the man was a drunk but that the Town Board and mayor had been ordered by the man's father, a wealthy resident of some power and influence, to install him in that very prestigious job.

After looking carefully around, Alex and Ainsworth parked their bikes and started the trek along the extremely long boardwalk, one that projected out about twenty to twenty-five feet over the water. It was beautiful, peaceful, and somewhat eerie, but the friends continued on, often having to jump over rotted wooden slats through which they could look down and see the deep water below. They walked three-quarters of the way across, but decided it was a little too dangerous to continue on the rotten pier. They decided to stick to exploring the hand railings, under which there were shallow alcoves where people could crawl in and sit to get away from the blazing sun or get shelter from the rain.

When they approached one of the alcoves, Alex stopped Ainsworth by tugging on his arm and putting a finger to his lips, motioning for silence. Alex thought he recognized a familiar voice, and out the corner of his eye, he saw a pink pump, one that he was sure he had seen an identical pair of in his mother's room. His eyes opened wide and, pulling Ainsworth down, whispered in his ear, "Shh, I think somebody's here. That shoe looks like one my mum owns. Look around the corner slowly."

Ainsworth did as Alex suggested and pulled back so fast he almost collided with Alex's head. "Hey, your mum's here. I think I see Albert's dad, Mr. Moss, too. Take a look!" He was breathing erratically, almost incoherent. Fearing that they would be heard, Alex pulled him out the way and looked into the alcove. What he saw made his heart stutter to a stop then resume pounding painfully. He motioned to Ainsworth that they should back away slowly and as quietly as they could.

Once they'd crawled backward a few feet, they both jumped up and raced helter-skelter to where they had parked their bikes. After Alex failed to mount his bike in two tries, he just grabbed the handlebars and raced as fast as he could, Ainsworth behind him, trying to get off The Jetty as fast as they could. They feared discovery at any moment, but apparently the watchman was either too drunk or asleep because, thankfully, nobody called out or tried to stop them.

After running about a quarter of a mile, Alex put his bike down and threw himself down next to it. Pale and shaking, he started dry-heaving and retching but was not able to empty his stomach or unsee what his eyes had seen. He put his head between his knees, sweating, panting, and shaking, and Ainsworth, afraid that Alex was going to pass out, said in a panicked voice, "Hey, Al, what did you see back there? Come on, tell me. Don't you dare pass out. Don't make me have to slap you!"

"Give me a minute, and don't you try to slap me!" Alex's voice sounded strange even to his own ears. He practiced some of his deep-breathing exercises he'd learned in diving classes and forced himself to calm down. "Ains, I saw them. I saw my mum and Mr. Moss. They were naked. I think they were having sex. My mum's cheating on my dad!" He wailed as his mind recaptured the images forever seared into his brain. He started gagging again, this time bringing up froth and saliva.

"Alex, you're scaring me. Don't you die on me, you hear? Are you sure you saw them doing it?"

"Yes. I wish I could say that I didn't, but I know what I saw. Poor Dad, he doesn't deserve this!"

"Alex, let's think about this. Please, you can't say nothing to your dad until you have real proof."

He put his arms around Alex's shoulder, attempting to calm him down. Alex allowed it for a few minutes as he got his breathing under control, then he shrugged Ainsworth's arm off and jumped up and climbed onto his bike.

Alex didn't say a word and just pointed the bike north and headed toward home. They rode together in total silence; once, when Ainsworth glanced over at Alex, he could see the tears flowing freely down Alex's face. Ainsworth's heart bled for his friend; he could find no words of comfort to offer to Alex. Alex was always the strong one who fixed everything and encouraged everyone else when they were feeling down or experiencing a crisis.

When they passed the bridge that separated the south side from the north side of town, Ainsworth forged ahead of Alex and detoured onto Front Street. Alex blindly followed, not asking any questions, which in itself was alarming because Alex always questioned everything. He was not the type to ever be a docile follower; he was always and foremost a leader. Once they'd gone another couple of miles, Ainsworth indicated that they should head for the beach. He forced Alex to follow him; when they got to the shed standing there, they dismounted, still silent, neither saying a word.

As they sat on the bench in the middle of the open-sided shed, Alex blurted out, "I'm not saying anything to my dad because I don't want to hurt him. Who knows, he probably already knows about this. Mum's not exactly been quiet about the fact that she doesn't care for or about him. He's only given her everything. I hope I never love so much that I give up my identity for somebody. And don't you snicker or say one word about Sherrette, Ainsworth, I mean it!" He balled his fists up.

"My mum does not deserve my dad. Did you know she's been back visiting that Booty Bunker place a lot lately? We should've known she was up to her old tricks with different men. You know what else is insulting? My dad says that my mum doesn't like sex, that most women don't really enjoy it, but she didn't look like somebody who wasn't having a good time. Maybe it's sex with my dad that she finds so distasteful!" He continued with dawning understanding and horrifying wisdom.

Tears welled up in his eyes and streamed down his face as he wiped them off. "I hate her. She's a cold-hearted bitch. We should leave her right here and go back to England, but I know Dad won't go, even though it's his home, which he left to be here with her. What am I going to do?" He was in such pain, he could barely articulate what he was feeling in that instant: a mixture of rage, anger, disappointment, and disgust, all fighting for dominance in this moment of utter betrayal.

"I don't know what to say, Alex. Normally, I would say that you shouldn't call her that horrible "b" word, but in this case, it's justified. I don't know what I'd do if I saw my mum in that kind of situation. Maybe you can talk to her once you calm down, but try not to say anything to your dad. Make her tell him what she did because he's so deep in love, he won't be happy with you ratting her out. What she did is foul, but maybe it's not the first time. You really should stay out of it, Al." Ainsworth looked at Alex directly in the face so he could stress how important this was. "Stay out of it!"

"I won't say anything, but I can't look her in the face right now. She makes me sick, literally!"

They remounted their bikes, and Ainsworth followed Alex to make sure he got home safely, then, as Ainsworth was about to leave for his own home on the other side of town, he came to a quick decision. "Hey, why don't you grab some clothes and come spend the rest of the weekend with us? My parents won't mind, and my little sister will be very happy to see you." That got a little smile out of Alex, but Ainsworth was really worried about what Alex would do when Cathlean or John came home. Ainsworth cared about his friend too much to leave him in such a volatile situation; he knew Alex needed a change of environment so he could clear his head and think things over. Alex nodded, agreeing that going to

133

Ainsworth's would probably help. He didn't want to face Cathlean at all today, so, moving like an automaton, he threw some clothes into a suitcase. They then exited the house together, side by side. The two young men had definitely done some growing up today.

When they arrived at Ainsworth's house, he quickly ran into the kitchen where he found his dad, Mr. Dennis, standing near the sink. "Dad, Dad, Alex needs to stay here for a few days. Please don't ask any questions. I'll explain later, but can he stay with us? He can share Robb's and my bedroom."

Mr. Dennis looked at Alex's troubled face and trembling lips; he noticed that the boy was trying his darndest not to cry—it was obvious that something was terribly wrong, but he trusted his son, so he turned to Alex with a big hug, and patting Alex on his back he said, "Welcome, son. It'll be fine. Let me talk to my wife, and we need to call your folks so they know you'll be staying over, but no problem at all. Ainsworth, go get some sheets for the spare bed in your room. Did you boys eat?"

"Thanks, Dad!" Ainsworth said, hugging his dad in appreciation. "We ate earlier. You hungry Alex?" At Alex's quick shake of his head, Ainsworth took him by the arm. "Come on, let's get settled in. I'm so glad you're here." They quickly left the room, heading toward Ains's bedroom.

Next day, after all the children got up and got ready for school, Mr. Dennis decided to drop the boys off after taking his daughter to school. Worried about Alex, Dennis thought it was the least he could do.

Later that day, Cathlean casually asked John, "Dear, why didn't Alex come home last night? I hope he doesn't plan to make that a habit." She had to work at affecting a concerned demeanor.

"I think he and Ainsworth are working on a project, which is why he spent the night. He'll be back tonight, don't worry," John said soothingly. "Will you need me for anything this week? I have to go on maneuvers in Mountain Pine Ridge with a platoon of the Belize Defense Force. As a matter of fact, if they need me more, I may be there for two weeks."

Cathlean raised a disbelieving eyebrow and glared at him. "What? Why am I just hearing about this?"

"Honey, I would've mentioned it but you didn't get home until late last night, remember?"

She flushed, turning guiltily away. "Oh, yeah, I remember now. Let me help you pack, baby."

John abruptly turned toward Cathlean, sloshing hot coffee on his thumb. He forgot the last time she had called him by a nickname like "baby." It was not her style to use loving, cute nicknames toward him; he wondered what she wanted from him now. Watching her as she sashayed away, hips swinging, he knew that whatever it was she wanted, he'd get and give to her. He couldn't ever deny her anything though he often detested his weakness where she was concerned. Cathlean, on her part, was oblivious to John's thoughts; she was just happy he'd be gone a day or maybe, if she was lucky, a whole week. There really *was* a God! She hurried along to their room to start packing John's kit bag.

John left an hour later, frustrated as hell and blue-balled. Cathlean had refused to give him any nookie even though he could be gone from her for up to two weeks. While she was leaning over the bed packing his gear, he'd made his big move, rubbing himself over her rounded bottom, temptingly displayed for his viewing pleasure. She'd suffered his clumsy attempts for a few minutes before pulling away, smacking him lightly on the buttocks. Even though John begged, Cathlean turned him down flat; she wanted some sex action but not from John—no, never from John, her loving husband.

John drove away thinking that he really needed a break from Cathlean. He was at home with her too much, but she wasn't sexing him the way he would've liked, so this outdoors maneuver was just the thing to get him away from what he lusted after. He would call Alex later and let him know he was at Mountain Pine Ridge. Alex was pretty astute, so John was sure that Alex would understand the occasional need for John to leave and get away from Cathlean. Alex was growing older and could already pick up on the nuances of John and Cathlean's relationship. John fervently prayed that Alex would find love with a sweet warm woman and not a coldhearted person like his mother Cathlean was.

CHAPTER 20

John made good time as he traversed the two hundred miles or so from Dangríga to Mountain Pine Ridge. The day was clear and beautiful; John could not help thinking that how cold and damp it would be in England at this time of year. He was a truly blessed "Adam" to be living in paradise; the only thing missing was his Eve. Within a few hours, John was pulling into the camp ground, where he was met by Captain Horace Gonguez, who saluted John sharply and hurried to help him unload his gear from the Mini Moke, John's favorite mode of travel. John breathed in the thin, clear air. Ah, he was where he felt most comfortable, in a military setting! He was ready to impart knowledge to another eager group of soldiers, whom he hoped would soak up what he had to say like brand-new sponges.

Maneuvers went very well; John called Cathlean on the second day to say that, as expected, he would be gone a full week. Cathlean protested vehemently, but John couldn't help but think that he also heard a sigh of relief from her because he'd be gone a while. That evening, John called Ainsworth's house to speak to Alex, hoping that Alex would've already gone home. Much to his surprise, Alex was there and quickly came to the telephone when Mr. Dennis called him. Mr. Dennis worked for the government so he, too, was also provided with a telephone to use at home.

"Hullo, Dad. I miss you, but I can't come home yet because we're still working on our project."

"I'm not there, Alex. I'm out on maneuvers for the next two weeks. You'll need to go home and keep Mum company." He listened intently for Alex's response; his son sounded strange to John.

"Well, we're not done yet!" he yelled, then, in a calmer tone, said, "Dad, I can't go home, okay? I'm not ready to deal with Mum yet." As he realized what he'd said, he added quickly, "Well, Dad, enjoy yourself. I have to go right now." John could hear him getting ready to hang up. Something was wrong; normally, regardless of how busy Alex was, Alex always looked forward to long conversations with John, but for some reason, Alex was rushing to get off the telephone tonight.

"Son, what's going on with you? What did you do?" Concern was heavy in John's voice.

"What did I do? Why does it have to be that I did something? Why don't you ask your wife what she did?" He raised his voice at John for the second time, then backed down, ashamed. In a quiet voice, he said, "Dad, I can't talk about this now and have to get back to my homework. I'm sorry. Please talk to Mum. Oh, by the way, Mr. Dennis just said I can stay here while you're gone."

"All right, I'll talk to her, but you should go home before I get back, Alex. Can you, please?"

"No, Dad. I'll come back when you get home. Good night." And with that, he hung up on John.

John, shocked, stared at the receiver buzzing in his hand. Alex had been borderline disrespectful while speaking to John. Something was wrong; John thought he should go ahead and return home immediately, but he'd given his word that he'd stay two weeks, and he was always a man of his word.

He shook his head as he hung up, hoping and praying that the issue would be resolved when he got back. For now, his boy was where he could continue with his schooling and not at home where he and Cathlean would fight without John there as a buffer zone between them. John's mind darted in different directions, wondering what Cathlean had done.

Anyway, John needed to concentrate on what he had to do; everything would work out during the next two weeks, and he was sure of it. Grabbing a jacket, he went down to the bar to get a couple of drinks before coming back to his room, where he would soon settle into a deep but troubled sleep. He would have an early start the next day, and he needed to be well-rested and at his very best. His soldiers would be looking to him for military leadership and combat survival techniques.

Alex continued to flourish at the home of his friend Ainsworth; his grades were as good as ever, and he enjoyed Miss Millie's cooking even more than Cathlean's even though Cathlean was no slouch in the kitchen.

Several times during the weeks that John was gone, Alex visited his house to pick up fresh clothes. He timed his visits to coincide with days when Cathlean was absent from home, which seemed to be all the time (he heard she was practically living at the Booty Bunker these days), so he could go in and out, picking up his stuff without running into her. He was still furiously angry at her and didn't want to have to speak to her.

Whenever he closed his eyes, he could see his mum writhing in the arms of Mr. Moss, Albert's father, and still had nightmares about it. He'd even taken to completely avoiding Albert when their paths crossed, but when Albert asked him what the problem was, Alex just told Albert to drop it, that there was nothing to talk about. The two of them hadn't been particularly close previously, so Alex didn't think he was missing much. However, he didn't want Albert or his siblings to experience the loss Alex himself was feeling regarding the liaison between Cathlean and Mr. Moss.

In the meantime, John was having a hard time applying himself to the military maneuvers. He couldn't stop thinking about Alex and Cathlean, but even though John wanted to question Cathlean when he spoke to her, he remembered Alex's pain-filled voice which seemed to suggest to him that the questions should be asked face-to-face. John's life took on a pattern: rise early in the morning, meet for maneuvers, break for lunch, continue in the afternoon, have dinner, then hit the bar for drinks every night before falling into bed drunk, then getting up next day and doing the same routine again.

Towards the end of the second week, John thought it would be best for him to leave a couple of days early. His concentration was shot; he missed his family, and he just wanted to get home to see what was going on there. He explained to Captain Gongora that he had a family emergency, then left Mountain Pine Ridge on a Thursday afternoon. John made even better time on the return trip, stopping only once for a bathroom break and gas; he didn't know why, but he had a sense of urgency that he absolutely needed to get home right away.

Over the years, John had learned to listen to the little voice in his head that he heard when there was impending trouble. He didn't know if this voice had first came into existence when he had been trained for the priesthood in his younger days, or if it had always been there lying dormant, but whatever the source, it had helped him out of many potentially sticky situations in the past. John's British troops often teased him about his "gift"; his Belizean troops called him "Obeah man" because they thought it was a magician's trick, the accuracy of which they'd often witnessed.

So John pushed on, passing through several picturesque villages and towns, as well as the fruit stands with delectable fresh fruit and roasted nuts set out for sale by farm owners, but not stopping to appreciate any of it as he normally would have. He was on a mission and just needed to get home. He was grateful when he finally entered at the Y-entrance to Dangríga, gunning the engine, and passing over the two bridges over the river running through the center of town, until at last, he approached his house. His other car was parked haphazardly across the driveway, meaning that Cathlean was home, but lights didn't appear to be on in the house even though it was just past dusk and already starting to get dark. John left his car on the street, thinking he'd go inside and surprise Cathlean first, then grab her keys and come back to park the car properly so he could safely pull the Mini Moke into the driveway.

CHAPTER 21

He made his way to the door, treading lightly so Cathlean wouldn't hear him and ruin his surprise. He turned the doorknob and stuck his key in the lock, but it wasn't necessary because the door was unlocked. As he stepped in, he noticed that the living room was pitch-black, but he could hear a strange noise coming from his bedroom at the back of the house. Puzzled, he approached the door, then recognized the sounds as low-pitched moans or groans. Thinking Cathlean was hurt and possibly needed help, John quickly grabbed his retirement gift musket from the drawer in the laundry room, where he'd left it temporarily after cleaning and polishing it before going out of town. Although it looked like a beautiful toy, the musket was a real gun, deadly and able to do some serious damage, as the British Army had informed John when they had gifted him with it at his retirement ceremony.

All of this ran through John's mind as he carefully took the safety off the gun and again approached the bedroom door, where he quickly threw the door open, snapping on the light at the entrance and cocking the gun as he entered the room. The sight that met his eyes was one he would never forget: Cathlean was completely naked, her sweat-slicked body sitting astride an equally naked and sweat-slick man—a *very* large, muscular man, John noted.

Both of them had their eyes closed, moaning, groaning, not in pain but in the throes of sexual passion and mutually shared bliss! Cathlean was making guttural sounds, moving in well-skilled downstroke motions on top of her lover as he held her by the buttocks and thrust up from the bed. John had never seen Cathlean that animated in bed before; as a matter of fact, he'd been led to believe that she was frigid or hated sex, so he couldn't believe what he was seeing or hearing. The loud click of the cocked gun must have penetrated Cathlean's sexual haze because she partially opened her passion-glazed eyes and looked straight into John's shocked, blue ones. Then she opened her eyes wider, but kept on moving on top of her partner, never pausing for a moment or missing a stroke.

As she became aware that John was standing there looking, she even smiled at him, a cold, evil little smirk which seemed to mock his lack of prowess in bed as she silently dared him to use the gun. Her lover, someone John recognized as Zeke, father of one of Alex's school chums, sensed a change in Cathlean's rhythm and slowly opened his eyes, as he strived mightily to achieve climax.

When he looked past Cathlean and saw John standing there frozen, cocked gun in hand, he pushed her up and off him, diving wildly over the back side of the bed. He put his arms up and uttered the words, "Hey, don'tchu shoot, white man. I'm leaving now. See you later, Cathlean. Got to go!"

He jumped up in all his naked glory, catapulting himself toward the open window. In a minute, he was hanging out the window, his legs and now-flaccid penis outside the window, buttocks still inside the room, while John's finger slowly came unstuck and he pulled the trigger, pointing the gun toward his rival teetering in the windowsill. Cathlean's lover quickly wriggled his way out, expecting to feel a bullet in his back or his bottom at any moment, but John pulled his aim at the last minute, intentionally missing the man. He didn't want to shoot the man's rear end but would've loved to have shot off that monstrous penis that Cathlean apparently preferred to John's little, pencil-sized one.

The size of the man's package and the fact that his Cathlean had been enjoying it in their marriage bed enraged John much more than the fact that he'd actually caught Cathlean being unfaithful to him. As they listened to the man fall through the window, then get up and run away, John slid the safety back onto the gun. He heartily wished that the clumsy fool had landed on the lid of the septic tank that sat mounted on the ground immediately below the Putnam's bedroom window. Most yards sported one of these disposal units designed to assist in keeping human waste contained. They were primitive, but they worked. John hoped that Cathlean's boy toy would have landed onto the septic tank and broke a hole in it with his monstrous penis so he could fall in and drown in its horrific contents.

John hardly ever wished ill of others, but this time was the exception and justifiably so. He turned to look at Cathlean, who'd carelessly presented her back to him, her naked body held away from him in rejection stance. She shrugged her shoulders carelessly then pulled on the sexy blue silk lingerie set that he had just bought her a few months before. John held himself still, watching Cathlean sadly. Afraid that if he moved any closer to her he would do her bodily harm, he reached deep inside himself for the discipline he'd learned, preached, and exhibited in his numerous years of military life.

His look was one of utter sorrow and defeat as he realized once and for all that he'd just been fooling himself for the last eleven years. He knew Cathlean didn't love him, but he didn't think she despised him this much as her ultimate disrespect toward him now indicated. He wondered if this was the first time she'd been unfaithful, how many times she had been, and with how many men. He felt hurt, stupid, and betrayed, and as emotions flitted across his face, all he could say to Cathlean was, "Why? And in our bed? I love you. I know you don't love me, but did you really have to do this?"

"Because you don't satisfy me and never have, pencil-dick!" she screamed in self-righteous rage. "All you care about is your damned military career. You're boring in and out of bed, and don't worry. I'll leave. You won't have to kick me out." She flounced to the closet, grabbed a suitcase from it, and started pulling clothing out the drawers, haphazardly throwing them into the suitcase. John could've stopped her because he'd bought the suitcase and all the clothes she was packing in it, but he didn't.

Fearing his legs would no longer support him, John sat down on the bed heavily, tears filling up in his eyes. "Why didn't you tell me how unhappy you were? I gave you everything. Go, I know you're going to that Booty Bunker whorehouse where I found you! And what are you going to tell our son? Did you forget about him?" He could barely finish speaking before giving into the tears. He wanted to use that gun to end his life and hers to shut up her lying mouth forever, but he knew he couldn't harm her because he loved her so much. He also loved Alex too much to make him a motherless statistic. Many crazy, disjointed thoughts swirled around in his head, leaving it pounding.

"I'm sure Alex will manage just fine. He can decide if he wants to live with you or with me, but I'm sure he'll choose you, Daddy. I'll explain to him later," she sneered. She turned and grabbed the telephone, calling for a taxi to come get her. In about a half-hour, good old Tooth, dependable cabdriver and friend, was there to pick Cathlean up. As he helped her off the porch with her suitcase, he was uncharacteristically quiet. He sorrowfully shook John's hand and walked away, then tipped an invisible hat toward John. In a few minutes, Tooth and Cathlean took off, the beat-up cab looking much nicer in the dusk than it really was, tail lights being quickly swallowed up in the darkness of the night.

CHAPTER 22

J ohn staggered back into the house, still in shock at what he had seen and not believing that Cathlean was gone. He wondered how he would tell Alex what had occurred, but now he wondered what Alex had been trying to tell him the week before. Had Alex found out about his mum's double life? John was proud of the fact that their boy was sharp and that not too much got past him.

John was anxious to talk to Alex, but when he looked at the clock, he realized it was a little late to try to call; it didn't seem like it, but it had only taken a full two hours for John's life to completely unravel. Alex was probably deep into his homework, so John decided he'd pick Alex up from school the next day and bring him home so they could talk. With a solid decision and plan in place, he got the keys and moved the car and the Mini Moke into their proper places in the driveway. Then he grabbed a blanket, got into bed in the spare bedroom, and soon fell into a peaceful, dreamless sleep.

The next day, John called out to Cathlean when he awoke, but when he got no answer, he looked up and saw that he was in the guest room. The horror of the night before crashed into his brain and caused him to struggle to get out slowly and painfully from bed. He felt old, used, and beat up, and he almost started to cry at the unfairness of it all. All he wanted to do was love his wife, but she had clearly chosen to reject his love. He thought of his parents back in England, how they loved Cathlean so, and he also thought about his brother, Geoff, who'd always thought that Cathlean was trash, couldn't be trusted, and was no good for John. *Well, brother, John thought, it appears you were right after all!*

John plodded to the kitchen and mechanically went about brewing himself a cup of Brooke Bond tea. Nothing fixed things like a cup of tea, he always thought. He really needed it today; he had to maintain that famous British stiff-upper-lip, but all he wanted to do was bang his head against the wall and wail. He remembered when his men would come to him with tales of heartbreak, how he'd always naively just told them to "buck up" and get past it, but he couldn't tell himself to do the same now that he was experiencing the situation himself. This was personal and hurt like a son of a bitch, but he would just have to deal with it starting right now, come hell or high water!

With that resolved, teacup in hand, he turned toward the bathroom, where he showered and shaved and had a long, leisurely morning. After all, he didn't have to pick Alex up until later that evening, so he had a whole day to get through, hour by excruciating hour. He decided he would go to one of the local restaurants to eat some Belizean food and take in the local flavor; that was always good for a little entertainment. Yes, that's what he would do instead of sitting around the house moping and hoping that Cathlean would decide to come back home. Even if she did return, he didn't want her thinking he was sitting around desperate and waiting for her. As a soldier, John knew that the best defense was a great offense, so he had to get a game plan or make it up as he went along.

So John jumped in his Mini Moke and took off for downtown Dangríga. He thought briefly of driving the car but could not bear the thought of getting into the car that transported Cathlean and her big-dicked lover to their tryst in his home. John was too raw to think that smelling Cathlean's scent and her perfume wasn't going to cause him to start blubbering like a baby, so the Mini Moke would have to do. Besides, that was his go-to vehicle anyway; John liked the feel of it, the masculinity of it, and the military feel of it, especially now that he felt he was under siege and at war with his unfaithful wife—and in his own camp at that!

CHAPTER 23

John slowly drove down winding, pothole-filled Commerce Street; it had rained early that morning, so the roads were wet and a bit muddy. Belizeans were used to the atrocious condition of their streets, so people walked around, jumping over puddles as needed, or lifting pant legs or frocktails to navigate through the mess. John had one destination in mind: he would go to Bluebell's, a little corner restaurant where he would be assured of a good, tasty meal and some great gossip.

As he turned at Commerce and Riverside and pulled into the parking lot, he saw Junior Reyes, a friend he had known since the first time he lived in Dangríga. Junior stood to the side, arms folded as he watched John park. As John got out the jeep and locked up, Junior approached him.

Throwing his arms around John's shoulder, he squeezed hard and slapped John on the back saying, "Man, John, I heard what that wife of yours did to you. I'm so sorry, but you know she don' deserve you right? Too bad it's so early. I would buy you a pint of Guinness to drown your sorrows!" He kept pace with John as they walked together, but John raised his eyebrows in surprise. John knew Dangríga was small and Belizeans loved to gossip, but this was absolutely ridiculous!

"Wait a minute, Junior, what are you talking about?" he bluffed, slowing down. He wanted to know how much people knew about his personal business, less than twelve hours after it happened. Maybe he needed to rethink going into Bluebell's if everyone was going to be this inquisitive.

"Oh, come on, Johnny, we heard you found Cathlean with that big buck she runs around with, heard she was sexing him in your own house. Always thought the woman was trouble, and she thinks she's too pretty for her own good." Junior looked John directly in the eye. "You sayin' it's not true?"

"Well, something happened," hedged John, "but, how did you hear about this already? Damn!"

"A friend called me last night after his friend called about Cathlean leaving you. You should've just killed her ass and that stupid man of hers. I would've if it was me. Doesn't that fool know the man code? You don't sex it up in a married woman's house!" He was righteously angry on John's behalf.

John eyes started filling up as he lost some of his appetite. Was he going to have to listen to this all day? It was not his idea of fun, and he wondered if he should've come out in public so soon.

"You know what, Junior, you seem to know everything that happened, so I have nothing to say. Matter of fact, I'm not hungry anymore, and I'm not going into Bluebell's." he started to turn back.

"Nonsense. You must go on with your life. Suck it up, man. Don't let her get her way and win too." Junior took John by the shoulder and turned him back toward the restaurant. He was not going to let John go home and lick his wounds by himself; he could feel John's shoulder, stooped and shaking, and he was worried about what John might do with himself if left alone. He always thought John loved Cathlean too much and had spoiled her rotten. The thing about it was that Cathlean was not worth it and had made it painfully obvious that she didn't appreciate John's efforts or took them for granted. Junior had himself been recently betrayed, so he knew what John was feeling.

John reluctantly turned and shuffled toward the restaurant, head down and eyes downcast. As Junior stepped ahead of him and pulled the door open, a hush fell upon the small crowd of ten or so people there. John could feel himself turning red, but as he tried to go back, Junior pulled him by the arm until he was all the way inside the door. As they walked toward an empty table in the back corner, conversation resumed, but when John looked at people, they wouldn't quite meet his eyes.

When John flopped down heavily in the chair, Mrs. Blanco, the plump proprietress and cook hustled forward, wiping floury hands on her previously pristine apron. "Oh, John-John, good morning and welcome! Although you may not think this is such a good morning, hmmm?" She raised her eyebrow over the tops of her glasses. "How about me bringing you your favorite breakfast, some flour tortillas or powder buns, scrambled eggs, and fried Spam or sausage? Oh, and a nice cup of Brooke Bond tea to wash everything down?" She ran out of breath as she motioned for her number one waitress, Juanita, to come forward with the teapot. John needed Mrs. B's best today.

John shook his head, gagging at the thought of all that food. "Please, no, Mrs. B. I couldn't eat anything. I'm just not hungry. And what do you mean it's not a good morning?" he asked grumpily.

"Nonsense, John," she said in a more serious tone. "You have to eat. Go ahead, Juanita, pour the tea and get Mr. John some o' that condensed milk he likes in his tea. Hurry, gial!" she ordered.

Without missing a beat, she pulled up a chair and parked it next to John. "Come on, John. I heard what happened, got me an earful when I went to market this morning. I heard that undeserving bitch-wife o' yours really showed her ass this time . . . literally! What that woman mean by bringin' another man into yo' house and bed?" Her Kriol accent thickened as she shuddered at the very idea. "I nevah liked that snooty woman anyway, walking around here like we didn't see her grow up po' and had to scratch her way till she wound up wit' you. You know you could've got a much better Garífuna woman, right? I know so many other women around here who would've been much betta for you!" She was so incensed, the spittle was flying from her lips as she spoke. "Juanita, pour di tea, gial. John, I don' want to get in yo' business—oh well, I already am—but Cathlean's a fool."

As John sipped his piping-hot Brook Bond tea, he wondered who in this town, if anyone, really liked his Cathlean. His Cathlean? He was going to have to stop thinking like that, he told himself. Everybody seemed to be saying the same thing: that she put on airs and carried on like she was better than everyone. He'd seen her act that way many times, but he always overlooked her actions because he'd been with her too long to be offended anymore. He knew she was mean to Alex and to others.

John tuned back in to hear Junior say in a hesitant voice, unsure if Mrs. Blanco was going to allow him to say anything: "That's exactly what I told him, Mrs. B." He pounded his right fist into his left palm for emphasis, "John's too nice to Cathlean. I woulda killed both her and her boyfriend." He looked at John who was forking up a big bite of scrambled eggs and sausage into his mouth. "You were, and still are, way too good for that tramp. I'm just worried about her nice, sweet child, Alex. That young man's got more brains in his head that his mamma does. You tell him 'bout this yet?"

"No, I'll tell him when I pick him up from school" John said, wiping his mouth as Mrs. B looked on approvingly. She always thought food was the answer to every ill in life, even when it came to getting over heartbreak—especially when it came to getting over heartbreak! She absently ran a hand over her well-padded figure; she'd experienced much heartbreak in her sixty-odd years on Earth and had the pounds to show for each experience.

Mrs. Blanco watched John take a bite of the powder bun, a sweet bread that she knew he always enjoyed whenever he visited her restaurant. She baked all her breakfast goodies the old fashioned way: a cast-iron pot set up on three bricks or large tin cans, with fire on top of the lid, and burning hot coals underneath the pot to ensure a lovely golden brown appearance all over, along with authentic Belizean flavor. She also loaded her powder buns with raisins and nuts so that they resembled dessert instead of a breakfast food. Her customers loved them that way, and she sold out every day by early afternoon. Those who wanted to be guaranteed Mrs. B's breads for evening teatime had to place orders by noon each day, no exceptions. Well, maybe John was the exception; he was special.

Pondering on John's response, Mrs. Blanco suddenly blurted out, "Oh, no, John! You betta go tell your son about his mum before somebody at school tells him first. You know how gossipy this town is." She ended on a scornful note, forgetting that she, too, was a gossip, part of the gossipy town. "Hurry up and eat, then pick yo' bwai up before lunch, because if no one's said anything to him yet, they will during the lunch break, you mark mi words," she said in a slightly panicky note.

"I thought I had time, but I didn't know everyone would know my business this soon," John stated accusingly, as he looked around the restaurant, and the other diners again lowered their eyes. "Okay, who in here doesn't know what happened at my house last night?" Not hearing a response, and seeing the guilty looks being exchanged between the diners, he jumped up in disgust.

"You're right, I have about a half-hour to get to Alex before lunch. Can I get my food to go, Mrs. B?" he said, turning to her. She turned with a smile and boxed up John's breakfast. For a man who hadn't been hungry, John had made a decent dent in the food. She added more powder buns, some flour tortillas and fried jacks, along with some items from the lunch menu, making a packet of food for a couple of meals for one man and a rapidly growing young man.

She shook her head, wondering when the next time would be that John and Alex would have a home-cooked meal. That's one thing Cathlean had gotten right: she cooked for her family most of the time, and, Mrs. Blanco thought grudgingly, Cathlean was a darn fine cook, good enough that she could open her own restaurant. Also, Mrs. Blanco heard that Cathlean had taught young Alex how to cook some basic dishes, so maybe he and John would be fine. Mrs. B poured John's sweetened tea into a thermos; she wouldn't have given up her thermos to anyone else, but she knew she'd get it back from John later. He had always proven himself a man above reproach, honorable even in the little things.

Thrusting the packet at John as he walked out, leaving Junior in the restaurant, Mrs. B said, "Go on now, John-John. No, you don't," she said as he tried to hand her some bills. "Go to your boy, and good luck, John. You'll need it, but God won't give you any more than you can bear. Trust Him!"

John hurried to his jeep, a little more of a kick in his step than when he'd arrived. These folks had adopted him, and it was obvious they loved him a lot, and he had seen it in the restaurant. He felt full, humble, and lighter of heart, happy to know that if he and Cathlean divorced, her people would not divorce him too. Now his main focus was to get to his Alex and let him know that Cathlean was gone.

John didn't have far to go to get to Ecumenical High. He'd come to tour the campus when they returned from England, so he had a good idea of where the principal's office was. He parked, quickly jumped out the Mini Moke, and walked briskly toward the office. There were few students wandering around, but classes would end in about ten minutes, at which time there would be hordes of students converging on the hallways trying to get to the cafeteria. John approached the school secretary, Ms. Lucas, who looked questioningly up at him. There was a hint of recognition in her eyes, then a look of realization as she saw who was standing there. John wondered if that look meant that she, too, knew what had occurred last night, but he chided himself for being paranoid.

"Uh, hullo, Ms. Lucas. I'm Alexander's father, John Putnam. I need to sign him out of school early today—actually, right now," he said, trying not to show his nervousness. John hated attention, and even more, he hated to have to explain himself. Explaining himself often felt like he was seeking permission, and he didn't like the feeling one bit. However, he realized he had to come up with a quick explanation, so Alex could be released from classes for the rest of the day. "I have an emergency, but not to worry. I'll make sure that Alex gets his assignments from one of his school chums. Can you please call him for me right now?" He blinked blue eyes behind thick-lensed glasses.

"Certainly, sir," Ms. Lucas said, picking up the intercom. She spoke softly into the receiver, often glancing up at him in a strange manner. To John, this confirmed that she knew about Cathlean, and though she seemed to be burning to ask questions, she held her peace as she turned the student log book around so that John could sign Alex out for the day. While John waited for Alex to appear, a few people sauntered causally by, making John feel like a spectacle on display. *One thing about small towns,* he mused, *everybody knows everybody else's business!* Soon, finally, he heard footsteps coming down the hallway, and Alex popped into the office, breathless and looking worried.

"Dad? What's going on? Mr. Gerard said you were here to pick me up. I have Chemistry next period, and you know that's my favorite subject. I hate to miss that class." He approached his dad.

"Alex, son, everything's fine." He saw Ms. Lucas look at him doubtfully. "I mean . . . let's go. I'll explain in the car, and you'll have to call Ainsworth or one of your chums to get your assignments."

They turned and walked out together: one young, tall, and black, the other pudgy, short, and white, but anyone looking at them could sense the strong love they had for each other. Ms. Lucas watched them all the way to John's vehicle, shaking her head, silently cursing Cathlean because, of course, as John had supposed, Ms. Lucas *had* heard what had happened last night. Her mum, Sandra, had told her that she'd heard it from Mrs. Blanco, the restaurant owner, when they'd met at market earlier that day. Sandra, a hot mess, had mentioned it to everyone she met on her way home.

An impatient Alex yanked open the front passenger door, while John got into the driver's seat in a much more sedate manner. As John turned on the ignition, Alex could see that John's hands were trembling and that his fingers were white, appearing bloodless as he gripped the steering wheel. As John looked over his right shoulder to back out, Alex thought he detected the sheen of tears in John's startling blue eyes. *Oh no,* thought Alex. *Dad's crying. This cannot be good!* But Alex waited until John had finished navigating out of the school's parking lot before he turned sideways to face him. "Now, Dad, please tell me what happened and why you've picked me up early. Mmm, I see and can smell food in here. May I please have some now, or must I wait till we get home?"

"Go ahead and eat, or you can wait till we get home because I'm not going to make any stops. We'll talk when we get there." John's voice broke on the last word—it was becoming hard to appear normal, even in spite of Alex's reaction to the food. In any situation, Alex would always be hungry, which would've normally cause John to chuckle, except that he didn't feel much like laughing today.

Alex grabbed a powder bun and some fried green plantain chips from the greasy white paper bag out of which they were peeking. He closed his eyes in bliss as he took a monstrous bite of the sweet treat and took a bottle of strawberry Fanta from the crate behind him. His hunger temporarily satisfied, Alex turned to look at John again, humming and munching on his food. He took a few gulps of his drink and decided he could hold off until they arrived at home, though he could sense John's misery. With that sixth sense gifted mostly to the young, Alex had a feeling that he wouldn't like what John had to say, so Alex planned to enjoy his lunch now and put off any bad stuff John had to say for much later. The balmy wind caressed their hot cheeks as they traveled along.

CHAPTER 24

Within a short time, they were pulling into their driveway, and John parked next to the car. Alex quickly snatched his knapsack, the bag of food, and balanced everything in one hand, while he opened the door with the other and shoved the door with his hip. He took the steps in two long strides and banged on the front door. "Hullo, Mum, please open up the door. We're home! Mum?"

John stepped up behind Alex and reached around him to unlock the door. "Wait, Alex, let me help you." He set his keys on the side table and grabbed the bag of food and took it to the dining room. He saw that Alex was looking puzzled, about to call out for Cathlean. John held up a hand, stopping Alex in his tracks. "Don't call out to her, Alex. Mum's not here. She left last night. That is what I needed to talk to you about." John started shaking as he opened up the thermos and with shaky hands poured out a half-cup of tea and added a healthy measure of One Barrel Belizean rum to fill the cup up to the rim. He picked up his spiked tea, blew on the concoction, and took a big sip.

"Dad, stop stalling. What happened to Mum? Is she sick?" Alex asked in a strange, little-boy voice.

"No, she's not sick—she's just fine! Me? I'll be fine, just not right now." He set his cup down and sat down heavily in the nearest chair. "Son, your mother's moved out. I don't think she loves me anymore, but don't worry, she still loves you." He wailed out loud and Alex quickly went over to him.

"Hush, Dad. It'll be fine," he soothed, marveling at the role-reversal of child comforting parent. "Can you tell me what happened?" He rubbed at John's back.

"I-I-I came home and, and . . ." John cried louder, remembering the horror, unable to go on.

Alex was not a straight-*A* student for nothing; he thought he had an idea of what John was not able to articulate. Especially based on his experience of seeing what Cathlean had been up to at The Jetty, he did some quick mental calculation. "Dad, was Mum here with some other man and you caught her?" John nodded his head vigorously, shoulders shaking as he struggled to contain his emotions.

"That sneaking, conniving bitch!" Alex spat, again remembering the impotent rage he'd felt when he'd seen Cathlean betraying his dad. "I didn't want to tell you this but I saw her a couple of weeks ago having sex with Mr. Moss. Ains and I rode up to The Jetty, and when we parked our bikes, I thought I saw a car looking like Mr. Moss's. Later, when we were walking on the pier, I saw them in a corner, Dad. I'm so sorry, but I didn't know how to tell you. That's the night I left here and started staying at Ains's house a lot. I can't respect her anymore, Dad. Sorry, but she's not worth it!"

John's eyes flashed at the insult to Cathlean. "You will not speak of your mother that way or call her vile names. This is between me and her, and I won't tolerate any disrespect," he roared, then he thought about what Alex had said. "Wait, did you say you saw her with Mr. Moss? Isn't that Albert's dad? That's not who was here with her!" His head dropped heavily into his palms as his shoulders and entire body began shaking violently. "Oh, Cathlean, what have you done to us?" he wailed pitifully.

Alex firmed his stance, prepared to do battle with John. "Dad, *she is* a bitch, a no-good whoring bitch who doesn't deserve respect. I will not apologize for what I said. I really hate that woman!"

John looked up at Alex, seeing his pain, the color of the pain of betrayal that they both shared. At least Cathlean had professed to have loved John, but she'd never acted like she loved or cared for Alex. John shook his head, realizing he would have to be strong and be there for his son. Alex was strong and self-sufficient, but he still needed his mum. John got up and grabbed the bottle of rum from the bar as Alex ran to the bathroom, tears streaming down his face, an unvoiced scream in his open mouth. Alex slammed the door behind him, so hard that the whole house rattled. How dare Cathlean do this to him and his dad? Alex had always known her to be selfish, but to have sneaked a man into their home where she lived with her husband? She'd been unfaithful with two men, and Alex wondered how many more there were. He thought back to occasions in which he had been out in public with Cathlean when, as usual, numerous males had been drawn to his mother. She always just smiled and flirted with them, but now Alex wondered how many of those men Cathlean was having a sexually intimate relationship with. He wondered how many cues he'd missed or had not been observant enough of, but now, so much more made sense. He'd always thought proudly that his mum was hot and irresistible to males, young or old, but perhaps she'd been sharing her goodies with many of them.

"Ugh, I hate this. I feel like a fool, but I know Dad feels like a bigger fool. Guess he always suspected she was up to something, and that's why he's been drinking." He remembered the two quick drinks John had just guzzled down back-to-back and decided he'd better go stop John from getting drunk in the middle of the day. Too late, because when he got to the dining room, he saw that John had moved to the living room, half-bottle of rum on the floor next to the settee where he was sitting. He raised glazed, unfocused eyes to Alex, already drunk and becoming incoherent.

"I guessh itsh just you and me now, shonn," he slurred. We don't need Mum. Itsh just us boys!"

"Dad, come on, it's the middle of the afternoon, and you're drunk. You get a pass today, but I hope you're not going to keep drinking. Think I haven't been seeing empty bottles at the bottom of the trash can, and that Mr. Tooth hasn't told me that he's been bringing you home drunk from the saloons? Mum's gone, but I will not lose both of my parents. You need to be strong just like I will have to. If you keep drinking, you're letting her win by proving you're the weakling she's called you." He deliberately made his words stinging and hurtful, trying to penetrate John's alcoholic haze.

Alex stood over John for the first time, really noticing the broken blood vessels on John's nose, the red eyes, the deterioration in John's appearance and general demeanor that Alex had missed, and that had nothing to do with Cathlean's departure. When had John aged? Alex felt such sorrow that John had been reduced to just a shell of his former self, no longer the strong soldier with the great military bearing that he'd always displayed. How was it possible that John had aged so rapidly while Cathlean just seemed to become more sensual and attractive as she matured? Life was not fair—or was it the fact that evil often appeared to triumph over good and that those who practiced it flourished? As a young man, Alex hadn't lived long enough to gain much wisdom, but he just knew this wasn't right. He resolved right there and then that as much as he already loved Sherrette, he wouldn't allow himself to became twisted up in a woman's diabolical schemes; he had already learned from the best.

Alex grabbed a sheet and threw it over the now-sleeping John, who was still sobbing in his sleep. A wave of tenderness and love engulfed him as he vowed to take care of his dad, Cathlean be damned. And if it took John too long to bounce back, and Alex had to call and ask Grampa Elton and Gram Beth to come from England to stage an intervention, then so be it. Alex was that ready for a fight, and he would not allow Cathlean to drag him and his dad down with her mess.

CHAPTER 25

Alex grabbed the car keys and jumped in the car; he'd go take a drive and clear his head before coming back and calling Ainsworth for tonight's homework assignments. He had gotten his driver's license as soon as the family had moved back to Belize because he had already sneaked and been taught to drive at the age of fourteen by his chum Ralph's dad, back in England. The great thing about the move to a British country was that Alex didn't have to learn how to drive on opposite sides of the roads; in Belize they drove on the same side as they did in Great Britain.

With no particular destination in mind, Alex meandered down the road, snacking on some of the food he'd brought with him from the house. He would enjoy a picnic for one and reflect on the changes in his circumstances and think about his life up to his great age of sixteen. Alex deliberately took the back way through the Melinda Airstrip, the landing area that served as an airport or landing field for the small Cessnas that transported tourists from Belize City's Phillip Goldson International Airport to Dangríga, Placentia, Gales Point, Punta Gorda, to the Cayes or to other popular points of interest.

He drove past the pristine whiteness and glitz of Pelican Beach Resort marveling at the contrived, touristy atmosphere of the place. He much preferred the raw, natural beauty of the white sand beaches, the black and white Mangrove trees encroaching on the swamps, crabs running here and there, and wild, beautifully colorful birds; this was peaceful, an unspoiled paradise. The whole country was full of natural wonders, which is why Jacques Cousteau, the French ocean explorer, had visited and explored the Great Blue Hole in his famous ship, the Calypso, in 1972; he loved Belize so much. The Belize Audubon Society had even been formed in 1969 to honor John Audubon, an American naturalist who painted, cataloged, and described birds of different lands, including Belize.

Alex parked, grabbed his food and blanket, and lay back to enjoy the calm tranquil waves as they rolled forward and then broke onshore. The lazy afternoon was just what he needed to calm his troubled soul, and it did much for reestablishing Alex's equilibrium before he headed home to deal with reality. John would need him, and he would need John; they would help each other.

Upon Alex's arrival home a few hours later, he saw that John was up, had showered, and was looking much like his normal self. "Hullo, Dad. How are you feeling? I left you a note saying I was borrowing the car. Did you find it?" John was bustling around heating up dinner and preparing dinner trays so they could eat in the living room. No Cathlean meant that they could be free to eat where they wanted and not in the dining room where she always insisted they eat when she was around.

"Yes. How was your drive, and where did you go? He seemed to be genuinely interested.

"I drove past Pelican Resort and relaxed, Dad. It was wonderful on a day where things were not so wonderful. You've got to go with me next time. It'll do you good." Alex enthused, washing his hands in the kitchen sink, another no-no when Cathlean was around. John only raised his eyebrows.

"Well, let's eat, then you can call your classmate for the homework." They dug into split pea soup seasoned with boiled salted pigs' tails served with white rice, stewed beef, coleslaw, and leafy spinach that John had picked from Cathlean's garden near the kitchen door. Not saying grace before their meal was another rebellion against Cathlean's rules in their small, unspoken way. It felt good to regain some small, childish measure of control. It was game on: Cathlean 1, Alex and John 1.

"Dad, what are you going to do? You can't give up, and you can't stay here drinking your life away. I think you should help out at the Belize. Defense Force (BDF) barracks more often. You know the military is your life, and any contribution you make will help you get on and stay on. If you don't do something like that, I'll really worry about you, and I don't need the distraction from school. What do you say?" He waited with bated breath, hoping that John would agree to this plan.

John blinked his eyes rapidly behind his thick glasses, pondering Alex's words. He could call in a few favors, and he knew the BDF would be happy to have him, either on a voluntary basis or for pay. John lived comfortably on his retirement income, so a paid position was not mandatory. He also recognized the wisdom of Alex's suggestion, knowing that if he didn't do something, he may be tempted to do something desperate to himself, even though in his early studies when he'd been training to become a priest, he knew suicide was never, ever the answer. Killing Cathlean or her lovers was not an option, either, so John knew he had to keep those dark thoughts at bay or act on them.

"Well, I can go back to Mountain Pine Ridge, where I'd been earlier this week, and I can go see General McDougall afterward to see how he can use my help. Son, I think you have the right idea. Ever since I retired, I've felt lost and not quite myself, which is why your mother was getting tired of me being underfoot all the time." He hushed Alex as he was about to say something unsavory about Cathlean. "Let me make some calls tomorrow, and I'll see what they say. Please go call about the homework, but Alex . . ." He waited for Alex to look at him, "I can't go into every detail, but I want to tell you, I really thought about killing your mother and the man she was in our bed with, but I thought about you and how disappointed you'd be in me, so I intentionally missed when I shot at him. I want you to know it was the hardest thing I ever did, letting that man escape."

He began to cry huge gasping sounds, shaking so much he had to put the dinner tray on the floor. Alex rushed over and pulled him up, then hugged John with all his might, salty tears pouring from his eyes too. "Stop, Dad. Please stop crying. We'll get through this. I know you love Mum, but you have to be strong. Once you get away from here and go to Mountain Pine Ridge, you'll be distracted enough." He held John until John quieted, still sobbing, but no longer in total meltdown. "I'll go start my homework now. Will you be okay? Maybe you should go visit some of your friends." John nodded in agreement, but he really didn't think he wanted to be around other people.

"Go on and do your work. I'll be fine." He stood up, and they took their trays to the kitchen.

Alex patted John on the shoulder then ran up the stairs to his room to call Ainsworth about the homework. He grabbed the telephone, dialing the digits while silently damning Cathlean to hell for eternity.

How could she do what she'd done to a sweet man like John—and in his own home? The utter gall of the woman! Ainsworth's mother answered the telephone. Her first words were, "Alex, I'm so sorry to hear about your parents. Tell John that my husband will call him tomorrow. Ainsworth, it's Alex!" Alex was stunned as he wondered how many people knew what had happened. Before he could ask her what she knew about it and how she knew, Ainsworth was on the telephone.

"Hey, Alex, man, how are you? I heard what happened. Everybody was talking about it at school, so just be glad you left early. Man, Miss Cathlean is cold. I know you remember when we saw her at The Jetty, but to bring a man to your house? Wow! Oh, Sherrette wants you to call her when you can. She was upset that you and your family was the topic of conversation. She defended you, man!"

"Ains, thank you. I'll call her. That's my girl. I know she'll set those hypocrites straight. I'm doing fine, but how did people find out so fast? Unbelievable! Dad and I are doing well, so can we please not talk about this anymore? I'm already coming to terms with the changes in my life, so please just give me the page numbers for the homework so I can get started on it," Alex replied rather abruptly.

Ainsworth, properly subdued by Alex's cool response, did as requested and gave Alex the information he needed. "If you need to talk, please don't hesitate to call me," he said before hanging up. He knew Alex was a private person and that all the attention was going to kill him, but Ains would be there to support his friend. He was glad that Sherrette was also in Alex's corner to support him, and he'd been pleased to see her stand up to the some of the folks who'd spoken negatively about Alex today. She was small and feisty but could be quite the scrapper, Ains thought fondly.

Alex worked hard on his homework for the next few hours. He could hear the deep rumble of his dad's voice on the telephone from time to time, and once, when Alex went downstairs for a snack, he found John sprawled on the settee, sleeping soundly. As he covered John up, he knew that they would both get better; it would just be a matter of time. He was happy that John was interested in becoming actively involved in military life again because if there was anything John loved as much as he loved Cathlean, it was the military and living a soldier's life. Take that away from John, and he was a ship without a rudder; the man John knew himself to be would be reduced to nothing.

When Alex got back to his room, he thought it would be safe to call Sherrette now, so he quickly picked up and dialed her number. "Hi, Sherr, it's Alex. And how is my fair lady-champion tonight?"

"English! Of course I know who it is, silly. Who else would be calling me? You know my mother will not let any males call me, remember? How are you?" Her voice became serious with her concern. "I was so worried about you after I heard what people were saying. I almost left school early this afternoon, too. Is it true that your dad found Miss Cathlean having sex with a man in your house?" Alex became a little annoyed, but he knew she wasn't asking to fuel the rumor mills but because she genuinely cared for him and wanted to know exactly why she needed to defend him.

"I don't know the details, but thanks for taking up my battle. I heard you're my superhero, Supergirl. Should I get a cape made for you, Super-Sherrette?" He chuckled even though it wasn't a laughing matter; he was trying to lighten the moment. "Don't get into trouble with anybody about me. Just ignore those people. That's what I plan to do!" he stated, wondering how he was going to get through the next few weeks until the next crisis consumed the town, eclipsing the Cathlean-John saga.

"I just can't stand these messy people in this town," Sherrette said, getting upset all over again.

"Hey, it's nothing," Alex said. "I have to get back to homework. I was just checking on you."

"Well, I love you, so I won't stand for their disrespect," she said, still not ready to calm down.

Alex went still, reviewing Sherrette's declaration in his mind. "What, you love me?" he asked, incredulous. "Wait a minute, did I hear you right? Would you please repeat what you just said?"

On her end of the line, Sherrette flushed a bright red, even though Alex couldn't see her. She couldn't believe she'd revealed what had been in her heart these past few months. "Yes, I just said I love you. Please don't go getting a swelled head!" she said worriedly, wondering if he reciprocated.

"Well, I love you too, Sherrette. I have since I met you, but was afraid to say it and scare you off forever," he declared joyfully, marveling at the fact that he was experiencing the highest of highs after the lowest of lows, all in the same day! The universe truly had a warped sense of humor, he mused. Needing to get back to his homework, Alex signed off, wishing a Sherrette a good night.

CHAPTER 26

The next day, Alex met with Sherrette at morning break; he thought he'd be embarrassed at the fact that they'd both revealed their innermost feelings over the telephone the night before. But as he kissed her cheek, hugged her, and held her hand as usual, there was no awkwardness between them, just the knowledge that they were going to be exclusive now and could possibly become an item.

Alex had prepared himself for the scrutiny from teachers and his peers, but even though people looked at him in a pitying way, they stopped whispering when he approached them in their little gossip clusters. Just as he thought scornfully, nobody was brave enough to approach him with questions about the situation or share opinions on the matter of his parents' breakup.

Directly after lunch, Alex was summoned to Mr. Diego, the principal's office. Alex's shuffled his feet as he approached the office, his heart skipping a beat as he wondered if something had happened to John. When Ms. Lucas ushered Alex into Principal Diego's office, his legs were shaking so bad he was happy to sit in the chair pointed out to him. Mr. Diego, tall, dark, and imposing, steepled the fingers of his hands together as he rocked back in his large leather chair. His eyes met Alex's, full of concern and care as Alex silently looked up at the ceiling in a nervous manner.

Soon, he stopped rocking and began. "Well, young man, I never had a chance to formally welcome you to our school, but now's as good a time as any, eh? Welcome. I know your mother well and have had the pleasure to meet your father many times. And a very fine man he is, indeed! Alexander, I understand you've had a bit of an unsettling event happen in your life yesterday. I'm very sorry to hear about your parents' problem, and I wanted to reach out to you to make sure you are all right. Are you?" At Alex's nod, he continued, "Please know that the faculty and I are here to do anything we can to assist you. We have both male and female counselors here for you to talk to should you need them. Just let Ms. Lucas know that you need to meet with one of them, and she'll get you in to see them. Breakups are always traumatic, especially for the children involved, so please let us know. We don't want you falling apart because you're keeping everything bottled inside."

"Thanks Mr. Diego," Alex said, overwhelmed, now suspiciously wondering just how well Mr. Diego "knew" Cathlean. Would he always wonder now every time a man said he knew Cathlean if she'd been intimate with them, especially if he appeared to be leering, winking, or even smirking when mentioning her? He sincerely hoped not! "I'll certainly remember that, but Dad and I are great right now. I'll let you know if that changes. And thanks for welcoming me to the school. It's a beautiful campus. It's great to be here, and I hope to do well here and make you proud. Is that all, sir? I have to get back to class." Only good manners kept him in the seat, but he wanted out now.

"That's it, son. Good luck to you. Heard you're an ace student, so keep it up. We don't want this issue with your parents to get in the way and distract you, right? Remember, my door and the counselors' doors are always open to you. Go on back to class now." He rose and shook Alex's hand firmly then picked up the sash-cord whip that he used to punish students with. It wasn't meant to be a menacing gesture, but Alex took it as such because he heard Mr. Diego loved using the "Tommy-Tickle," as he called the whip, on pupils who arrived at school late or misbehaved in class.

As he opened the door, Alex stepped out quickly, anxious to get back to class. He was missing too much class time between John's picking him up early yesterday and this meeting just now. Alex was smart and could easily catch up, but he loved the time he spent in school and hated missing out. He could always get lecture notes from other classmates, but Alex's note-taking style was very different from others: he doodled in the margins of his notebooks and noted off-subject asides or comments made by lecturers. He had a voracious appetite for facts and information, gobbling it up like a starving man at a buffet, his appetite for knowledge only being rivaled by that for real food.

163

CHAPTER 27

Meanwhile, while Alex's and John's lives were falling apart, Cathlean was settling in at—where else?—the Booty Bunker! Like a duck to water, she wholeheartedly dived back into the single life just as if she'd never left it. In all fairness, Cathlean had thought about moving into a small house by herself, but there were two problems with that: she didn't have much money of her own, and she was scared to live by herself without John's steady and dependable presence to make her feel safe and protected. Funny how she took that safety and protection for granted when she had lived with John.

As devious as Cathlean was, one would think she would've socked a lot of John's money away over the years, since she'd never had any meaningful income of her own, but in her arrogance, she never expected John to catch her committing her dirty deeds, nor did she expect to have to leave once he caught her. However, Cathlean only had a few thousand Belize dollars and a thousand British pounds to her name. She realized she would have to use her money sparingly until she could hire a good attorney to relieve John of some of his funds to keep her in the style to which she'd become accustomed.

There was also the adultery angle that a judge would have to consider before Cathlean could get any money; furthermore, she was the perpetrator of that particular crime, so who knows what would happen? In the meantime, she would enjoy and have fun, fun, and more fun. Yes, she could now catch up with all the men who'd given her the eye before her departure from, and return to, Dangríga and give them *herself*—for a price, of course. Cathlean wasn't a prostitute, just a smart businesswoman.

Betty and Bridgett, two of the original inhabitants of the Booty Bunker, welcomed Cathlean back with open arms. To show their delight at her return, they threw a huge party, inviting single women recruits who might be considering moving in, along with many single men and former johns who had taken pleasure within those walls at some point or another. Cathlean thoroughly enjoyed the party, which had actually turned into an orgy as couples, threesomes, and other groupings—daisy chains being the new thing—sexed openly, inhibitions thrown along the way via the use of marijuana, LSD, uppers, and downers flourishing in Belize in a big way, just as they were doing in other parts of the world.

Cathlean's one sex partner of the moment was none other than Zeke, the man she'd been caught with by John. She was and had previously been a true love-'em-and-leave-'em kind of woman, but there was something about Zeke that made her reckless to the point of inviting him into her home and bed she shared with John. Zeke may have been pea-brained, but he was certainly big where it counted. After all those years of being only with smaller-than-average John, Zeke was a nice change.

Word got back to John on a regular basis about Cathlean and the goings-on at the Booty Bunker. After returning to Mountain Pine Ridge for a week, he had gotten a position volunteering at the local BDF office. He was provided a free breakfast and lunch with the soldiers in the mess hall every day, and he was kept so busy he didn't have time to dwell on the reports about Cathlean and her activities. Every evening, though he was not a cook, he got home in time to throw dinner for himself and Alex, not gourmet fare but stomach-filling food that provided needed nutrition for them. A couple times a week, depending on the mood or weather, they'd go out to dinner, but they couldn't linger because Alex always had tons of homework to do, so he had to get home to get it started.

Alex ignored the gossip about his mother, throwing himself into schoolwork and sports activities and ignoring the stories. As a result of his parents' breakup, he often experienced dark periods, bouts of helpless rage, and major depression, nausea, and headaches, but he refused to seek counseling with school counselors or with the pastor of his church. Since many of the locals kept their ears peeled for any updates on the salacious John-and-Cathlean show, Alex didn't trust that they or any counselors would keep what was discussed in strict confidence. He refused to give the rumor mills any help.

Sherrette, surprisingly mature for her age, was there for him during the bad times, soothing him, making him feel loved and wanted.

Naturally, she and Alex became very close; the fact that she was a popular cheerleader and he was the star of all the sports teams didn't hurt either. Together, they made a beautiful couple, a match upon which people couldn't help but comment.

At the same time, Sherrette was also struggling with math, specifically geometry, and since Alex had aced that subject back in England, he decided he'd help to tutor her to try to improve her C grade. When Miss Ida heard about this, she reluctantly allowed the tutoring to take place in her home where she could chaperone the young couple. Even though they kept giving each other sultry looks, they never acted inappropriately in her presence, so she soon relaxed her guard around them.

Miss Ida became more comfortable with the idea of her precious baby girl being with the tall, serious British young man with the military bearing, and when she saw how he treated her daughter as if she were the finest crystal ever made, she started seeing him in a new role: that of potential suitor for her daughter. Of course she knew they were too young, but she wouldn't object to their dating in a few years after they were done with school. Emboldened by Miss Ida's tentative acceptance of him, and knowing she was feeling bad due to his parents' situation, Alex grasped the opportunity to set out to charm and win her over. Little did she know that he planned on working on her so she'd agree to him and Sherrette dating now rather than later.

Alex sat with John at the dinner table a month or so later, strategizing with him. After all, John was a master military strategist, so who better to help Alex launch this offense? John was happy to help and grateful to have a "project" with which to distract himself. They laid out a very simple plan on paper: Alex would visit Sherrette and tutor her as he normally did, but at the same time, he'd ply Miss Ida with flowers and her favorite sweets each time he visited the house. The lady was known to love attention from any member of the male sex, especially one bearing gifts.

John was still hearing unsolicited reports about his wife and the Booty Bunker shenanigans, but like an accident he couldn't look away from, he still kept listening. Although his heart broke to hear what Cathlean was up to, and he cried himself to sleep almost every night, John was getting used to her being gone. He and Alex were closer than ever; his new semi-military life was exactly what the doctor ordered, and he was thriving. Women often gave him the eye, but he wasn't interested.

Three months had flown by unbelievably fast, but so far, neither he nor Cathlean had started divorce proceedings. John promised himself that if he ever ran into her, he'd tell her that if she wanted to end things permanently, she'd need to initiate such action. As far as John was concerned, he was married for life, and he took his vows before God and man extremely seriously. He was also not ready to join the ranks of the "divorced club"; he'd never aspired to be a member of that loser group. Besides, he'd no intention of ever remarrying, so who really cared about getting a divorce?

CHAPTER 28

John was still drinking heavily, especially on the nights when Alex was out of the house. He was careful to keep the levels unchanged in the One Barrel and the Caribbean rum on the bar because he bought additional bottles and stashed them in the yard, the hibiscus hedges, and other such places for easy access as needed. He always had cases of Guinness beer and Stout, Heineken beer, and Belikin beer that he purchased at discount prices from the BDF base and kept in the house, supposedly to entertain his few friends who stopped in to check on him. To be honest, he drank more of the alcohol by himself than he shared with any visitors who might have come by.

Sometimes, John saw Alex sniff the air when he came into the house, nostrils quivering at the odor of alcohol on and around John; he'd raise his eyebrows in a disappointed manner but wouldn't say a word. At times like that, John vowed he'd stop drinking, ashamed, because he never wanted to disappoint his son. John also worried that word would get to Alex that John was not really coping as well as he pretended to and was getting drunk in the saloons. Tooth had to bring John home so often that he even joked that he'd appointed himself John's security detail and designated driver! John continued to offer Tooth pay for cab service, and Tooth continued to refuse the money but reluctantly accept it. Somehow, they'd formed an alliance that worked.

Two weeks into the "charm Miss Ida campaign," Alex decided to approach her about taking Sherrette out on a real date. Since they had declared their feelings for each other, he was having the hardest time keeping things platonic between them; the few stolen kisses they'd shared brought out a yearning in Alex that he couldn't try explain to John even though they were extremely close.

He knew about biology, sexual chemistry, the birds and the bees, but these new feelings were a little too much for his virginal body to handle. He woke up with painful erections in the middle of the night, and his morning wood refused to go away even after he urinated. Many times, much to his chagrin and shame, he actually woke up in the mornings, dream sexual encounters completed, with cold, wet sheets to show for his efforts. On those mornings, he quickly got up before John, stripped the sheets off the bed, and washed an emergency load of laundry. However, once his arousal calmed, he just had to be near Sherrette during the day only for the problem to return with a vengeance.

On a bright Saturday morning, with these shameful thoughts in mind, Alex drove to the market and picked up some fresh flowers and a giant Cadbury's milk chocolate, then headed over to Sherrette's. Upon his arrival, he found Miss Ida struggling to open the door, hands full of purchases, having apparently just come from the market herself. "Oh, Miss Ida, please let me help you before you drop something." Hiding his items on the bottom step, he took the stairs two at a time as he trotted up to take a few of the packages from her arms. "By the way, good morning. How are you?"

"I'm well, and you? Thank you. You're such a nice boy," she replied, unlocking the front door.

"I'm fine, doing better, and my dad's fine too," he said hurriedly, anticipating her next question.

"That's great to hear, but what brings you out this early on a Saturday?" She looked at her watch.

"Oh, wait, I forgot I have something for you." He ran back down and grabbed his bribe items. Handing the chocolate to her, he said, "Here, for you. Please give me a vase in which to put these."

"Right there, underneath the sink," she pointed as he opened the door and pulled out the vase. She opened the refrigerator, rooting around in it. "Thank you very much for the gifts. You shouldn't have." She glanced at him as he avoided her eyes. She could clearly see how uncomfortable he was to be there. "But thank you anyway. Now I was about to fix a snack. Are you hungry?" She threw eggs, cheese, onions, and green sweet peppers all together in a pan and proceeded to whip them together to make an omelet. She poured the concoction into a frying pan sizzling on top of the stove, then grabbed the spatula and lifted the edges. At the same time, she started buttering slices of whole wheat toast as they popped up from the toaster.

"I need to ask if Sherrette's home?" he asked, unwilling to beat around the bush any longer.

"No, she spent the night at Miss Millie's last night. The girls had a slumber party. She'll be here soon. Pull up a chair, sit down. What flavor of jam do you like? I have guava jelly, blackberry and strawberry jam, and marmalade."

"Surprise me," Alex said, pouring himself some tea and sweetening it with condensed milk in the Belizean style to which he'd become accustomed. He cleared his throat and started to speak, but it came out as a high-pitched squeak. Embarrassed, he tried again. This time, his voice was more normal. "Miss Ida, I came to ask you something." He wrapped both hands around the cup of tea and sipped, enjoying the warmth as it slid down his throat. "You know how much I care for Sherrette. As a matter of fact, I love her. She's beautiful, sweet, and kind, but I don't have to tell you that. You know her—she's your daughter!" He chuckled nervously. "Miss Ida, I wanted to ask if I can take her to a movie this afternoon? I won't keep her out late." He ended in a rush and gulped his tea.

"Don't you think you are both too young? From what I've observed, you're a nice, mannerly young man, but I've told you my daughter shouldn't date until she's out of high school and in college." She frowned at Alex suspiciously, wondering if she was being played for a fool. "Well?" she added sharply when he didn't answer immediately; he hadn't thought her question required a reply.

"It's not really a date. We'll be back before dark. You can come along to chaperone if you'd like."

"I don't think so, and it's a date. Let's not play word games. I don't want my daughter on a date this early in her life. I want to keep her innocent as long as I can do so," she said, pursing her lips.

"I'm not asking her to marry me, at least not yet," Alex quickly assured her. "We'd go to a matinee. We both want to see the new Bruce Lee movie, *Enter the Dragon*. That's all we'll do. What do you say? I want to give her a treat for being so supportive through my recent ordeal." He looked at Miss Ida sadly as he delivered the final line, the one designed to elicit Miss Ida's sympathy.

"Sorry, I don't think so," she said, irritated. She pulled out her chair, starting to get up.

"Please, Miss Ida. She'll be safe with me, and I need a break to clear my head. Or please come with us, we'd be happy to have you. Remember when we went on that class trip? I kept her safe, and she came back in one piece, right?" He was making it up as he went along since he'd never asked a woman for a date with her daughter before. Touching her hand, he looked directly into her eyes. "Look, can we please just ask when she gets here, see what she says? If she says no, I'll accept that."

Miss Ida sat back down, saying slowly, "I'll think about it. Now let's eat this food while it's hot!" So they dug in. The food may have been delicious or tasted like sawdust, but Alex couldn't enjoy it; he was nervously excited, his stomach in knots. Miss Idea hadn't said a firm "no" yet, so he could still hope. He considered turning up the charm a bit more to push her in the right direction.

Either way, Alex would get his answer very soon because about five minutes later, he could hear light footsteps running up the stairs, then the door was flung open. In came Sherrette, bright-eyed, fresh-faced, and beautiful, a breath of fresh air in blue jeans, a bright gold eyelet-lace top, and matching gold patent leather sandals. She stopped short upon seeing Alex in her kitchen but quickly recovered her composure as she leaned over and kissed her mum on the cheek. "Morning, Mother, how are you? Hi, Alex. What are you doing here so early?" She came over and gave him a quick hug.

Alex, always the courteous one, immediately stood up, returning Sherrette's hug, then pulling out a chair for her. She lowered herself into it gracefully, and in one deft motion, buttered a slice of toast, liberally added guava jelly and piled eggs on top. Taking a delicate bite, she looked curiously from her mother to Alex as she delicately chewed the mouthful of food.

Alex realized that Sherrette was still awaiting an answer, so he cleared his throat and said, "Well, I came over to see you and your mother because I wanted to ask her a very important question." He looked at Miss Ida, trying to read her expression. She'd briefly acknowledged Sherrette's arrival and had hugged her back but, so far, hadn't said a word. Alex waited; afraid of offending Miss Ida, he decided to defer to her lead, but inside, he was bursting to tell Sherrette exactly what he'd asked.

"Darling, I'm so happy you're home. How was the slumber party with your friends? I missed you!" She was all smiles as she looked her daughter over. "What, didn't Millie feed you breakfast?"

Sherrette took a big sip of papaya juice, chilled just the way she liked it. She closed her eyes, blissfully savoring the tangy salty flavor. "I had fun, Mother. The girls were nice, and we ate so much last night, I didn't want breakfast this morning. Now, I'm absolutely starving! Why's Alex really here?"

Miss Ida looked uncomfortable, not sure she should say anything about Alex's request. Then she decided to go ahead and be honest to observe Sherrette's reaction. Pursing her lips, she said, "The young man came by to ask me for a favor. He wants to take you to a movie. What do you say?"

"Really, Mum?" she jumped up, squealing, turning to look at Alex. "Really Alex? Is this a date? When are we going?" She was so excited she couldn't stop talking and couldn't stay in one place, nor could she decide whether she should sit or stand. However, she picked up on her mum's vibe that she wasn't too pleased about the request, so she dialed back on her enthusiasm. The surest way to blow this date before it happened was for her to act too eager, so she pretended a nonchalant attitude.

"I didn't give my permission yet, missy, because I think you're too young to date at fourteen. This boy also said he loves you, but what do you know 'bout love?" she scoffed, shaking her head.

"Sherrette, I asked your mum if I could take you to matinee at Joyland Theatre to see *Enter the Dragon,* the movie we wanted to see. I even invited her to come along if she wants to." Alex resented being referred to as a boy, and he especially hated being talked about as if he weren't there.

Miss Ida was the one who'd left the door open for him to still ask for that date with Sherrette. He guessed it couldn't hurt to restate his request and be damned for it since Miss Ida was messing the whole thing up. Clearly she didn't want to give her permission, but Sherrette clearly wanted to go! In full strategist mode, he figured he'd overstayed his welcome for the moment, so he decided to leave mother and daughter to hash it out. He quickly pushed back from the table, saying, "I'll go ahead and see myself out. Please let me know what you decide. Miss Ida, if you give us your permission, we'll go on a weekend, so the outing (he intentionally didn't use the word "date") will not affect school. Thank you for the tasty food. I enjoyed it. Sherrette, I'll talk to you later." He hugged her, and taking off in a rush, he tore down the steps and jumped into his car before speeding away.

"Bye," Miss Ida growled, glaring at Alex's back and closing the door in full Mama Bear mode.

CHAPTER 29

Alex could not wait to get out of there and go talk to his dad about the latest development. He wondered if he's been so pushy or forward that he'd messed things up with Miss Ida. *Man, this falling in love and dating thing is hard. How do people make it look so easy?* he wondered. Upon his arrival home, he found John in the driveway with a water hose in his hand, bleary-eyed but determined to wash his Mini Moke. Alex pulled in next to the jeep, and after getting out and hugging his dad, he took the hose away and greeted John. "Morning, Dad, or is it afternoon yet? How are you this lovely Saturday?" John nodded slowly, trying not to move his head more than necessary. He was a bit hungover and didn't want Alex to guess what was going on. He stepped back as Alex sprayed water over both vehicles and started soaping them down. "I'll wash 'em, Dad."

John sat on the bottom step of the kitchen, content to let Alex do his thing. "Fine, son, thank you for washing the vehicles. You got here at the perfect time." He chuckled at his pathetic attempt at a joke. John had never been good at jokes; he had too serious a demeanor to pull it off. "You were out early today?" he asked, turning the sentence into a question. "What's happening?"

"Dad, I just came from Sherrette's." He saw the flash of concern in John's eyes. "No, don't worry, it's okay. Miss Ida was there. I went to ask her to let me take Sherrette out this weekend. She's been nicer to me, Dad. She even fed me!" he boasted, smiling mischievously. "I'm waiting to hear back from her or Sherrette. Miss Ida doesn't seem so keen on the idea, said we're too young, but Sherrette wants to go. If her mum says yes, we'll see *Enter the Dragon*. Heard it's a great movie!"

"What? You asked her, and you're still in one piece?" He struggled to his feet, came over, and slapped Alex on the back. "That's my boy. Guess you got that courage and attitude from your mum. Way to go, son!" Alex, warmed by his dad's approval, went into some detail regarding the conversation, mentioning that Sherrette had arrived home right after he and Miss Ida had talked. "I'm waiting to hear back from them, but I don't know, Dad," he said worriedly. "Miss Ida's tough."

"Ah, but that girl o' hers has a mind of her own, and she likes you a lot." He laughed slyly, sitting back down. "As a matter of fact, I'm sure she loves you, so I know she'll work on her mum. I'm not going to say this because you're my son, but you're a catch: tall, smart, handsome, and a gentleman. Plus, I know we raised you right, so Miss Ida should be happy to have you courting her daughter. Sherrette could do worse, but as I said, she's smart, so don't worry so much." He looked up at Alex.

"Okay, Dad. Let me hurry up and finish, just in case I need to use the car this evening." He rinsed off the vehicles and began drying them rapidly. As he applied wax to each, he saw John disappear into the house. He wondered what was going on until he saw John coming back outside with the telephone in his hand. John had attached the extra-long cord to it so he could put the telephone next to the area where they were working. "Oh, thanks," Alex said with a smile. "I hadn't thought of bringing the telephone out, but you're right, that makes sense. Now, if Miss Ida or Sherrette calls, I won't miss it."

There was a bounce to his step as he finished the task of washing, waxing, and buffing both vehicles until they shone. John grabbed a rag and started wiping down the dashboards, windshields, and other parts of the interior of each. Father and son worked like a well-choreographed team, anticipating each other's need until, about an hour later, both cars stood glistening and clean in the bright afternoon sun. Alex and John stood back and admired their work; they were impressed at the appearance of the cars. If Alex was going out that day, he and Sherrette were going to do so in style!

By the time Alex and John had gone into the house and had both taken long showers, Alex was disappointed because he still hadn't received a call. He figured he'd wait a few more hours, and if he still hadn't heard from Sherrette, he would go hang out with Ainsworth and his brother, Robb. They hadn't gotten together in a while, so they could pick up some food and play cards or listen to the BBC programming broadcast from England on Radio Belize on Saturday nights.

Alex was sure Miss Ida was going to string him along before agreeing to let him take Sherrette out, so he needed to come up with some alternate activities with which to occupy himself until he got the word that it was a go. He knew the answer was going to be yes, but he also knew Miss Ida was not just going to hand her daughter over that easily. So he and his friends would play cards, listen to the BBC program, or chill out with some country-western usually broadcast from America on one select radio station on Thursday and Saturday nights. Alex really loved country music, but he didn't think it was cool to admit so, so he always tried to hide his interest by acting nonchalant about it.

If the lads were especially bored, they would find out if anyone had died that week and would plan to attend the wake, which was always a good place to meet up with friends and score some good food. In addition, going to wakes also provided a fascinating opportunity, especially for Alex who was still new to this Belizean culture, to watch some "entertainment," as mourners performed for their audience, they fell out screaming over their dead relative's coffin, much to the delight of the older crowd and to the shame of the younger. Oh, yes, Alex decided he would find other creative things to do while he played Miss Ida's cat-and-mouse game. After all, anything worth having was worth waiting for, however long it took, and Sherrette was worth it to him every day, any day, all day!

When Alex finally left home around eight that night, he and his friends had settled on getting some food and hanging out at their house, playing cards instead of going "wake-hunting." The one death they'd heard about, and for which there would be a wake that night, had occurred "up the road." This description covered an area from about the four-mile point outside of town, south to "twelve miles," specifically Alta Vista and the Pomona Valley, more commonly called "The Valley."

Although Alex had transportation and could drive his friends to the wake, Dangrigans were clannish and didn't often associate with those "bushies" or "bush people." The townsfolk, or "townies," thought they were better than the bushies because they lived in town, while the bushies had to come to town to sell their wares (crops, fishhooks, carved tops, game meat etc.) and buy supplies. Their children also had to be bussed into town for school every morning, objects of ridicule and disdain, and they were loaded off the buses near the school gate. Most townies thought bushies were wild, untamed, and pitiful.

What the townies conveniently chose to forget, but what Alex had laughed about to himself and when discussing with John, was that "The Valley" was one of the most fertile areas in Belize and was the location of the heart of the citrus industry. It was a bustling area to which townies had to be transported to work in the factory and to contribute to the processing of the largest export of which Dangrígans could boast. Banana plantations in Big Creek and Independence also claimed their share of townie workers but maybe not to the same degree as the citrus industry did.

Miss Millie, Ainsworth's and Robb's mum, had fried green plantain chips and red snappers and left the food for the boys, while she and her daughter went visiting a social with one of her ladies' groups. Mr. Dennis had gone to the local saloon to play Chinese checkers and dominoes, so Alex and his friends had the house to themselves. As Ainsworth forked the Habanero peppers-and-onion sauce over his piece of snapper, he noticed that Alex seemed a bit preoccupied. It wasn't like Alex was quiet or totally uncommunicative; it just seemed like he didn't want to be engaged much.

He knew Alex too well, so Ains decided to have some fun at Alex's expense. "Hey, Alex," he began, taking a bite of fish. "What's going on with you? Your body's here, but you're not here."

"Nothing's going on, Ains. What's going on with you and Robb? We hadn't gotten together in a while and I really missed you." He took a couple of chips and stuffed them into his mouth as he took in a forkful of coleslaw. "This food is good. Miss Millie's such a great cook!" he said as he chewed happily.

"Look, don't try to change the subject. Something's going on. You're like a cat on hot bricks."

"Don't know what you're talking about. I've been busy with school, so I haven't come by, that's all." He looked Ainsworth and Robb directly in their eyes and could see the concern in Ainsworth's. He knew Ains was a "fixer"; he always wanted to know what was going on just so he could fix it. "What the heck," he said, coming to a decision. "Man, I asked Miss Ida if I could take Sherrette out."

"Like on a date? Wow, Alex, that's big! What'd she say, what'd she say?" He set his food down.

"Hold on. She didn't say yes yet, but I know she will. I went to their house and asked her this morning, and I am now awaiting an answer. Man, I hate this waiting," he said as he angrily pushed his plate away.

"What, Alex, did you say you went to Miss Ida's house?" Robb asked, fork halfway to his mouth, eyes opening wide in alarm. "Weren't you scared?" He turned to his brother. "Ains, your friend's a crazy man!" He went back to his food, looking from Alex to Ains, waiting for one of them to speak.

"Hush, Robb. I'm sure Alex will tell us how this all came about." Ainsworth looked at Alex expectantly.

"There's no great mystery," said Alex. "I love Sherr and she loves me. That gave me the courage."

"Hear that?" Robb asked, teasing Alex with his mouth full. "He used the *L* word. He loves her!"

"Yes, and she loves me, so I decided we should go out. Besides, she's been there for me during the last few months of my parents' breakup. She's a keeper, and even though she's young, she's mature in her thinking. I don't want her to get away from me," Alex declared earnestly.

"You think Miss Ida will allow you to date her precious daughter? Dream on!" Ainsworth said.

"I know she will. I just have to be patient," he said, looking miserable because he was not a patient person. "I thought I'd hear from her by now, but so far, nothing. I know Sherrette wants to go because I went around her mum and asked her directly if she would go, and she screamed 'Yes'!"

"Really? You're my hero! What's the rush anyway, gettin' blue balls?" This came from Ainsworth.

"Funny you should say that." Alex blushed, lowering his head. "I've been having wild, sexy dreams about her." He looked around to make sure nobody else was there listening to their conversation. He continued in a whisper, "I've been having these wet dreams and having to wash the sheets. I want her so bad. We're both virgins, and want to give our virginity to each other."

"Just be careful, man, and if you get with her, always wear a French Letter. No mistakes allowed. You don't want any *pickney* (Belizean slang word for child) at your age. Mek sure you know what you're doing," cautioned Ainsworth gravely.

"Man, come on. I know you're still a virgin too! You trying to tell me you're that experienced?"

"Not saying if I am or not, but these little girls are hot-crotched, so I know a thing or two. Just do what you can to service yourself and deal with your wet dreams. Believe me, that'll keep you out of trouble!" Ainsworth saw the hurt look on Alex's face, so he came over and slapped Alex on the back. "Sorry to make fun, but all of us males, even your dad since Miss Cathlean left, well, we have to deal with our sex drive ourselves, right? Especially if we don't have a female around, know what I mean? Good luck with Miss Ida and Sherrette. It'll work out. Now, can we change the subject?"

He deliberately reached out and turned on the radio on the shelf above the table so they could listen to the country-western station. That night, it featured music by a special artist, Johnny Tillotson, singer of some of their favorites: "Heartaches By The Number," "Send Me The Pillow That You Dream On," "I'm So Lonesome, I Could Cry," "It Keeps Right On A-Hurtin." As they sang along, they realized how sad the lyrics were; these were not songs three teenage boys should be listening to on a Saturday night, especially when one of them was pining for a girl he loved but didn't quite have.

They turned off the music, pulled out the card table, and Robb started dealing fast and furious. Pitty Pat was the game of the hour, and so they ante'd up their bets: a shilling a hand, a shilling for each side-bet like "highest diamonds," "holder of the six-of-clubs," etc. Alex lost all his money to the two brothers because his concentration was shot to hell; he was busy thinking about Sherrette and what Ainsworth had said about "handling" his sexual frustration. It was kind of funny, he thought, that Ains bragged that he was getting plenty of action from his girl, Mia, but apparently that wasn't true. Alex didn't want to call Ains out on it in front of his brother, Robb, so Alex decided to leave it alone.

CHAPTER 30

Around eleven, Alex took off, but instead of heading home, he decided to stop at John's favorite saloon to see whether he was drunk and needed a ride home. However, Alex couldn't find John, and after being denied entrance to that saloon or the next because he was underage, he just headed home.

John had not yet arrived, but soon after Alex had put on his pajamas, brushed his teeth, and had gotten ready for bed, he heard a car pull up and park in front of the house. When he peeked out, he saw a man who appeared to be Mr. Tooth struggling to help John out of a beat-up car. Alex rushed to the door and plucked it open, going outside to help with John, who couldn't hold himself up or walk in under his own power. John grinned up at Alex drunkenly, eyes bloodshot, not their usual shiny blue.

"Hey, Mr. Tooth, how are you? Let me help you with him," said Alex, holding John by one arm.

"Hello, Master Alex. I'm fine, but I t'ink your dad had one too many tonight," said Tooth with a chuckle.

"Tonight? Mr. Tooth, I know what's been going on, and it's not just tonight. Please do not encourage my dad. He's just using Mum's absence as an excuse to drink." Alex replied, disgusted.

"Ohh, hullo, shon," slurred John. "Tooth's my pershonal taxi-man, aren'tchu, Tooth?" He leaned heavily on Alex, reeking of alcohol fumes, as Tooth pushed the door wide open. "I'm going to shleep. P-please pay the man, Alex. 'Night, Tooth. Time for my beddy-bye-bye," he belched.

"Not yet, John. Let me help you into bed," said Tooth, as he and Alex loosened John's clothes and tucked him into bed. Alex was a little embarrassed, but he realized Tooth was like a family member now, and he was always coming to their rescue, so there was no need to hide. Alex pulled some bills from John's wallet and handed them to Tooth, who turned and walked out without taking the cash. "No, keep it, Alex. I'm happy to help your dad. He's a good man who got a very raw deal."

Tooth drove off in his rattling cab as Alex locked up and made the house secure for the night. He shook his head reflecting on what Tooth had said. Cathlean—damn her—really had a lot to answer for.

As Alex sat there watching John sleep, he could feel the rage building in him as he reflected on the many colors of pain. As usual, his pain seemed to stem from one person, and as he thought about Cathlean, he wondered why he gave her so much power over his life. One of the people he loved and who was most important to him was lying here, semi-comatose and smelling like the local distillery; the other was snug in her bed, separated by a few little miles that felt like a river that Alex had to ford to get to her. Miss Ida was the bridge that would allow, or not allow, passage to that river.

Alex was hopeful that Sherrette's love would offset the color and hurt of his pain, but he also recognized that it was wrong of him to expect a fourteen-year-old to be able to accomplish much. It was a tall order and not fair of him to want it, but he couldn't help himself. After wearily pulling the covers around John, Alex stood and stretched, feeling like a grown man, aged beyond his years; he was going to have to be the man and take care of his dad. Day by day, it was becoming clear to Alex that the color of John's pain was overwhelming him. It was devoid of any warm colors of love he'd previously felt for Cathlean: it was pitch-black, totally eclipsing any love he'd once felt for his wife.

The color of Alex's pain was a crushing weight, causing him to feel helpless and unsure of himself at times. The loneliness of Cathlean's desertion and the utter despair he felt at times would have destroyed a much weaker person, but Alex had learned one good thing from his upbringing in England: Brits were always proud and kept a stiff upper lip. So Alex kept his head up in public, never letting anybody see his vulnerability; only John knew that when Alex got home, he allowed his weakness to show. Before, he and John had been united in their pain; now, he felt like John had found a new companion—alcohol—beautiful, deadly, and alluring but capable of destroying him.

Alex shuffled off to his room, feeling so sad; he thought his heart would break. As he closed his door, he felt something running down his face, and when he rubbed at it, he was shocked to discover that he was crying. He supposed he was crying for lost innocence; crying because John had been his friend, and he had no siblings with whom to share the pain of abandonment; and crying because he had never, ever cried for his mum's withheld love—he never even cried when she'd left. It all poured from him, purging the poison from his body; soon afterward, he fell into a deep, healing sleep.

The next day, Alex woke up refreshed; he felt like Superman—like he could handle anything. He decided to get up and fix himself and John breakfast, that is, if John could enjoy food at all with a hangover. Maybe he could also talk John into going to church; he realized that they hadn't gone since Cathlean had left, but maybe now was a good time to go back. Only God knew that they both needed some divine intervention right then: Alex to get in with Sherrette, and John because he'd started loving the bottle way too much.

Alex jumped up and showered, then headed for the kitchen, where he whipped up a batch of eggs, and began sifting flour, salt, and baking powder together to knead some dough. Cathlean, a great cook and baker, had forced Alex to learn how to knead dough for bread, sweet buns, flour tortillas, and powder buns. For example, he knew enough to remember that yeast was used for leavening of bread and sweet bun dough, but baking powder was used for johnnycakes, fried jacks, powder buns and tortillas.

He had become a much better baker than a cook, finding the act of kneading and pounding the dough a very therapeutic endeavor. Of all the foods he was expert at baking, he disliked kneading powder buns most of all even though he really enjoyed eating them. Because sugar was the main ingredient in the preparation, he found it difficult to mix the dough, as the sugar melted under his hot hands while the dough was being kneaded. Whenever Alex and John wanted powder buns, and they wanted them often, they would pick up them from Bluebell's, as Mrs. B made the best ones in town. Alex knew his limitations and would just leave the kneading of powder buns to the experts.

As he was taking the last batch of golden brown fried jacks out the frying pan and placing them on tissue so they could drain, John stumbled into the kitchen, pale as a ghost, bloodshot eyes no clearer than they had been when Alex had looked into them the night before.

"Good mornin', Dad" he said, feeling very proud of his breakfast preparation. "Ready to eat?"

"Eat? Oh no, couldn't eat a thing," he said, turning green at the thought. "Got any tea ready?"

"Yes, tea's ready, but you have to eat, too. I fixed your favorite breakfast." He placed a steaming cup of tea in front of John, black and unsweetened, hoping it would clear John's hangover so he could eat a little food. John picked up the cup with trembling hands, blew on it, and took a small sip.

After a few sips, he started looking like his usual self, so Alex fixed a small plate with a couple pieces of fried jack on it and a small serving of eggs. He also poured himself and John a nice tall glass of grapefruit juice. Fixing a huge serving for himself, Alex dragged a chair out and sat down. John cringed and covered his ears. "Too loud, son. Can you please keep it down?" His head ached.

"Oh, sorry, Dad. Let me get you some aspirin." He got the bottle from the top of the fridge and shook four into John's hand. John gulped them down gratefully with a large sip of his juice. As he reached for his plate and tentatively took a bite, he chewed slowly, determined to keep it down. "Dad, we have to talk about this. You have a drinking problem, but I know I don't have to tell you that. Don't you think you should talk to someone, try to get some help? I love you. I hate to see this destroying you, and it is destroying you. I'm worried that one day it'll kill you." Alex's voice cracked.

"Son, trust me, I have it under control, but I'm so lonely. I miss your mum!" He began sobbing.

"Hush, Dad, please don't cry," Alex said, getting up and rubbing John's back. They both looked out the window at a small group of children playing jump rope; the action stopped because the children were busy arguing about whose turn it was to jump and whose it was to turn the rope. *Ah,* they thought, *to be that young and carefree again for just a few hours would be wonderful!*

"I cried enough for both of us last night," Alex continued. "I don't want to start again. Can you hurry up so that we can go to church this morning? I think it's time we went back, don't you?"

"Church?" John asked, as though it was a totally foreign concept. "I don't want to go to church!"

"It was just a suggestion. We don't really have to go, but you should make an appointment to talk to Reverend Goff at the church. I think he can help." He sat back down and resumed eating. Breakfast was good even if he said so himself: the fried jacks were light, crisp, and fluffy; the eggs were just right; the black tea perfectly brewed and sweetened; and the juice cold and tangy. Alex hungrily cleaned his plate, often checking on John, who'd managed to eat most of what he had on his plate. They could still hear the children in the background, louder now, but not enough to stop them from savoring their food. They ate in companionable silence, lingering over breakfast, slightly hesitant to face the day and what it may bring to their little lost world but knowing they had to venture out.

After Alex had cleaned up the kitchen and done the dishes, he got ready for his day. The fact that Sherrette or Miss Ida still hadn't called was not far from his thoughts, but he would not let it ruin his day, so he decided he'd go round up a few friends, male and female so Sherrette could be included (Miss Ida wouldn't object to that, right?), then go bike-riding to one of the friends' farms. It was the perfect time to go mango-picking; Dangríga had gotten quite a bit of rain in the last six months, so the harvest would be rich and plentiful.

One of the great things Alex appreciated since leaving London was that he could have farm-fresh fruit: bananas and citrus, of course, plus mangos, custard apple, mamee, papayas, plums, soursop, any kind his heart desired, any time he wanted it. Many of his friends' families dabbled in farming; they often grew just enough to eat and share with friends and neighbors but not necessarily enough with which to make any kind of substantial living. Of course, this suited Alex just fine; it was great to eat succulent fruit year-round—and at zero cost, the eating was that much sweeter!

The dads considered themselves "gentlemen farmers," meaning they'd inherited farms from their fathers and grandfathers, but they didn't like to get their hands dirty. Besides, many of them had full-time jobs, so they did just enough to keep the ground tilled and primed to ensure an annual crop, and that was the height of their involvement. Teenagers, on the other hand, thought farms were just a fun place in which they could go hang out, and the beauty of it was that the farms were located a distance from town so the teens could feel like they were getting away from the adults. As long as they watched their steps and didn't get lost or snake-bitten, they were allowed to visit the farms.

CHAPTER 31

When Alex called Sherrette, she picked up the telephone instantly. When she heard Alex on the line, she relaxed. "Hey, English. How are you? What's going on? Hope you're not calling to bother my mum, 'cause you know she won't be rushed into making a decision about us going out, you know?"

"Hullo, Sherr. Nothing's gone on. No, I'm not trying to bother your mother yet. I can be patient, believe me. Hey, listen, why don't you call two or three of your friends while I call a few of mine? We want to ride our bikes to the farm. You interested? Please say yes." He held his breath, unsure if she was in the mood for something gritty like farming on this beautiful but hot, sun-soaked day.

"Oh, yes, that'll be fun. Mum should be fine with me going because we already went to early mass this morning. She's usually mellow on Sundays after she's visited church and been touched by Father Cecil. I know she loves that man and wants to try to corrupt him!" She giggled. "Now get off the telephone so I can call the girls. I won't tell Mum I'll be seeing you today, because I don't want her to say that I can't go out at all. And you know she would stop me . . . I'll call you back very soon!"

Alex hung up the telephone excitedly. "Yesss!" he yelled, then called up four friends, including Nick and Earl, with whom he hung out sometimes, and, of course, Ainsworth and Robb. After Sherrette had called back to say that she and her friends could go, Alex checked on his dad once more to convince himself that John could be left alone. John was laying low today, headachy and still a bit hungover, so he promised that he was not going to leave the house or take a drink from any of the liquor bottles. Alex made a show of marking the levels of alcohol in the bottles before leaving.

Satisfied, Alex got on his bike and rounded up his friends, then rode to Princess Margaret Park, so named after the younger sister of Queen Elizabeth, II, and designed to look like an English garden with manicured hedges and a great profusion of assorted flowers. This was the area on Front Street, near the center of town where children gathered to play on the swings, where bands performed from the huge bandstand during the summer, or where schools had their annual "Battle of the Bands". They would meet the girls before heading to the farm of choice that day, one simply called Flores's Fancy.

Nick Flores's family owned a huge spread about five miles southwest of town; the friends especially liked this farm because it was a nice, energetic ride, not too far away, and the caretaker was a nice young man. Fabian was just a few years the friends' senior, but he was a responsible young man who took his duties seriously while the owner of the farm, Police Chief Flores, performed his peacekeeping and law-and-order duties. Fabian always welcomed visitors, proudly taking them on mini-tours of the farm, especially when he wanted to show off a new plant hybrid with which he was experimenting or to show some new bird or animal he'd tamed. Alex and his friends were special, and he hadn't seen them in a while. Besides, he didn't get company too often, and he was lonely.

As they arrived and dismounted from their bikes, Fabian came out the farmhouse, hand shading his eyes; he squinted, looking serious, until he recognized his visitors. "Ho, who do we have here? Master Nick, Master Alex, and company. Welcome, welcome. Long time no see!" He hugged the girls and shook the young mens' hands, very happy to see everyone and relieve the monotony of his day.

"How've you been, Fabe? It's so hot today! You know Nick, and these are my chums. I think you've met a couple of them," Alex said. "So, how's the harvest? Plant anything new? Fabian's a master, a degreed botanist who studied at Cambridge, England—a clever wizard with a green thumb!" he boasted, showing off. He was very really proud of Fabian's English connection.

Fabian ducked his head, squirming uncomfortably; he hated praise and attention of any kind. He was just happy that people loved the variety of fruit grown on the farm, amazed that it could all be cultivated in one place. Visitors or would-be reapers could pick bags of any one type of fruit or a combination of many different types. In addition, there were several varieties of cashews, considered a double treat because not only was the fruit sweet and succulent but one could also twist off the green cashew nuts at the end of each fruit and stash them separately to be dried for a few weeks and roasted to yield the popular cashew nut snack that they all enjoyed, but was way too costly to purchase from the store. Fabian would be happy to share; Chief Kenji Flores, his boss, wouldn't mind.

"The crop's good since we had some rain. I haven't been experimenting too much with anything lately, so all I got is plain, boring old fruit, just the way that God created 'em. Come in and have some mango-papaya juice. I just made some rice pudding, too." They eagerly entered the house. Fabian was a great cook who loved making goodies with items grown on the farm. The friends knew they were in for a treat, so they washed their hands and sat at the table as they were served the rich, creamy rice pudding and ice-cold juice. After they ate, they thanked Fabian and headed to the orchards to pick fruit from the overloaded trees. They could smell the winelike odor from fruit on the ground fermenting in the heat as drunken flies hovered, sluggish and full from over-indulging.

When the friends got tired of picking fruit and had stuffed themselves, they sat under a large tree, leafy and green, which provided ample shade from the sun, that was now beating down mercilessly from a clear blue sky. Sherrette's friend, Arva, had had the foresight to pack a few bottles of cold water, and everyone thirstily drank some. If anyone wanted more water, they just had to ask Fabian, who would lead them to the well near the back of the property to get their drink. There was a bucket for drawing up the water which flowed sweet, pure, and clear in the bottom of the well and tasted like nectar to anybody who drank it. Everyone had worn shorts to try to stay cool, so they took the opportunity to slap sunscreen on their exposed skin to avoid burning while sitting out in the sun.

Coincidentally, or maybe by design, there were five females and five males, so everyone paired off, the couples sitting a little apart from each other. Alex sat with his back against the sturdy tree trunk with Sherrette's head on his thigh. Content to be in the moment with his lady love, he stroked her closed eyelids and played with her hair. He didn't think about the pain of the night before and just wondered how he'd gotten so lucky that this girl had fallen for him, but he didn't want to think at all. This was a lovely day for relaxing, communing with nature, and celebrating life and youth, and to just be.

When Fabian came out to check on his guests a while later, he found them asleep, so he gently woke them, knowing it was getting late and they had to go back to get ready for school the next day.

"Thank you for everything, and for taking care of my friends," said Nick. "I'll tell Dad you said hello. Come on, everybody. Let's grab our bags and head out." He held his friend Karole's hand. Alex raised his eyebrows as he looked at their linked hands; he was glad that Nick seemed to have made a love connection. Nick was a great person, fun to be around; he would be good for Karole.

"Yes, thanks for everything, Fabe-man," Alex teased. "We'll be back to see you soon." Everyone grabbed their bag of fruit, tied it across the handlebars of their bicycles, and rode out. They didn't speak, unwilling to break the peaceful spell from the wonderful afternoon and outing they'd enjoyed.

As they hit the Y at the entrance of town, the couples separated, and heading in different directions, they were conscious of gossipmongers milling around on a Sunday evening, eyes darting around, ready to run and tell what they saw, or thought they'd seen, or just to start trouble. These people had no lives; their one purpose was to sow dissent and problems, so savvy people doing things they shouldn't exactly be doing, and in company they shouldn't be in, knew to stay away from the gossips like the plague. Alex knew he shouldn't be with Sherrette, especially while waiting for Miss Ida to decide if she'd allow him to take her daughter out, so he and his male friends quickly headed home, happy to have had their memorable time together with the girls at Flores's farm.

CHAPTER 32

As Alex got home and pulled into his yard, he was happy to see both the car and jeep in the driveway, so at least John was at home—unless he'd called Mr. Tooth to take him to a saloon. Alex's heart was in his mouth as he ran up the stairs and unlocked the door. "Dad, are you here? D-a-ad!"

"I'm here. Why are you shouting?" John came out the kitchen with an apron with the words "Kiss the Soldier-Cook" tied around his waist. Alex could smell food cooking. "You're just in time. Dinner'll be ready in an hour." John had a big grin on his face as he turned and led Alex into the kitchen. Alex was pleased to see that John seemed clear-eyed and sober, the very picture of health. What a difference a few hours and the departure of a hangover makes! Whatever had brought on the changes, Alex was extremely grateful for it, so he decided he'd play along and tease John.

"What're you doing, Dad? You don't cook. What do I smell?" Alex asked, sniffing suspiciously.

"I cooked meatloaf, and I'm baking potatoes which I dug up from our potato patch outside. What, don't you believe me? Please wash up and cut up the vegetables for the salad." He laughed.

Alex stared, mouth hanging open, "You're joking. You can't cook that well. Come on, what's up?"

"Ha, ha, I'm pulling your leg. Of course I can't cook well, but I can heat up a mean pot of food, which is what I'm doing. I ordered meatloaf and baked kidney beans from Rhys's restaurant, but I really am baking potatoes, and I still need you to make the salad. You should see your face!" he added.

"Whew, you scared me, Dad! All right, I'll go clean up. I'm not too hungry, but I'll eat a bit then go do my homework." He was glad to see John happy, almost back to his old self, which, in itself, was a miracle. Alex skipped off to the bathroom, where he stripped, took a quick shower, then headed back to the kitchen to fix the salad and tell John about the fabulous outing at the farm. It was a great finish to a great day; the only thing marring Alex's pleasure was the fact that he still hadn't heard from Miss Ida, and it was the end of the weekend. Well, there was always next weekend!

Alex awoke the next morning, cheery and anticipating his next encounter with Sherrette at school. No doubt about it, he had "Sherrette-on-the-brain-itis"; just the thought of her had his erection tenting the sheets in a shameful way. Alex thought back to what Ainsworth had said about staying away from physical contact and "handling" himself to alleviate the problem, but Sherr was all he could think about during every waking moment. She even invaded her dreams, and if he was not such a smart person, he was sure his grades would be in danger of slipping. Concluding that lying in bed daydreaming would do him no good, he got out of bed and made his way to the bathroom to take a cold shower, which didn't help (another myth, he thought), and prepared for his day at school.

CHAPTER 33

The next couple of weeks passed without incident; people weren't gathered in groups whispering about Alex, then going quiet when he approached, like they used to do right after Cathlean had left over three months before. As Alex had hoped for, and like his friends had predicted, new gossip had taken the focus off him and his dad. Mrs. Bucknor and Mr. Meggs were both on temporary suspension status, having been caught by Janitor Jamie in a very compromising position. Rumor said that they had been getting it on in a broom closet when Jamie was cleaning up one evening.

Supposedly, they'd been partially undressed, and rumor had it that Mrs. Bucknor's husband, Vernon, had moved out of their home and was staying at his mother's. Mr. Meggs had temporarily left town because he's heard that Vernon was looking for him armed with a machete, ready to do some serious damage. When Vernon couldn't find Mr. Meggs, he'd put a hex on Meggs, which caused Meggs to immediately become sexually impotent. *Amazing how much gossip surrounded that little tryst!* thought Alex; he shook his head thinking about people in this town and how many of them knew what the lovers had done and weren't afraid to gossip about it. Alex was so happy to get people's eyes off himself and John; he could kiss the couple, but that would only add to the rumors!

Alex continued to see Sherrette at school and shared a few stolen kisses with her, but she never had any update from her mum regarding his request to take Sherrette out. He didn't dare ask, figuring that if Sherrette had anything new to report, she would initiate that conversation. Either way, Miss Ida was being awfully quiet, much to Alex's chagrin. He resolved in his mind that if he didn't hear anything within the next week, it would be time to visit Miss Ida and plead his case once more.

That Friday night, as Alex was preparing to go to a soccer game with John, the telephone rang. John picked up, and Alex could hear him speaking in low tones, and he was giggling. "Now, what's that about? Sounds like things may be looking up for Dad. Good, it's about time!" He hoped John had met someone and could start getting over Cathlean. Alex was in love, so he wanted others to be in love too. "Alex," John called out, "it's for you. Pick up the telephone, please."

"For me, but who is it?" Alex asked, picking up the receiver with a puzzled expression on his face.

"Just pick up, please, and don't ask any questions," John shouted, a little irritated.

"Hullo," Alex said hesitantly. "Oh, Miss Ida, h-how are you?" He stuttered as he recognized her voice.

"Hello, young man," she responded in a brisk, no-nonsense voice. "And how've you been?"

"Fine, Miss Ida. To what do I owe the pleasure of this call?" He twirled the telephone cord nervously.

"I've been giving your request some thought and have decided that Sherrette can go to the movies with you. I don't need to go with you as chaperone, but you'd better not disappoint me."

"What? Thank you, Miss Ida! I'll take care of her. You can count on me," Alex replied.

"I still think you're both too young, but I appreciate that you've helped her with her math, and she's improved her grade a lot . . . Let me know what day you're going out, and I'll have her confirm."

"All right. Sunday afternoon may be a good day to go to a matinee. Please ask her to call." He hung up, filled with joy. "Dad, Miss Ida said I can take Sherr to the movies. We'll probably go on Sunday! I can't believe she made me wait, but she said yes, she said yes!" He lifted John off his feet.

"Put me down, Alex. I'm happy for you. We're going to be late for the game if we don't leave right now." John headed for the door, with Alex trailing behind him and a stunned expression on his face. The planets must have aligned for Alex because their hometown team, the Grigans, who had had a horrible record all season long, routed their opponents, beating them with a score of 11-0. Alex was on cloud nine all evening, nodding to a few acquaintances, happy and excited, planning his first official date in his mind. He couldn't wait, and he wondered how he'd survive the next couple of days.

Alex got up whistling on Saturday morning. He drove to Bluebell's and picked up a bag of johnnycakes, stopped by the market and got some fresh fruit, then returned home to fix a great breakfast for himself and John. After breakfast, he changed bed linens, gathered the other dirty laundry, and did a load of it. As John helped to hang the laundry on the clotheslines, he and John talked about nothing in particular until Alex suddenly blurted out, "Dad, how old were you when you lost your virginity? If you think that's inappropriate, please say so. I'll understand." He watched John turn red with embarrassment.

"I would say you're being inappropriate, but you'll be seventeen this year, and you're mature for your years, especially after the last few months we've had. I'll be honest—I was a virgin until I met your mum." At Alex's look of surprise, John went on, "Remember, I had been studying for the priesthood. I wanted to remain pure for my life in ministry, but things changed and I became a soldier."

"Dad, I'm not studying to be a priest, so I don't think I can wait until I marry to lose my virginity. All the young men my age at school are having sex and boasting about it, but I want Sherrette to be my first. If we start to date, I'm sure it'll happen. What do you think?" Alex asked.

John had always encouraged Alex to confide in him about anything, but this one really threw him off. As he looped a sheet over the line and pinned it in place, he handed Alex a clothespin to secure the middle of the sheet, then rubbed the grey stubble on his chin thoughtfully. "I know you're a sensible person, but please, if you indulge sexually, always, always use a condom! Matter of fact, after we finish the laundry, we'll go to Shipley's drugstore to pick up a big box. You and Sherrette have a lot of great years ahead, so be careful to prevent pregnancy and disease. Look at me, promise me!"

Alex looked directly into John's blue eyes. "I promise, Dad, but we don't need condoms yet."

"But you'll go get them today—no ifs, ands, or buts about it," John said sternly. "Let's finish up."

So they finished the laundry in silence, a little uncomfortable, but both were happy that they had talked about it. Alex wanted to hurry up so he could wait for Sherrette's call, even though they had brought the telephone outside, and it was sitting nearby so they could hear it if it rang. After they were done, Alex went into the house to sweep, mop the floors, dust, polish the furniture, and pick out his outfit for the date. He would be dressing casually in jeans and a button-down Oxford cloth shirt, but those clothes would be nicely pressed—of that, there would be no doubt!

CHAPTER 34

Alex measured out some starch powder, made from the milk of the cassava plant and dried to a fine powder, then went about preparing the starch for use. He slowly added some powder to a pot of boiling water, stirring briskly so it wouldn't become lumpy, and, as the starch cooked, it thickened into a transparent gel. Next, he set it aside to cool, got a large tub, and filled it with water that he could mix with the gel to make a watery solution. When the mixture was at room temperature, he dumped in jeans, shirts, and a couple of John's fatigues. After the clothes had become saturated, he lightly squeezed them out, then went outside to a different clothesline to hang them to dry.

Everything would be properly dried within an hour—up to two hours for the jeans—so John seized the opportunity for them to go to the pharmacy to pick up the condoms. John wasn't trying to embarrass Alex, but just in case Mr. Shipley, the druggist, had a problem selling condoms to the young man, John wanted to be there to purchase them if he had to. They drove the Mini Moke to the drugstore, parking in a spot directly in front of the store. As usual, Mr. Shipley was doing a brisk business at the counter; people were lined up waiting to pick up prescriptions; and everyone had their full consult time with him regardless of the complaint: constipation, ringworm, toe fungus, or dandruff.

Mr. Shipley was not a native Belizean, but he loved the townsfolk, and they loved and accepted him in return. The fact that he often waived payment from those who couldn't afford their medicine or extended credit terms and deferred payments to those who needed help didn't hurt at all. John and Alex awaited their turn, John standing in line, nodding to people he recognized.

Alex nervously paced, browsing the potions, ointments, and medications available for sale. Mr. Shipley's assistant, Pete, along with two Shipley grandsons, attempted to handle the over-the-counter sales, finding everything in record time and moving the crowds out to ease the overcrowding. It didn't really seem to work because, as two or three left, five more entered to replace them. Whenever Alex was there, he wondered just how the employees knew where everything was; they were able to put their hands unerringly on things that people wanted, even boxed-up ones. This was an amazing feat, so he concentrated on it to distract himself and not dwell on the reason why he was there.

The place was hopping, as usual, on a Saturday, because people had gotten paid and could come get their medicine. In the entire country of Belize, free inoculation shots and free medication were provided by hospital dispensaries for most ailments; drugstore prescriptions were only written for specialized or terminal illness that required managed care. Other reasons for the crowds that day included the fact that Shipley's didn't open on Sundays, so this was the last opportunity for pickup before Monday, Shipley's was also a welcoming and social meeting place. However, some simply came in to gawk—to see what they could see, to gossip about certain over-the-counter medications they saw people buying, and to wonder who was picking up birth control pills (they were only prescribed to married women) or buying birth control pills (too many people had too many children and were too poor to afford them!), who had a sexually transmitted disease, who was pregnant, or who was incontinent. These were deadly people who never hesitated to poke their noses into others' business!

As John's turn arrived, Alex joined him at the counter, where he furtively looked around to see who was watching before he approached Mr. Shipley and said. "I-I need some French Letters, Doc. A whole box, please." He nudged John in his side. "My dad is here. He can vouch for me if needed."

"No, young man" said Mr. Shipley. "I don't need Dad to say or do anything 'cause you're a man." He pulled out a box of condoms. "Let's see what size you need, hmm . . . regular, magnums?" He looked Alex over. "I think you need magnums, the largest I got. You don't want them babies breaking on you and making babies!" He cackled at his feeble attempt at a joke, while Alex cringed.

"Whatever you say, sir," he said, looking at John, who nodded in confirmation, and handed over a $10 bill to pay for the purchase. Mr. Shipley dropped the box into a brown paper bag, took the money, and wrote out a receipt, which he handed to Alex. "Next time you come in, you'll know what to buy, son. Just come straight to my counter, give me the sign, and I'll take care o' you. Don't need folks gossiping about your purchase, do we?" Alex shook his head. "Okay, we're done." And they were.

As Alex and John drove home, Alex was quiet, so John said awkwardly, "Do you know how to put them on, son? You start from the tip, then roll the condom downward until you're fully covered."

"Da-ad, we have sex ed classes at school and practice with a cucumber. I know what to do!" He was blushing all over. Won't be using these anytime soon. I know, you want me to be prepared."

"Yes, I do. If you have anything you need to talk about, I want you to continue to come to me."

"Thanks. I appreciate it, and I love you," Alex responded, as they pulled into their driveway. He bounded out of the jeep and ran to grab his clothes off the line; it was time to iron them now.

John unlocked the door, marveling at Alex's energy, while Alex entered then folded a blanket and sheet on one end of the table to use as an ironing board. He placed the iron on a metal trivet over the burner of the stove to heat; many people heated their irons in glowing hot coals, but John, concerned about safety, wouldn't allow Alex to do so. While the iron was heating, Alex lightly sprinkled the stiff, starched clothes with water, rolling them up in bundles to prepare for ironing.

John watched proudly as Alex precisely creased his jeans and began ironing them. He'd taught Alex to iron back in England (where they'd used an electric one), using military-style creases, by the age of ten, much to Cathlean's dismay. John was very tickled when his men would remark on the perfect creases in his fatigues and dress uniforms. He always gave Alex credit, who, as he got older, took delight in pleasing John by getting those creases just right. Alex had been the only child in primary school whose little knee shorts maintained their knife creases even after nap time, when all the other children's would appear appropriately rumpled, wrinkled, and limp.

Once Alex became a teenager and started high school, getting those proper creases in his uniform became even more important a goal as he ironed his uniforms for the week on Sunday afternoons. Whereas other teenagers and classmates appeared to have thrown themselves together before school each morning, Alex stood out and always looked well-groomed and put-together; even his P.E. gear was always on-point. Now, as he got those creases perfectly pressed in the legs of his jeans, he also made sure those in the sleeves of his shirt were perfect; he needed to make an impression on Miss Sherrette for their first official outing. Afterward, Alex ironed John's fatigues so that they, too, seemed like they could stand on their own without a body in them. Just as Alex was finishing up, the telephone rang. John picked it up, nodded, and silently handed it over to Alex.

Sherrette was on the line, gushing excitedly. "Guess what, English? We're going to the matinee tomorrow. I still can't believe Mum agreed! We can get tickets now so we don't have to stand in line tomorrow." Alex couldn't see her, but he could hear her heels clicking as she paced, unable to sit.

Feeling like he could relax a bit now, he responded with a laugh. "Yes, I'll go get the tickets, miss. Can you be ready tomorrow by two? Show starts at three." She responded in the affirmative. It was on, and all was right with Alex's world! He planned on taking Sherrette for a hamburger after the show, but he'd surprise her with that later. "So, I'll see you tomorrow," he said as they hung up. He turned to John. "Dad, I need to take the car and go pick up tickets for the matinee tomorrow."

"No problem. Be careful, I know how excited you are," said John, smiling at Alex's demeanor. Sherrette was the only person who could ruffle Alex's cool; she didn't know how much power she held in her little hands. John hoped and prayed in his heart that she never realized or it could be bad for Alex—could be his ultimate downfall. Cathlean had held John's heart in her hand since the moment he met her, and look how that turned out! John shook off the dark thoughts; he was going to stay positive and just wish the young couple the best. Also, Sherrette was not a conniver like Cathlean!

Alex went out to pick up the tickets, and while out, he stopped and made dinner reservations at an upscale restaurant, Yang Chew's. Sherrette's favorite food was Chinese, but she also loved burgers, so he figured he would book a place that catered to both of her tastes. Alex was in a great mood, so he decided he'd fix John a wonderful meal that night to thank John for his steady, dependable support. He stopped by the meat market to pick up some beefsteaks, then at Joseph's grocery to get Irish potatoes and corn-on-the-cob; he would cook the steaks and serve them with mashed potatoes, gravy, and roasted corn. Lastly, he stopped by Bluebell's to pick up a freshly baked lemon cake and some sweet buns for Sunday breakfast. He and John would eat their favorites for dinner and breakfast because this weekend was a time of celebration—Alex couldn't contain his elation; he felt as if he'd won a large jackpot! He had to pinch himself to make sure he was awake.

CHAPTER 35

Sunday dawned bright and clear. Anxious to get the day started so that afternoon could come much quicker, Alex got up to fix himself and John breakfast, just as he'd planned to on Saturday. Feeling the need to attend church to thank God because Miss Ida had said yes, Alex talked John into going along. He wanted John to take a moment to request a counseling session with Reverend Goff, so he was going to force John to speak with the minister about the alcohol drinking and the frustration of their being without Cathlean. It was time for an intervention before things spiraled out of control.

So they headed to the Stann Creek Methodist Church, where they were treated to the beautiful sounds of the choir, accompanied by a six-piece orchestra. Reverend Goff, a Barbadian, a nonconformist, had shaken up the church since his arrival during the Putnam family's time in England.

When the Putnams left Belize, the Holy Heart Catholic Church was by far the most popular, with its American and Canadian priests and nuns and young church staff whom the people adored. The Methodist Church had been stuttering along, but the arrival of "the Soulful Rev," as Reverend Goff was called, had changed the status quo, spearheading tent and summer-revivals, vacation Bible school, and youth and young adult summer camps. His sermons set the church on fire, and even though a few of the older conservative members left in disgust, most stayed to enjoy the changes.

As usual, Reverend Goff didn't disappoint; his sermon, appropriately entitled "Patience and Faith in God" spoke directly to Alex and John—Alex, because he had had to be patient and wait on God (and Miss Ida) the last couple of weeks, and John, because he felt like he was being tested like the biblical Job, since Cathlean had disrespected him in his home and left him in a huff as if he was the one in the wrong. Unlike the biblical spouse of Job who told Job to curse God, John had picked up a nasty alcohol habit, which he felt was a direct result of Cathlean's bad behavior. Truthfully, if John wanted to be honest with himself, he recognized that he'd already started indulging way before his wife left.

After the service, Reverend Goff stood at the exit shaking hands with his parishioners, asking after loved ones by name and comforting those whose family members were experiencing specific illnesses. He had a formidable memory, which endeared him to all because they were made to feel special that he singled each out to cheer up and encourage, personalizing their problems and showing that he cared. As he spied John coming toward him, Reverend Goff shook his hand and slapped him on the back. "Well, hello, Mr. Putnam. I'm very happy to see you. Thought I was going to have to stop in to see how you're managing." Lowering his voice, he continued, "So sorry to hear about Mrs. Putnam's departure, but God knows all, yes He does. Let me know if you need to talk. You too, young Alex!" he said, turning to Alex, including him in the three-way embrace. "Really, please make an appointment with the office to come see me, or if you want to keep it private, come directly to the parsonage."

John nodded, not trusting himself to speak; he still fell apart when people sympathized with him about Cathlean—it was a bit too much sometimes. Alex, reading John's mood, answered, "Thanks, Reverend. I'll make sure we come see you, either separately or together. Dad really needs to talk to you!"

Feeling that they'd taken up too much time, and because a few of the elderly church gossips were straining to hear what was being said, Alex pushed John along toward the door until they exited the church and drove home, being sure to use the shortest route, Gumágarugu Road. Today was not the day for stopping to socialize with friends on the way or for cruising home—no, it was date time!

John was very quiet on the way back, while Alex reflected on their grand return to church; he felt good, thought things had gone as well as expected, but now it was time to get ready for his outing.

Soon, they arrived home and entered the house. Alex went to the kitchen to prepare lunch for them: Spam sandwiches and chips were on the menu. John seemed to be over his sadness because he ate two sandwiches, washing them down with a large glass of grape Kool-Aid. Alex ate sparingly, just a half of a sandwich; he was saving his appetite for snacks at the movies, to be followed by dinner afterward. As soon as he could politely leave the table, and at John's nod, Alex headed for his room to change into his well-pressed blue jeans, shirt, and loafers, striving for a casual, but semi-dressy look. Sherrette was a sharp dresser, so he wanted to match her without eclipsing her style.

It was about 1:30 p.m., and the movie was starting at 3:00 p.m., so it was time for Alex to head out to pick Sherrette up. As John hugged him good-bye, he stuck some money in Alex's shirt pocket, along with a string of five or six condoms. Alex burst out laughing. "What're you doing, old man? I told you I don't need those today, but I'll take the money." He pulled out the condoms.

"Take them. I'll feel better if you do." He pushed them back into the pocket. "Go on, have fun!"

Alex asked John to call Sherrette to let her know he was on his way, then ran down the stairs, whistling softly to himself. His car gleamed in the sunlight—a chariot fit for picking up a princess. As he drove down Front Street, he saw people entering the stadium because there was a baseball game that day, and the hometown team was expected to win. Their record this season was perfect. Alex waved to a few people he knew but didn't slow down to talk. Soon, he was crossing Havana Bridge, the halfway point which let him know he was getting closer to Sherrette's residence.

After another fifteen minutes, he arrived and parked in front of the house. He looked up as he felt eyes on him; Miss Ida stood there looking out the window. Alex, feeling like a condemned man heading for the gallows, walked up the stairs, looking carefully at his feet to make sure he didn't trip. Before he could knock on the door, it was opened by Miss Ida. "Good afternoon, Alex. Come in!"

"Good afternoon, and how are you today, Miss Ida?" He looked behind her but didn't see Sherr.

"I'm fine, but it's a little warm today. Sherrette will be right out. Sherrette, Alex here now, gial!"

And Sherrette stepped out, looking like a vision in her powder blue ruffled blouse, flared white skirt, and blue strappy sandals. In her hand, she held a little clutch, the exact color of her blouse and shoes.

Breathlessly, she said, "I'm here, Mum. Hello, Alex. You're a little early. Please sit down." Alex looked at his watch and saw he *was* early, so he sat across from Sherrette as Miss Ida handed him a glass of water. Suddenly feeling the saliva leave his mouth, he gratefully took it and took a big gulp.

"Young man, a few rules before you and my daughter leave: You will be respectful toward her, you will not buy her or give her anything alcoholic, and you'll bring her home immediately after the movie's over." She winked at the last instruction because Alex had already told her about the surprise dinner to which he was taking Sherrette. "Okay, it's 2:30 p.m. Time for you to leave now."

"Yes, I'll do as you ask, Miss Ida. You can count on me. We should go. Ready, Sherrette?"

"Yes, I am," she said, as they both stood up. Miss Ida noted what a striking couple they made; Alex's shirt coordinated, matching Sherrette's even though they hadn't consulted each other about how they would dress or what colors they would wear. It was just one of those "in sync" things.

As they headed for the car and took off, Miss Ida watched until they disappeared around a bend in the road. She suddenly felt old; her baby was growing up, and she was going to have to let go soon. In the meantime, Alex and Sherrette arrived at Joyland Theatre by the riverside. There was quite a crowd of would-be karate enthusiasts who couldn't wait to see Bruce Lee in action. It was good that Alex had had the foresight to pick up the tickets on Saturday because people watched them, irritated that they hadn't got their tickets in advance too, as they walked straight into the entrance. The usher took their tickets and showed them to their plush, velvet seats in the raised section of the theater; the section not quite orchestra or mezzanine but better than the regular seats and cost quite a bit more.

It was still ten minutes to showtime, so Alex went to buy a couple bags of roasted peanuts-in-the-shell and a large drink that he and Sherrette could share. He smiled when he heard some folks in line grumbling that they couldn't buy tickets to this movie with Brooke Bond tea labels. Usually, people could collect ten labels to purchase one ticket, but that special deal did not work for new movies. *Enter the Dragon* had just arrived in Dangriga about a month prior, and because of its popularity, it would be a while before any discounts would be offered. The theater owner, Mr. Wallace, was going to make as much profit as possible, especially since people were willing and ready to pay a full price!

CHAPTER 36

As the lights went down promptly at three, Alex held Sherrette's hand, only letting go to shell peanuts and put them in her mouth. She even made eating peanuts a sensual experience to watch. As they sipped their drink and ate peanuts, and Alex placed her hand on his thigh, he felt like he could burst with happiness. He couldn't believe he was actually here; regardless of what anyone else called it, this was a date, and the way Sherrette kept looking at him from lowered eyelids, he could tell, or at least he hoped, that she was happy to be in his company too.

Alex settled back to watch Bruce Lee do his thing; the man had skills and was clearly a martial arts expert! Many children had been hurting themselves trying to copy Bruce's moves, but Alex had read that those moves had been perfected over many decades even though Bruce had died at the young age of thirty-three, just before the posthumous release of the movie. Alex found a kindred spirit in Bruce Lee, who'd been born in America but had moved to Hong Kong as a child. As a teenager, Bruce had been taunted by British students for his Chinese background, just as Alex was taunted in London for being a Belizean, a "coconut" who spoke English with a Caribbean accent.

The movie was two-and-a-half hours long, full of great nonstop, action-packed adventure. Amazingly, the audience was quiet and engaged, which was unusual because they were the type that usually spoke back to the characters on-screen, berating them loudly whenever they did something with which the viewers didn't agree. Ushers didn't have to throw anyone out for tossing peanut shells in the crowds as they were known to do at least two or three times per movie screening.

Anyway, the storyline was typical: good, in the form of Bruce Lee in collaboration with up-and-coming martial artist Jim Kelly, triumphing over the evil Mr. Han and brawny antagonist Bolo. Everyone was kept enthralled and entertained, for which Alex was extremely happy. The mood in the theater helped relieve any stress about his date with Sherrette, dinner, and how the afternoon or evening would end. Sherrette, for her part, cutely clutched his hands or arms, squealing though the tense parts of the movie, making him feel manly and protective toward her. It was a great time!

When the movie ended, she pouted, letting him know that she wasn't quite ready to head home. That's when Alex surprised her with the news about their dinner reservations at Yang Chew's, but she fretted about her mother's being upset that they were going to dinner. Alex shared the second surprise: Miss Ida knew about dinner and had already given her blessing. Sherrette couldn't help herself; as she got into the car, she leaned over and gave Alex a big hug, careful not to make it too long or inappropriate. She didn't know who Miss Ida's spies were or where they were hidden. Alex left the crush of folks leaving the theater and drove to the restaurant just about ten minutes away.

As they entered the restaurant and the aroma of all the good food greeted them, inspiration struck. He approached the host's corner, where tiny doll–like Mrs. Yang ruled with an iron fist. She pushed her glasses up on her nose and beamed as she spotted Alex. "Young Mr. Putnam," she gushed. "Right on time for you reservation. I hope you ready to eat. Hello, miss." She looked at Sherrette. "She's a pretty one, you lucky boy. I know, no menus. You already know what you want."

"Hullo, Mr. Yang," he said, looking toward the kitchen. "Mrs. Yang, how's your arthritis?" Alex said hugging her briefly, towering over her. "There's been a change of plans. Can we get everything packed up for takeaway? I need to borrow a hamper because I'm taking my girl on a picnic."

Sherrette glanced at him, but he stayed focused as Mrs. Yang clapped her hands, ordering Mr. Yang, the cook, and a couple of the kitchen staff to pack the food in cartons to go. Alex had pre-ordered hamburgers plus other Chinese fare: fried rice, chicken wings, sweet-and-sour pork, stir-fried vegetables, hot-and-sour soup, and pot stickers. These were Sherrette's favorites, but he had to admit they were his too. To wash the food down, he ordered cold ginger beer, and for dessert, he bought almond cookies and strawberry-filled cake. Seemed like a lot of food, but he'd take John the leftovers. He'd even ordered a separate entrée— teriyaki chicken and steamed brown rice for Miss Ida.

As he peeled some bills off and handed them to Mrs. Yang, she folded them and gave them back. "No, you keep!" she said. "Don't want your money. Go picnic, enjoy!" She pushed them toward the door. Mr. Yang came out the kitchen, wiping his hand on his apron and squinting at the couple. He took Sherrette's hand in his and slapped Alex soundly on the back.

"Yes, you bring hamper back later, Alex," he added to his wife's comments. "Say hello to Mr. John. Tell him to come for lunch or dinner soon. Sorry to hear Miss Cathlean gone." He looked sad.

"Thank you, Mr. Yang, Mrs. Yang. I'll tell Dad what you said. We have to go now," Alex said, leading Sherrette out the door before too many "lookie-loos" saw them and called Miss Ida. He had the ideal place in mind for their picnic: they'd go to "Y-Not Isle," near the river-sea bar-mouth. There were picnic tables they could set the food on, or if they wanted to, they'd set up closer to the seashore on a blanket he had in the car trunk; either way, they'd be alone and away from prying eyes.

They headed toward the island, about fifteen minutes from the restaurant. Alex was pleasantly surprised to note that no other cars were parked nearby; the place seemed completely deserted. He figured everyone was either at the baseball game, at the movies, or at home enjoying their Sunday. Sherrette delightedly agreed to beachside dining, so she helped Alex to spread the blanket out and set everything up on it. She was very happy to be on a grown-up date with her Alex; regardless of what anyone thought, this was their first date, so she planned on making it a memorable occasion. As Alex served her plate and she poured their drinks, she marveled at how beautiful the day was.

"To us, English, and to many more dates." Smiling, she clicked their plastic cups together.

"I second that, Sherr," he echoed, holding her hand around the cup and pulling her closer. "I haven't told you I love you today, have I? Well, I do, I love you. Thanks for saying yes to this date." They both drank some ginger ale, then started enjoying the very delicious Chinese cuisine. Alex could hardly concentrate on his food; he was so entranced watching Sherrette chow down. She was small but had a healthy appetite. Like him, and being an avid sports player, she loved vegetables, so she dived into the stir-fry and nibbled on small bites of chicken and pork.

"Mmm, this is so good. Thanks for getting my favorites." She bit into a hamburger. "But, you know, we'll need to hurry up and eat so we can get back home early. I don't want my mother telling me I can't go out with you again." She shrugged her shoulders, not seeming too concerned at all.

"Ssh, don't worry so much," Alex said between mouthfuls of his food. "I've got this, trust me."

So Sherrette relaxed, folding her skirt demurely under her thighs. Alex looked at her lustfully, hoping that his lascivious thoughts wouldn't scare her off; to his surprise, she met his eyes boldly and even winked at him. He was a little surprised but relieved that things didn't feel too awkward because if he had his way, he would get pretty close to Sherrette today; it was time to take things to a whole new level. So far, she seemed to be ready for whatever the afternoon brought.

Comfortable as they dined, they laughingly chatted about the latest gossip in Dangríga, who had gotten into trouble at school lately, John's drinking, and Miss Ida's campaign of pursuing her priest. The elephant in the room and taboo subject that they refused to touch was Cathlean and what she was up to. Alex had stopped listening to gossip about his mother; it was just less painful that way.

The waves rolled peacefully onto the shore, their quiet echo a wonderful backdrop to the two young lovers' picnic. As they finished eating and wrapped up leftovers to take home, Alex took the bags back to the car while Sherrette disposed of the trash. When he returned from the car, he had a flask of rum, which he opened and poured into their cups and added ice and ginger ale. "What are you doing?" Sherrette exclaimed as she watched him mix the drinks. "Hey, Mum said no alcohol!"

"Relax, baby. See, I added ginger ale, no big deal. Taste," he ordered, putting the cup to her lips.

"No, I don't want any." She swallowed, then looked at him in surprise. "This tastes really good." She took the cup and sipped greedily, while Alex smiled, happy that she liked the drink. He wanted her relaxed so she wouldn't reject his advances; he planned to seduce her or to go as far as she would allow him to. He wanted her fully compliant so she couldn't say later that he'd forced her.

On her part, Sherrette was feeling totally relaxed, stomach full and building up a little buzz. She was not a lightweight where alcohol was concerned; most Belizean children weren't since many families made their own wine from readily available fruit, rice, potatoes, or sugarcane. People often joked that if someone wanted to, he or she could make wine from anything at all; just as long as they could add sugar to it, cover it up, and allow it to ferment, they could drink or serve it as wine!

CHAPTER 37

Alex carefully made sure that his drink was heavy on ginger ale and light on rum, while Sherrette's drink was heavier on rum than ginger ale. After all, he did have to drive home at the end of the date. He reasoned to himself that getting Sherr tipsy was not his only reason for abstaining. As she leaned her back against him, he started running one hand up and down her leg, from ankle to knee, over and over. Sherrette held her breath as his hand went above her knee a couple of times, fully prepared to slap his hand away. But Alex was no dummy, he knew just how far to go to keep her in a trusting state of mind; however, his girl had other ideas because she turned around and embraced him fully, planting a huge kiss, all tongue, on his surprised lips. As Alex reared up to see what she was up to, he felt one of her little hands stroke his crotch not once, but twice. He couldn't believe his little tigress! He looked at her to see if she was drunk, but she was clear-eyed and sober.

"What's the problem, English? I've been wanting to touch you there. My friends say their boyfriends like it. Do you?" She rubbed a little more vigorously, laughing at his shocked expression.

"Sherr, do you know what you're doing?" Alex asked, praying she wouldn't stop touching him.

"No, but we can learn together, right?" She giggled. "C'mon, lighten up and enjoy, will you?"

"Oh, I'm enjoying, but you're playing with fire. You don't know how often I dream of you like this, sprawled across me. But in my dream you were wearing less clothes. He ran his hand up her leg, but this time didn't stop until he was rubbing her damp crotch. Her skirt was no barrier; it allowed for easy access, which he was very happy about. Sherrette squirmed as he slowly stroked her.

208

As her eyes opened wide, she increased the pace of her hands on Alex, while moving sensuously against him. He was in blissful agony, afraid he would burst at any moment; her touch felt so good! As she closed her eyes, he held her hips and ground against her, but it was frustrating because their clothes were in the way. She was making little sexy, moaning sounds in the back of her throat, while he was trying to hold back so he wouldn't embarrass himself and spill in his pants like the virgin that he was. As she stiffened against him and groaned against his neck, he could feel her detonating, so he held her tight as she shuddered through the climax, head thrown back, wanton, dazed, and sated.

As Sherrette calmed, she opened her eyes with a dazed expression on her face. Without missing a beat, she pushed her hands into Alex's pants while he loosened his fly, allowing her more direct access to his manhood. She reached in and started rubbing him more vigorously than before; his skin felt taut, becoming hot and flushed as he thrust himself up into her palms. She was good: her untutored hands quickly bringing him to completion as he grabbed a bunch of napkins to catch his ejaculate. Soon, he felt the top of his head blow off as he burst in her hands; he quickly spread the napkins around, and on her hands, wiping up trying to avoid a mess on her skirt or on his pants.

Alex then fell back breathless. "Whoo, thank you. That was something!" he said, not believing what they had just shared. Right there and then, he resolved to himself that when they went all the way next time, it would not be on a beach, but in a big comfortable bed worthy of Sherrette's virginity. As their heart rates normalized, they both straightened their clothes, grabbed the blanket, and walked to the car. After stowing it in the trunk, they looked at each other. "I need to . . .," Sherrette started, then headed for the bathroom. Alex understood and went to the men's room too; they needed to wash up as well as they could so Miss Ida wouldn't suspect what they had been up to.

As they met back at the car, Sherrette refused to look at Alex, so he took her chin in his hand and turned her to face him. "Hey, what's wrong? I'm sorry that happened, but I'd be lying if I said I didn't enjoy it. Please don't tell me you're sorry about it!" He noticed that tears were filling her eyes.

"Can we please not talk about it, Alex? I can't believe I was so forward wit' you. You mus' think I'm a loose girl," she wailed, accent thickening in her distress. "Let's just go." They got into the car.

"I promise, you are not loose. I love you. What we shared is sacred. Sorry it wasn't in a bed."

He put the car in gear. "Will you go out with me again? I'll keep my hands to myself next time."

"It's not your fault, and there won't be a next time," she said, but Alex knew better. The genie was truly out of the bottle now; his Sherrette was a beautiful girl who hid her passionate nature very well behind a calm exterior. There'd be much more physical interaction between them in the future, but he knew not to say so right at that moment. It was about 8:30 p.m. as he held her hand and quietly drove her home. He wondered if he would have to start from scratch to win her over again. God, he hoped not! He didn't have that kind of patience; he just knew he wanted Sherrette again, breathless, panting, detonating in his arms, and soon would not be soon enough to satisfy him!

He pulled in front of Miss Ida's, got out, and came around to open Sherrette's door. He grabbed the bag with Miss Ida's food as he observed her looking out her window, watching them as they came up the stairs. Before Sherrette could put her key in the lock, the door was thrown open and Miss Ida stood there; she looked her daughter over, trying to see if anything was amiss. Satisfied, she stepped back so they could enter. "Good evening, Alex. Thank you for getting Sherrette home on time since you have school tomorrow. Did you have fun?" She directed her question to Sherrette.

"Yes, Mum. Thanks for letting me go. Here's your food." She turned to Alex. "Thank you. I had fun. Good night." She shook his hand coolly and closed the door, almost slamming it in his face.

"You're welcome. I had fun too. Good night, Miss Ida." He saluted smartly and ran down the stairs. He was a little disturbed at how cold Sherrette was acting, but he figured he would let her chill out before approaching her again. Inside, he was bubbling with joy, and as he bopped along, singing along with the radio at the top of his lungs, he was thinking that everything was right with the world! He'd had his first climax with his girl, and in spite of what his friends had discussed, that girls didn't really enjoy sex, he was sure Sherrette had enjoyed herself too, since she had also experienced climax.

John wasn't home. Alex was a little disappointed that he couldn't share his experience with his dad, but he figured he would do so later.

Alex skipped through his shower and homework that night so he could get to bed to re-live his incredible evening. He analytically re-lived the events to see if there was anything he could've done better and came to the conclusion that everything had gone as well as they could; the one sour note was that Sherrette seemed upset that they'd gone that far.

CHAPTER 38

Next day dawned bright and clear. Alex jumped out of bed with a spring to his step. He couldn't wait to see Sherr at school later that day. He could only pray that her attitude had changed overnight. Alex met with a few classmates to go over a presentation they'd be doing that morning, so he didn't see Sherrette until assembly; she was sitting near the front but had not saved him a seat as she would've usually done. "Hmmm, guess that means she's still upset," he mused. "Oh, well . . ." But he couldn't speak with her after assembly because it was time to go do his presentation, so he made a mental note to catch her at lunch time since he would be busy at morning recess.

She must have been truly upset with him or disappointed with herself because he didn't see her all day. When he finally had a minute to ask her friend about her, the friend said Sherrette had left school early. Alex became very concerned, deciding that he was going to call her that night. If Sherrette still didn't want to talk to him, even on the telephone, he was going to drive over to her house to check on her. With that decision resolved, he tried to finish out his day, but it wasn't good. Some of his friends were talking about *Enter the Dragon*, having seen it over the weekend too. Normally, Alex would've joined in discussion of parts of the movie, but he was just not in the mood to be sociable. He would catch himself daydreaming about the more pleasant aspects of what had occurred the previous day and then be struck with guilt and sheer terror that he and Sherrette were over.

Finally, the day came to an end, and he grabbed his bicycle and broke all speed records getting home. John had just arrived and looked up in surprise as Alex strode in. He was used to Alex staying at school for sports or extracurricular activities; rarely did he come straight home each day. Alex threw down his knapsack as he said, "Hullo, Dad. How are you? Can I talk to you?" He came toward John, step faltering just a bit. That little lag in step concerned John—what was wrong?

"Hullo, son. I'm fine, but the more important question is how are you? How was your date?"

"I'm not so good, but my date was great. You weren't home when I got here," he accused. "But even though the date was good, Sherrette's angry with me. Why are females so difficult, Dad?"

"Ah, so, if you can answer that question, you would solve the question of the ages. Sit, tell me!"

"The movie was absolutely wonderful, dinner was great, but it's what happened afterward that's the problem." He sat next to John, a sad picture with arms hanging between his knees. "Dad," he started, blushing, "Sherrette and I . . ." He held up a hand to stop John. "No, I didn't need condoms." He hesitated, then blurted out the whole story of what had happened between him and Sherrette. John listened in silence, never once interrupting; he realized Alex had to get everything off his chest. Once Alex ran out of steam, John patted him on the shoulder.

"Congratulations and welcome to manhood, son. If I were you, I'd leave Sherrette alone until she comes around. You didn't do anything wrong. And no, I would not call her either, unless a week goes by and you haven't heard from her. I know you care and want to check on her, but you're walking that tightrope not knowing exactly what to do. Her friend can tell her you asked about her, but don't do anything else. Oh, keep those condoms handy, sounds like you'll need them. Now, let's have a wee drink to your success!"

As Alex sipped on the rum that John poured, he looked John directly into his bleary, bloodshot eyes. He felt a little guilt at the thought that while he'd been out the day before, John had been probably sitting at home, wallowing in an alcoholic stupor, but today, John seemed clear and sober as he doled out advice to Alex, which Alex wholeheartedly decided to embrace. Thanking John, Alex stood up to go wash before dinner. He wasn't very hungry, but he'd eat a little, then he'd get to his homework soon instead of making that telephone call to his grandparents in England or to Sherrette like he'd also planned to do earlier. He figured tomorrow would have to take care of itself, just like the Sherrette thing would eventually resolve itself, and things would get back to normal very soon.

All week long, Alex tried to ignore Sherrette when he saw her at school. At times, when he turned abruptly and caught her staring, he saw the wistfulness in her eyes and was encouraged; at least she wasn't looking at him in a hateful way. He even waved at her, and she tentatively waved back once, a half-smile on her lips before she remembered that she was supposed to be upset with him.

He figured if he didn't talk to her by the weekend, he'd go ahead and contact her; the separation was killing him, not to mention he was anxious to move the physical relationship forward. That was the problem with having had a taste; now he knew what he was missing. Friday mercifully dragged to an end, and Alex rejoiced because he hadn't had any difficult exams that week or he would've done horribly. It was all Sherrette, all the time, saturating his brain. Ainsworth teased him a few times and even had to poke him in literature class when Alex's mind was wandering away from the classroom and Mr. Tillett had called on him twice to answer a simple question about Shakespeare.

Alex headed straight home intending to spend time with his dad, but when he got there, he found out that John was going to the movies with Mr. Tooth and Mr. Yang. The two had just arrived to pick John up, and Alex had to laugh at the sight of the three friends: one tall, black, and toothless except for that one glistening gold tooth; Mr. Yang, small and timid-appearing; John, round, pasty, and white. *Just goes to show,* he thought, *friends can be found anywhere.* He was happy that John was getting out the house and not heading for the nearest saloon. As they left the house, the telephone rang, and Alex ran to get it. "Hullo," he said and almost dropped the receiver when he heard Sherrette on the line. "Hey, how are you, Sherr? I missed you!!!" he said.

"Hi, English." She sounded subdued. "I wanted to apologize for the way I treated you this week. I'm so ashamed of myself. No, let me finish this while I'm brave enough to talk about it. I'm more disappointed in myself than I'm upset at you. I couldn't talk to anyone about what happened, not even my friends, but as I thought about it, I was angry because I thought you would think I'm easy. You know I've never done anything like that before. Okay, please say something now."

"Sherrette, I'm not judging you. You know I love you, and I was happy we shared what we did. I'm angry at myself that I didn't seduce you in a better setting, one more suited to your virginal state. It won't happen again. Next time we'll get a proper bed! And there will be a next time, but I'll wait until you're ready, okay? Sherrette, if we ever, ever have a problem again, please do not shut me out."

"Well, I don't know 'bout next time, but all right. Mother's coming, but can we meet at the netball game tomorrow? I miss my English . . . Kiss, kiss, I have to go!" She disconnected quickly.

CHAPTER 39

On his end, Alex turned a couple of cartwheels and whooped it up; he was so happy! He would hang out at home tonight and finish reading *Heart of Darkness,* the gritty book by Joseph Conrad on which he was writing a book report, then go to bed a little early—even this was strange for a Friday night because he usually stayed up late. However, he didn't know if he'd be able to sleep that night, since he was seeing Sherrette tomorrow. He was happy: looks like they were back on track and better than ever. That telephone call from Sherrette had really made his day and his week too!

So Alex jumped up bright and early Saturday morning and fixed breakfast for himself and John, who had arrived home around 1:00 a.m., slightly tipsy and stumbling around in the kitchen until Tooth had laughingly put him to bed and left the house. Now John covered up his eyes as Alex opened the curtains. "Nooooh, please turn off the lights. They hurt my eyes!" he wailed, squinting at Alex.

"Dad, it's morning. The sun is out. Let's go to the netball game by Holy Heart Church. Time to get up, c'mon, Dad!" Alex shouted. He couldn't wait to see Sherrette and wanted to leave right then.

John grabbed the covers trying to pull them over his eyes. He looked like a mischievous boy as he burrowed his head under one of the pillow, buttocks in the air. "Don't want to get up. Go away. Leave me alone!" Alex shook his head, deciding to let John go back to sleep; Alex would go to the game by himself and meet Sherrette there. Whistling, he grabbed his keys and ran down to the car, figuring he'd drive just in case Sherrette needed a ride home afterward. It was going to be comfort all the way for his girl—he enjoyed spoiling her so!

When Alex arrived at the open field in front of the church, he saw Reverend Miguel, the netball coach working with a few men as they checked the equipment in preparation for the game. There was already a crowd gathering: families walking around, people holding cups of strong black tea or fever grass (lemongrass) tea to wash down the bread, johnnycake, or powder buns just purchased from Mr. Belisle, who'd set up his table to sell his wares next to the wooden bleachers at half-court. As Alex nodded at some of those standing in line to buy their breakfast, he caught the scent of a subtle, light, flowery perfume. It tickled and teased at his nostrils in a most pleasant way.

He pivoted slowly to his right and saw Sherrette standing there, a lovely vision, even dressed down in blue jeans and a black T-shirt with the name of the hometown netball team emblazoned on the front. She was arm-in-arm with her little friend, KiKi, Ci-Ci—what was her name again? Didn't matter anyway; his girl was here. Turning, he gave her a quick hug and a little kiss, not trusting himself to do more, as he was aware that the gossipmongers were out in full force that morning.

"Sherr, morning. I'm glad you're here. How're you this fine morning?" He held on to her hands.

"Mornin', English, good to see you too! Of course I'm here. I wouldn't miss it for the world. We're going to beat somebody's bottom today! Remember my friend Ki-Ki? Ki-Ki, Alex, Alex, Ki-Ki," she introduced with eyes gleaming as Alex and Ki-Ki shook hands. "So, let's go get our seats. Game's going to start in a few minutes. I cannot wait for us to kick somebody's batty!"

"Sounds good to me!" he said with a laugh. "You ladies hungry?" As they shook their heads, Alex took them by the arm, and they climbed the bleachers to their seats. Within a short time, the teams came out mid-court; the GrigaNets, the hometown team, decked out in their dazzling white shorts, paired with yellow jersey shirts and black tennis shoes, and the Cuban Invaders in red shirts, blue shorts, and white shoes. Soon the game began in earnest; the GrigaNets were heavily favored to win, but by halftime, they were down by fifteen points! Annoyed and grumbling, people got up to walk around and stretch their legs. Alex and the girls stopped several times to chat with friends and acquaintances in attendance. It was tough going; somehow, it seemed like everybody wanted to talk to them today!

Turned out Ki-Ki had brought a small hamper with fruit, ham sandwiches, cups, and a thermos of hot tea, so they didn't have to stand in the long line with other people trying to buy food. They munched on their food and chilled out as they waited for the second half of the game to start. The break was supposed to be ten minutes only, but in the laidback way of Belizeans, it wound up being closer to twenty minutes before the two teams came trotting back on the court to continue the game.

Things got hot and exciting about midway through the second half when Dorothy Antonio and Bittie Gongora seemed to have gotten it together at the same time, both deciding it was time to trounce the Cuban Invaders. They became a two-woman wrecking team, pounding the court relentlessly, as they ran up and down making much-needed killer points. At the end, it was the photo finish play in which Dorothy made the final point that gave the team a one-point win. It didn't hurt that the crowd went totally wild in support of the GrigaNets; everyone was on their feet, and thundering applause rocked the bleachers causing the Cubans to lose their cool so much that they lost the game!

Their team captain, JoJo, even lost her sportsmanship right there on the court after the game. She had to be forcibly ejected from the area because the umpire had made what she'd considered a bad call. When Dorothy snickered at JoJo, JoJo came after her with a piece of wood she'd picked up from the ground. She was screaming expletives in English and Spanish at the top of her voice and had to be forcibly restrained from physically attacking someone.

CHAPTER 40

After all the excitement had died down, the crowd started heading out, and Alex offered his companions a ride home. KiKi didn't live too far from Sherr, so Alex would drop her off first. As the three of them piled into the car, they laughed together as they remembered funnier moments of the game and of the morning they'd just shared. Good thing it was a morning game, so there had been no alcohol served. Nobody needed to drink anyway, because the GrigaNets had won, so everyone was happy and giddy with hometown spirit. They could hardly wait for the upcoming award ceremony and parade to honor the team; those festivities would be taking place the following week. It was a great start to what everybody all hoped would be a wonderful weekend.

After Alex dropped KiKi off, it was just him and Sherrette, and they drove the last few minutes to her house in companionable silence. He was content to just glance at her profile every so often to just enjoy her beauty and the scent of her perfume. They soon parked near her house, and as he came around to open her door, she turned to him with a secretive smile on her lips. "Hey, guess what? I have a surprise for you. Mum's not here. She went out of town to see her sister, who's ill. She won't be back until later this evening, so we can spend the whole day together if you want to."

"If-if-if I want to?" Alex stammered. "Of course I want to! But are you sure? This is a lovely surprise!" His head was spinning with erotic possibilities. Alone with Sherr—how'd he get so lucky? But somebody had to be sensible; how would it look for his car to be parked at Miss Ida's all day, making it obvious that they were inside together? He decided he'd go home and leave his car and return by bicycle; he had an obligation to try and protect his girl's reputation, so in spite of the fact that she pouted a little when he explained his plan, he helped her into her house, then headed home.

Alex must've broken all kinds of records getting home, going into his room to grab condoms, and pulling his bike out. John was not home, which saved Alex from having an awkward conversation about sex and birth control. Soon, he was on his bike, pedaling as fast as he could, heading for Sherrette's home. This time, when he arrived, he was sneakier in his approach; he even stashed his bike in the little shed under the house. He took the back stairs two at time to get to the door Sherrette opened for him, as quickly as possible. Looking around, he slipped inside, hoping no one had seen him. She stood just inside the door, looking virginal but sexy in a lacy, sleeveless nightgown that hung just past her knees. She had taken her hair down, and it now hung in dark, shiny waves around her shoulders. "Come on in, English. I was worried you wouldn't come back."

"What, and miss the chance to be with you? Rubbish!" He pulled her toward him and kissed her, then smoothed her hair back from her forehead. "So, what's it going to be, Sherr? Want to play cards or watch TV?" He wanted to get right to intimate time with her but didn't want to spook her.

"Sit, let's play cards," she said, pulling him down to the settee. "I'll deal the first hand of "War.""

So he sat down next to her, and they played a couple of hands, of which they each won. Soon, she got that wicked gleam in her eye and looked at him through her lashes. "Hey, I know. Let's play 'Strip Me Naked,"—the Belizean version of strip poker. The idea was that whoever lost had to remove an article of clothing after each loss. Alex suspected that Sherr was trying to move things along because she was usually a cut-throat card player, but now she had lost three hands in a row!

He was no dummy; after the third loss and she was sitting there in a half-slip and bra, he just pulled her down and started kissing her collarbone, her neck, and the dimples behind her knees. Sherr was ticklish, and as she giggled and squirmed, he removed his clothes until he, too, was down to his underwear. Next, he lay on top of her, started stroking at her, touching her sensitive areas and licking at the shell of her ear. She was unaware that he'd removed the rest of her clothing until she felt cold air and she felt her nipples pucker. She helped Alex remove his underwear and grabbed ahold of his manhood, stroking him repeatedly.

Things got hot very quickly, and Alex was afraid he's detonate in her hands like the last time, so he quickly rolled a condom on, and they got down to serious business. A few short rapid strokes and he felt very close to orgasm, but he patiently worked Sherr, trying to make her first time the least painful he could. She had her eyes tightly shut as she tensed up.

"Come on, baby. Trust me and relax," he coaxed as he continued rubbing and caressing her.

"But I'm afraid," she whimpered. "Please stop. It's too big. It hurts." She stopped moving.

"You really want me to stop?" he groaned, hoping she'd say no. If he stopped now, he'd die!

"Yes . . . no, just keep going," she said, relaxing a bit. As Alex patiently moved on her, he broke through her hymen. She gasped; he was so scared that he stopped moving, but soon, she grabbed him by the hips and began meeting him, thrust for thrust, stroke for stroke. In a few minutes, as Alex felt he was about to burst, he stroked her magic button with his thumb, rubbing vigorously, which seemed to have been the right move because in another minute, she was reaching for completion.

He was just waiting for her to get there with him because, honestly, he'd been ready at insertion! As she moaned in his ear and tightened around him, he let go and joined her in their perfectly timed moment of mutual sexual completion. As sweat dripped off Alex's brow onto Sherr, he moved off her and quickly jumped up, heading for the bathroom. There, he removed the condom and was about to flush it down the toilet when he re-thought it and decided to just wrap it up in tissue and put it in his pocket. He was probably just being paranoid, but he had this vision of the condom somehow coming back up when Miss Ida flushed after using the toilet!

He then found a washcloth on the side of the sink and quickly soaped it and ran warm water over it, then went back to the living room, where he gently cleaned the blood from Sherrette. She opened her eyes with a look of wonder and touched his face. "Thanks for making that special," she said shyly. "I'd heard I couldn't have an orgasm my first time, but I guess that's not true."

"I wouldn't know, but thanks for the special gift you've given me," he said, humbled, loving her. "Let's get a snack, then maybe we can do this again?" He wiggled his brows at her. "Got to hurry before your mum gets home." They got a few cookies and a glass of juice and watched a silly show on the TV while they rested. Soon, Alex took the glass from Sherr's hands and started tickling her.

Tickles soon turned to hot caresses, and very soon they were going for sexual encounter round two. They were not as relaxed this time, and Sherrette was a little sore, but that didn't stop them from experiencing simultaneous orgasms: Sherrette first, then Alex immediately after her. As they lay cooling off, he realized that the shadows were getting longer, and it was getting late, so he quickly went to the bathroom and cleaned up. He also bundled up all the evidence of the afternoon's activities—towels, washcloths, the sheet that Sherrette had lain on, and used condoms; he didn't want to leave anything for Miss Ida to find when she came home— he only hoped she didn't miss her linens! After hastily kissing Sherrette good-bye, he tied the bundle on the handlebars of his bike, jumped on his bicycle, and pedaled home. His mind dwelled on the pleasant and idyllic afternoon he and his love had just shared. If possible, he felt as if he loved Sherr even more; she was the one who completed him, someone whom he could even see himself marrying when they get older.

CHAPTER 41

This time when Alex got home, John's Mini Moke was in the driveway, so Alex quickly threw his bundle in the trash box so it could be picked up early on Monday. The town board trucks came by at the ungodly hour of 5:00 a.m., which Alex always hated, but in this case, he welcomed the idea that the evidence of his Saturday afternoon tryst would be gone as soon as possible. Alex washed his hands at the faucet outside the kitchen door, dried them, then lightly trotted up the stairs and pushed the door open. He startled John, who was heating a pot of something on the stove and humming a catchy little tune. John had a great voice that he'd planned on using in God's service as a priest, but it hadn't happened. He still had skills, though, but he was humble about his gift and kept it well hidden.

"Hullo, Alex, me boy. How goes it?" he greeted in a hearty voice.

"Hullo, Dad. What smells so good? Mmm, fresh bread too???!!!" He broke a piece off a warm loaf.

"I'm heating up some cow's hoof soup that I bought at the market. Look at the okra and all the other vegetables. I swear, we never had vegetables like these in England!" He smacked his lips.

The soup smelled mouth-watering, but Alex could do without the okra. Thank God they were still whole and hadn't burst open to spill their slimy contents into the soup! That slime always reminded him of snot dripping from a nasty, runny nose, but he was too happy to let anything bother him. He was waging an inner battle with himself regarding whether he should tell John about what had occurred that afternoon. Then he made a decision: this was John, the dad he loved, who loved him, and who never judged. Of course, he would go ahead and share details of the special afternoon—just not *all* the details! Alex cleared his throat.

"Dad, I've got something to tell you. Let's put the food on the table so we can talk." They got busy taking the pot and bowls to the table; Alex dipped up the soup, while John cut up a loaf of bread, liberally buttering the thick slices. Alex could see that John's curiosity was killing him, but John would wait as he always did. John always seemed centered; Alex envied his calm demeanor.

As they dug into the food, Alex said, "Well, Dad, we did it! Sherr and I had sex for the first time. It was wonderful, Dad!" He blew on the soup as he talked and became more animated as he remembered the encounter. "Miss Ida was away, and Sherr had planned on today being the big day. Thank you for talking me into getting the condoms, you're a wise old man." He tapped John playfully on the arm. "But seriously, Dad, it was incredible!" He bit into the butter-smeared bread.

"Son, now that you've tasted the forbidden fruit, promise me you'll be careful, please. You know Miss Ida can't find out what happened, or she'll come get me right after she goes to her priest and has gone to the police. She's no joke. Doesn't matter if Sherrette gave consent, she's Ida's baby girl." "We don't want her obeah-ing your arse, either."

"I know, Dad, Miss Ida frightens me, but I'm so very happy; Sherrette knows not to say anything. Anyway, I wanted you to know because I know I can trust you with anything, thank you for listening, as usual. Now what are we doing tonight? Do you want to play cards? I can still beat you, though I know we haven't played in a while." He pushed back from the table, picked up his dirty bowl, then went around to collect John's. As he piled dishes into the washpan, he reflected on the fact that they had no kitchen sink, which was a luxury only rich Belizeans could afford. He rolled his sleeves up and started washing the dishes. John hated washing dishes, while Alex found the ritual somewhat therapeutic; he'd often resolve issues while elbows-deep in soapsuds. He watched John hesitate in front of the liquor cabinet, look longingly at the bottles in it, but, thankfully, he didn't stop.

The excessive drinking appeared to be under control for the moment, but Alex knew John was still fragile; those bottles would always call his name in an intimate manner with their sweet seductive voices. John and Alex would play cards tonight until they were tired, and Alex would do his best to keep John distracted because if there was anything that Mr. John Putnam thrived on, it was competition. Alex may beat him at cards as he invariably did, but by God, John wouldn't go down that easy! So with the radio broadcasting the "Saturday Night Serenade" program in the background, they settled down to a lively couple of hours of cardplaying. Alex must've been more distracted than he thought, or John had been practicing with Tooth and other friends, because John surprisingly gained the advantage for a short period of time. Ultimately the big winner of the night was Alex, but it was not an easy victory; he'd won by the narrowest of margins and had to fight for every bit of it.

The next afternoon, Alex was happy to get a call from Sherrette. "Hey, English. What's going on?" she asked in a rushed, breathless voice.

"Sherr, how happy I am to hear your voice! The question is how are you feeling?" he asked.

"Well, Mama came back about two hours after you left, and she was sad because her sister's not doing well. I'm glad she was distracted so she didn't notice anything out of order. I just got back from church. She's still there talking to the priest about my aunty. At least that's her excuse today!" She laughed naughtily, knowledgeable in the ways of man-woman interaction now after her carnal encounters with Alex. "Anyway, I'm still feeling very sore, so my friends and I are going swimming in a few hours. I feel like a soak in the saltwater will do me good, you know what I mean?"

"Absolutely, that sounds good!" Alex exclaimed. He was happy she was going to the sea to bathe; it would soothe and heal her much-used body after yesterday's sexual encounter. And Miss Ida wouldn't query the action as anything unusual. Dangrígans strongly believed in the restorative powers of the Caribbean Sea, which flowed on the eastern side of town. It is more affectionately known as "Sea," and somebody could always be heard saying, "Bwai (or gial), I'm going to Sea to take a bath," or "I'll go set nets at Sea so I can catch some crabs for my dinner tonight."

"Oh, I have to go now, but please don't come over by Sea to check on me. I don't want the girls asking any questions. Okay, bye. I love you, Englishman!" And she was gone just that quickly.

As Alex hung up, he smiled, shaking his head and wondering if he should round up a few of his friends and "wander" over to crash Sherr and her friends' party anyway, but he talked himself out of it. She needed a little space, and he respected that, so he decided he'd clean the house and wash clothes, tasks neglected the day before in pursuit of the much more exciting Miss Sherrette.

The rest of the weekend crawled by; Alex could hardly wait to see Sherrette at school, but he knew that when he did, they'd have to act cool and pretend that nothing had changed between them. He didn't want her reputation sullied in any way, so he'd be in full protective mode. It was lunch time before they finally met; for some reason, either by accident or design, their paths hadn't crossed at recess. As he and Ainsworth grabbed a table in the corner, Sherrette and her friend approached. Alex took her tray and kissed her on the cheek as she and Tanzie sat down.

"How are you ladies this fine Monday?" he asked, locking eyes with Sherrette as Ains looked at Tanzie. Alex knew his friend was interested in Tanzie and had often expressed in vulgar terms what he wanted to do to with her. Ainsworth could have her; she was definitely not Alex's cup of tea!

"We're doing well. The swim was wonderful yesterday. Just what I needed," said Sherrette.

Alex correctly interpreted this as code for "I'm fine. I'm doing better physically," so he breathed a sigh of relief. "So, does anyone have exciting plans for Easter break?" They would get out of school for two weeks: Easter Week, which began on Palm Sunday, through Easter Monday (the day after Easter Sunday, a holiday in the United Kingdom and all British colonies), and the following week.

Christian influence and a strong Catholic presence in Belizean culture demanded that Easter/Holy Week be kept sacred, so there would be church activities all week long, including "The 14 Stations of the Cross" every night that week at Holy Heart Catholic Church. Anglicans and Methodists later joined in with Holy Thursday and Good Friday services of their own. The women would bake sweet potato pound (pudding) and hot cross buns; they'd prepare their salt fish and the cassava-ginger drink called *hee-u*. All this would be consumed Good Friday afternoon, at which point all stores, banks, and official businesses would be closed until Tuesday, the day after Easter Monday; no cooking was allowed Good Friday afternoon—starting at noon, the time at which Jesus had died, according to the Bible. People would take time out that day to solemnly and quietly reflect upon Jesus's crucifixion and his sacrifice for mankind.

Late in the day, around 6:00 p.m., some of the more adventurous youth would create a "man" from straw and dried banana leaves, and they'd dress him, nail him to a cross made from wooden posts, then noisily carry him through the streets to the beach—a loose simulation of what had been done to Jesus Christ, as the story in the Bible described. Upon arrival at the seashore, they, and the midsized crowd following them by then, would take turns beating the "man" with sticks or weapons while singing songs about payback to Judas, *Hu-ree-iu* in the Garífuna language, for his betrayal of Jesus.

Once they'd beaten him to a pulp, they ceremoniously set him on fire, continuing to sing and mock him to repay him in a joyful, bloodthirsty way, for causing Jesus to be crucified. This was a barbaric custom, considered harmless but frowned upon by some; it was part of the Easter tradition in Dangríga and other Garífuna communities. People would awaken early on Holy Saturday morning, attend early mass, then return home to fix a breakfast of hot cross buns and tea. Soon, you would hear the sound of their machetes as they killed and dressed squawking chickens, cooked red beans, grated coconuts, and squeezed milk from the pulp to prepare rice-and-beans. They also boiled eggs, Irish potatoes and chopped up their onions and vegetables for potato salad; no Belizean Easter meal was complete without rice-and-beans, chicken, or potato salad, staples for special-occasion dinners.

These food preparation activities were often accompanied by transistor radios loudly blasting updates on the big annual cross-country Holy Saturday bicycle race which went from Belize City to the Cayo District and back to Belize City, a rough, gravelly, and hilly course not designed for the faint of heart. What Belize's local Tour de France lacked in finesse, it made up for in spirit: people rooted loudly for their favorites, and it was all they could do to keep up with their cooking responsibilities and stay on schedule as they became more and more excited about the race. It's a good thing the race was usually over by about 2:00 p.m., the first-, second-, and third-place winners having been crowned immediately afterward, empowered with bragging rights lasting throughout all of the next year.

On Easter Sunday morning, everyone dressed in their Sunday best: girls wore their frilly, lacy, pastel-colored dresses with matching hats and baskets, and boys wore their white shirts, nicely starched black or white pants, and neckties. Parents woke up, tired from attending Holy Saturday dances the night before; they were bleary-eyed and grumbling as they attended Easter sunrise service at their various churches. The children, decked out in their finery, attended the 9:00 a.m. service. They lined up at the back of the church to process in, excited and ready to proudly recite their Easter speeches that they'd been painstakingly rehearsing over the last few weeks. After church, some people went home, while others visited, sharing and enjoying their lovely and delicious Easter feasts. All the children cared about was that after today, they would be out of school for another whole week!

PART V

Cathlean's Story

CHAPTER 1

While Dangrígans were happily preparing for Holy Week and Easter Sunday festivities, Cathlean was experiencing her own private hell. What Alex and John hadn't seen on that day six weeks earlier when they visited Shipley's was that she had also been visiting the drugstore. She'd almost run smack into Alex and John, but quick thinking had saved her from having to see or speak to them. She didn't want them asking her about her trip to Shipley's, so she'd deliberately hidden from them.

Cathlean had begun to have breathing problems; the first time it happened, she thought Zeke had been the cause of her breathlessness. After a particularly lusty romp in her bed one afternoon, she must have passed out because she awoke to the feel of water being splashed on her face and Zeke straddling her, performing mouth-to-mouth resuscitation. After she had been stabilized, things were fine, but she was deathly afraid of dying, so she, at Zeke's and Betty's urging, had visited Mr. Shipley to see what was wrong. There'd been too many people in the store, as usual, so Cathlean had quietly whispered her request for a private consultation to Mrs. Shipley. These one-on-one private sessions were costly, but Cathlean would get one of her men to pay; she always did, so she didn't even hesitate. Nothing but the best for her, as usual!

So, at 9:00 p.m. that night, she covered up her face in an attempt to disguise her appearance and shuffled along to meet with Mr. Shipley in his personal sitting room. While Mrs. Shipley served tea and cookies and made small talk with Cathlean, Mr. Shipley prodded and poked at Cathlean as he tried to examine her with a minimum of fuss. As he listened to Cathlean's heart with his stethoscope, his demeanor went from jovial to worried in mere seconds. "What is it, Doc?" Cathlean asked. Being the sensual creature that she was, she was concerned about problems that would threaten to curtail her bedtime activities. "I know something's wrong, so please tell me, what!" She pushed her plate aside and tried to stand up, but Dr. Shipley pushed her back into the chair.

"Take it easy, Mrs. Putnam," he said. "Let me finish examining you!" Mrs. Shipley grasped Cathlean from behind, stroking Cathlean's shoulders, then she looked expectantly at her spouse.

"Thanks, dear." He smiled at his wife. "I don't like the sound of your heartbeat, Cathlean. I'll ask Dr. Rivas to order some tests for you, then you can go from there. He's discreet and will keep your confidence. But . . . you'll have to go see him in Belmopan, so let me write up the request." He scrawled illegibly on a blank page, then folded and handed it to Cathlean. "Take care of yourself."

Cathlean grabbed it and stood up in a daze, and an uneaten cookie slid off her lap and onto the floor, but she was totally unaware of it in that moment. "I-I-I'll go this week," she promised in a tremulous whisper, appearing beaten as she exited the door. The entire visit had taken no more than twenty minutes; now her mind was buzzing with questions like: Was she dying? Would she be okay? Should she tell John or Alex anything? Maybe she was imagining it, but she thought she felt her heart racing right then, so she made herself breathe slowly as she crossed the street and headed for the Booty Bunker. As she strode along, she pondered her fate and considered her options.

She decided she'd go ahead and get a ride to see the doctor tomorrow; no public bus or transportation for her—she was too good for that! Besides, people would stare, and though she liked attention, she was afraid that people would be able to see that she was sick, unwell, and tainted somehow. The trick now was to figure out who'd be her chauffeur to the doctor. Let's see, whom would she ask? Zeke? No, she didn't want him to see her weak or helpless. John? He would take her, but then he would become clingy. Alex? No, he wouldn't want to do her any favors. She'd figure it out later, but now it was time to have dinner and get some good sex so she could re-affirm life in the most basic of ways. Regardless of what anyone said, she was still in the land of the living and would make damned sure she remained there until such time as she was dead and buried.

CHAPTER 2

The next day dawned bright and sunny. Cathlean woke up, energized and determined to go see the doctor as soon as possible, so she started making telephone calls to the men she knew who owned cars, but unsurprisingly, nobody was available to help her in her time of need. What to do? *Hah,* she thought. *I'll find Tooth. He'll help me without asking a lot of questions.* So she wrote a note and sent a boy from the Booty Bunker to find Tooth by Riverside, the place where he usually hung out awaiting work. Of course, he immediately dropped everything and agreed to pick her up. When he rattled up in his wreck of a cab, Cathlean had second thoughts as she wondered if the poor excuse for a car would get her to Belmopan and back. As she sashayed out in her pumps, Tooth couldn't help but be impressed: the woman was gorgeous even if she seemed a little off at times.

"Good day to you, Miss Lady," he greeted. "Sorry if I took a while. I just dropped Aunt Lottie off after her trip to market. Can you believe that woman can't even get her son to take her shopping? *Magóliti,* lazy (he translated the Garifuna word), ungrateful wretch! Now that she bought food, she still has to cook it for 'im. Unbelievable how she spoils that man." Tooth was irritated. "Let's go!"

"Are you sure this wreck will make it? Uh, I mean this car," she said as he glared at her. "Seems to be in so much worse shape than last time I rode with you." She climbed into the front seat.

"You let me worry about that, Miss," Tooth said, going around and climbing into the driver's seat. "I'll get you there safe and sound. Now, which doctor did you say you visitin' today?"

"Dr. Rivas, let's see, his clinic is at 3245 Government Walk in Belmopan," Cathlean said, looking at the note in Mr. Shipley's almost-illegible scrawl. "Do you know long it'll take us, Tooth?"

"I know where that street is, we'll be dere in one-and-one-half hours. Please sit back and relax."

They took off, and as old friends do when they get together, they started talking and catching up non-stop! Cathlean subtly tried asking about Alex and John without actually asking, and Tooth carefully shared some information with her. He was still upset with her for stepping out on John with Zeke, so he really didn't want to talk about her family. Instead, he tried to question her about her doctor's visit. "So what's really going on? You don't look sick to me at all," he said.

"Just 'cause I had a breathing problem a few days ago, Shipley said I need to go see Dr. Rivas, who's a cardiologist. I passed out last week while Zeke and I were having sex." She laughed nervously.

"What? That's not even funny, gial," scolded Tooth. "Really, that's what happened? How?"

"How do you think? We were doing the deed, I got excited, I passed out. End of story!"

"Well, let me get you to see the doctor so you can get better soon. You know I care 'bout you."

They drove along in silence, each lost in their own thoughts. Tooth wondered if Cathlean was being punished for what she'd done to John; Cathlean wanted to know just what she'd done to deserve to be sick. In her arrogance, she couldn't even own up to her bad actions toward John and Alex. She shook her head in denial, then pulled out ham sandwiches and 7-Up bottles to share with Tooth. As she handed over the food, she finally admitted in a trembling voice, "I'm really afraid, Tooth; if it's something serious that I have? I'm too young to die!" she wailed, dropping her sandwich in her lap. "Please, Tooth, lie to me, tell me that I'll be fine." She hastily wiped tears from her eyes.

"Gial, stop that right now and start praying! Where's your faith? You know this is just a trial you're going through. Now eat your lunch, then lay back and take a nap, we're about halfway there."

Cathlean opened her mouth to say more, but seeing a stern look from Tooth, she sat back and ate. They traveled the rest of the way in silence, soon pulling into the driveway of a quaint, white clinic, proudly advertising in black type, "Dr. Dan Rivas, M.D. of Cardiology and Family Medicine."

"Well, this is it," Cathlean said, reluctantly exiting the vehicle. She had a very bad feeling about this. She thought back to the episodes of breathlessness that she'd been experiencing and ignoring these past months. If she hadn't passed out while sexing Zeke, would she be here now? She doubted it very much; it was easier to live in the state of denial when she didn't want to deal with reality.

Tooth, always a friend, took her lightly by the elbow in a strong, silent show of support as they walked through the door. The office was small, sparse, and clean; the scent of antiseptic was overpowering but subtly comforting. Colorful plastic chairs lined both walls, and there were a few people sitting, waiting to be called. Cathlean went to the reception window on rubbery legs; she was terrified to find out what was wrong with her, but the friendly "Nurse Dorla," as her name tag read, smiled reassuringly as Cathlean handed her the note from Mr. Shipley. "Thanks, Mrs. Putnam. Here, take this clipboard and fill out the forms. Doctor will call you in a few minutes."

Cathlean walked back and chose a red chair to sit in; she needed something bright, hopeful, and positive at that moment. In a short time, she'd completed the forms, and just as she started squirming, becoming restless, a side door opened, and a thin, bespectacled young man in a lab coat came toward her. *Hmmm, he's not bad-looking,* Cathlean thought, loving his clean, intelligent look. *I wouldn't mind getting myself a piece of him!* She actually licked her lips.

He stopped in front of her with his right hand extended to shake hers. "Mrs. Putnam, thank you for coming in. Doc Shipley already told me about you. Come on, please follow me." He had a deep, sexy voice. He led her from the waiting room; Cathlean would've loved to walk ahead of him so he could admire her bountiful assets. Oh well, no problem—she would work it out later.

"Dr. Rivas, I should be the one thanking you. I'm glad you could see me this soon," she said breathlessly, not sure if she was short of breath again or just excited to meet the doctor.

"Oh, Shipley sends me intriguing cases all the time. He's a smart man, and you're in good hands." He led her into a cubicle and instructed her to remove her top and bra. By the time she had done that, a Hispanic-looking

235

gentleman in a lab coat had joined them. "Mrs. Putnam, this is Dr. Garay. He'll assist me and consult on your case. Dr. Garay, this is Mrs. Cathlean Putnam."

"Please call me Cathy, both of you," she said flirtatiously. "I know you're young, but I feel old if you call me Mrs. Putnam. Besides, I'm not married!" she said, stretching the truth a little.

"All right, Cathy. Please sit here so I can check you out." He placed a blood pressure cuff on her arm and wrote down the reading, then listened to her heart using his stethoscope. He held up a finger requesting silence and motioned to Dr. Garay to step up and listen too. A look passed between them, which made Cathlean nervous as she looked from one to the other. Dr. Rivas shook his head, putting a finger to his lips when he saw she was about to question him.

"Hold on, Cathy," he said, "Dr. Garay and I will be back. Please put your blouse back on and wait." They turned and walked out step-for-step, with military precision, which reminded Cathlean of John. For one quick moment, she wished that he could be here to support her during this ordeal. After about ten minutes, the doctors returned, a plump nurse they introduced as Nurse Nuñez accompanying them. "Cathy, I'm sorry to ask you, but please take your blouse off again. We'll need to do an electro-cardiogram, or EKG, along with a stress test. I need to check your heart a little more. Please go with the nurse. Relax, I assure you, we'll be right in."

CHAPTER 3

Cathlean became more alarmed—what exactly was going on? The doctors were concerned about something, but they weren't talking . . . at least not yet. She followed Nurse Nuñez into a cold, sterile room, and as she was hooked up with several electrodes all over her chest and back, she found herself praying to God, bargaining with Him, something she hadn't done in a very long time. If only He made everything okay, she would turn from her evil ways and do the right thing; she made the promise silently, sincerely meaning it in that very scary and lonely moment.

Soon, the doctors came in and read the printout from the EKG machine, pointing to certain parts of it, nodding their heads but still not making any comments. As the nurse helped Cathlean to put her bra and blouse back on, Cathlean wondered if she was being paranoid because it seemed like neither doctor nor the nurse would look her directly in the eye. Irritated, Cathlean blurted out. "Well, doctors, what's going on? Will you please tell me? I'm not patient. I need to know right now!"

"Cathy, calm down, please," said Dr. Rivas. "We wanted to be sure of our diagnosis before we spoke to you. You have an enlarged heart, your blood pressure is elevated, and you have a small heart murmur. You can go on a waiting list for a new heart right away, but for now, we'll have to start you on some heavy medications. If we don't fix this problem, we can't guarantee you'll be here longer than one year. You're in relatively good health, and that should help, but it's not the best news . . . I'm so sorry." He held Cathlean as she swooned without warning, almost falling to the floor. It's too bad, he thought with pity, holding her close. *This is such a beautiful woman. What a pity!*

"Oh, my Lord, are you sure? Is that why I've been having problems breathing? I'm too young to die," she said selfishly, then remembering Alex, "Oh, no," she wailed dramatically, "my son's way too young to be motherless! You know what, Doctor, maybe I'll just have to get a second opinion."

"Do what you think is best, but I'll give you a prescription to fill at the dispensary downtown. I'd suggest you get the medication before you leave for home, whether you get a second opinion or not. Nurse, please take Mrs. Putnam to see Nurse Dorla so her name can be added to the waiting list for a transplant. 'Bye, Cathlean. I'll write up an order to see you for a follow-up visit in three weeks."

He was talking to her back since she'd already turned, plodding down the corridor behind Nurse Nuñez, her head down as if going before a firing squad. All thoughts of flirtatious behavior completely left her mind; she was in shock, facing her own mortality for the first time. She could not believe she was dying; she wondered if she'd get a second opinion, but for now, she was confused. And where was John when she needed him? As usual, he was missing in action; she sneered, needing a target for her anger. Thank God he or Alex weren't there, or they would feel the brunt of her rage!

After snatching the prescription from Nurse Dorla and stepping smartly through the outer door, Cathlean headed toward Tooth's car. He came running behind her, almost yanking the door off its hinges in his haste to open it. He quickly closed and secured it and jumped into his seat. Tooth looked at her sitting as straight and unbending as a statue. "Cathlean, where to? What happened?"

"Can you believe that damn doctor said I have a heart problem? The nerve! I will just get a second opinion, thank him very much. Drive, Tooth, let's go to the dispensary. Know where that is?"

"Yes, I shore do. A heart problem? What's that exactly? Let's go get the medicine then head back home to Dangríga. Sorry to hear your bad news." Predictably, he was already solidly in her corner. He took off, and after a few quick turns and a six-block drive, they queued up in front of a medium-sized, warehouse-style, unpainted brick building. They knew they were in the right place because people were standing in line, empty bottles in hand (they needed to bring their own bottles for liquid medication), complaining about the long lines and that the dispensary should hire more staff to keep the lines moving. Some children with runny noses played hide-and-seek through their parents' legs, while others and some adults appeared listless and sick, patiently awaiting their turn to get their much-needed medicine. Before Cathlean could add her irritated voice to the noise, Tooth touched her arm, motioning her to go wait in the car while he held her place in line. He promised to send someone to get her when it was their turn, and she was only too happy to comply.

After she'd waited in the car about twenty minutes, she must've dozed off, because she was awakened by a tap on the car window. She jerked awake and saw a young teenaged girl who told her that Tooth was calling her back in. Cathlean straightened her clothes, wiped the sleep from her eyes, and joined Tooth. Within ten minutes, they were through the line; somehow Tooth had managed to get two empty bottles for the tonic the doctor had prescribed. The other four medications were in pill form, so they were easily measured out into small envelopes, labeled, and handed over to Cathlean. She ungraciously snatched the medicine from the clerk in attendance, and, just like that, it was time to go.

"Whoo-ee, I'm glad that's over," she huffed as they re-entered the car. "Tooth, let me give you a treat. We'll go down to Roaring Creek and get some good fattening food to eat on the way back. And some strawberry jam rolls, we have to get a dozen of those. If I have to die, I might as well go fat and happy!" She was babbling, but she didn't care how she sounded; if she kept talking, she wouldn't have to think about the death sentence hanging like a dark cloud over her head. Tooth silently drove ten miles in the opposite direction to accommodate Cathlean's request. He knew she was still processing the horrible news, but they'd really have to discuss her options on the way home.

In short order, they arrived at the Halfway-Point Restaurant, located on the Hummingbird Highway, almost exactly half-way between Dangríga and Belize City, hence the name. Cathlean knew the proprietress of the restaurant, Mrs. Lily Roboteau, so they were served rather quickly, the best of what was available at that moment, for the lunch crowd had just left the restaurant, having gone through most of the menu. They headed home as Cathlean handed Tooth a container of food, and then she tore into hers as if afraid it would be snatched from her if she didn't devour it quickly.

"Hey, slow down or you'll choke!" cautioned Tooth as he watched Cathlean shoveling food into her mouth. "You must be rattled, gial. I nevah seen you eat like that befo'. Want to tell me more about it now?" he asked, stepping on the gas, determined to make it to Dangríga within two hours.

"No, can we please wait? I promise I'll tell you, but I want to enjoy my food," she said as she held up a hand.

"All right, but you're going to tell me everything, you hear?" he replied. They ate in companionable silence; Cathlean licked her fingers after chomping on an especially juicy chicken leg. "That lady can cook. This is good, but I know I can still do better," she smirked at Tooth. After she ate most of her food, she had a jam roll and a coconut tart, then rubbed her stomach. "Aahh, that's sooo good!!!"

CHAPTER 4

As she cleaned and packed up the debris from their lunch, she abruptly started talking. "Tooth, I have a heart murmur and an enlarged heart. I have to go on a waiting list for a transplant. If I don't get a new heart, I won't last another year. I still don't know if I believe Doc Rivas, but something is wrong with me. I can't breathe properly, I get tired easily, and I feel chest pains. I can't sex up my man without scaring him by passing out," she said, chuckling. Becoming serious, she continued, "I'm thinking about getting a second opinion, but I'm sure I'll get the same result. I may just go see the local healer, or *Buyei*, and request a Dugú ceremony to cleanse and heal my sick self. I have to find out how much it'll cost, but he's my mum's cousin, and my aunty works with him, so maybe I'll get a discount. I don't want to have to live at the Dabúyabah (Temple) for a whole month, but I'll do it because I am way too young and pretty to die!" She chuckled, but at the same time, she was angrily wiping at new tears pouring down her face.

"Cathlean, don't talk crazy, woman! I have faith that you can beat this thing, but you have to fight and hang on till you get a new heart. I also think you should tell John and Alex," he said as she shook her head. "That's not fair, why not tell them? Yet you're willing to go to Temple to see the Buyei???!!!" He was puzzled by Cathlean's reaction; you would think she'd want her family's support.

"No, I won't, and don't you dare either! We've been apart six months now, neither of them has tried to visit me or checked on me," she pouted. "I don't want their pity, they don't need to know!"

"Yes, ma'am, I promise," he replied, a serious expression replacing the jovial one he usually wore on his face. He wouldn't initiate the conversation, but if it ever came up and John or the boy asked him, he would tell what he knew. "For the record, I don't agree 'cause this is serious, but I'll let it go. Just take your medicine, get that second opinion, but stay away from that Dabúyabah—it's a bad idea. Oh, be sure you go to your next appointment. You need me to take you, let me know so I can leave my day open." Tooth secretly cursed himself for being a fool to be used by Cathlean.

She nodded in agreement; Tooth was caring and concerned, and he would keep her confidence. She felt better for having shared her diagnosis with him, but she doubted she'd tell Zeke, fearing his reaction. She didn't want him to pity her or treat her like an invalid; she still wanted to enjoy their rough sex play. She also decided she wouldn't tell anyone at the Booty Bunker because somehow, word would get out. They finished the trip in silence: Cathlean contemplating her next move, and Tooth determined to be there for her, a strong, supportive presence for as long as she needed him.

PART VI

Alex's Story

CHAPTER 1

A week or two after Cathlean had gone on her jaunt to the the doctor's office, Alex was still scheming to find ways to get together with Sherrette. Having had two sexual encounters with her had only stimulated his appetite for more. He dreamed about her at night and thought about her constantly during the day. They sat together holding hands at recess, and they ate lunch together most of the time. He felt like she was an obsession, a fever he couldn't cure, but he wouldn't trade the feeling for anything else. He was lucky because he could see her every day without having to sneak around.

Alex had long talks with John about relationships, asking about specifics of John and Cathlean's marriage and tips about treating a woman, so he could apply them to his situation. His plan was to be so attentive to Sherr that she would fall even more head-over-heels for him and that she would be as obsessed with her as she was with him. In English Literature, Alex's favorite Shakespeare classic was *Romeo and Juliet* because he could relate to their story. This time, though, his and Sherr's love would not end in tragedy; he would see to that as long as he had anything to say about it. Miss Ida didn't scare him much; at least that's what he convinced himself of!

The young lovers were extremely lucky because they seemed to fly under Miss Ida's radar, and somehow, she didn't know how deeply involved and in love her daughter and Alex were. She still thought they were experiencing "puppy love," nothing she needed to worry about; therefore, she relaxed her guard somewhat. What she didn't know was that her sweet little Sherrette had become adept at deception and that sometimes, on days when school let out early for planning or staff meetings, the couple would go picnicking past the Pelican Beach Resort, or at The Jetty, make-out spots where they were becoming more comfortable at expressing their love in a physical manner.

Sex was something they were starting to indulge in on a regular basis, so when Alex asked John to take him back to the drugstore to replenish his condom supply, John became a little concerned. "Son, don't you think you should slow down? You and Sherrette both have plans for college and great careers. Don't let an unplanned pregnancy sideline you," he cautioned as they drove to Shipley's.

"Dad, you worry too much, nothing's going to happen," Alex scoffed. "Besides, we're safe; Sherr and I are watching her ovulation cycle closely." This time, when they entered Shipley's, Alex asked John to purchase double the largest box of condoms. John raised his eyebrow but made no other comment to Alex, but he was a little alarmed.

"Fine, if your girl gets pregnant, your mum will kill me first then you, so guess you'll need these." He shoved the black bag of condoms into Alex's arms as Mr. Shipley chuckled knowingly. He could sense that Alex was no longer a virgin, a bit more comfortable with the purchase this time than the last.

"Well, Master Putnam, back again?" he teased. "Better safe than sorry, I always say. Good luck!"

The Putnams exited, hoping that their transaction had gone so quickly that even the inquisitive folks present hadn't seen too much. John was blushing a bright red, while Alex just strutted out the door. Alex dared anyone to make a comment, but nobody said a word to either of them; a few nodded at John, who totally avoided all eye contact. As they got into the car, John muttered, "Next time, you're coming to Shipley's by yourself. If you can have sex, you buy your own condoms!!!"

"You're right. Sorry to embarrass you, Dad, next time I'll come see Mr. Shipley and get 'em at night to avoid the gossips. But we bought a lot, so these should last a while," he said, grinning cheekily. John just grunted, and they drove home in silence, each lost in his own thoughts.

After John dropped Alex off at home, he told Alex that he was going to a saloon to get a quick drink. John hadn't done that in a while, preferring to drink at home, so Alex didn't make a comment as he entered the house and looked back as his Dad drove away. He wished that John could find a nice woman to love him the way Alex loved Sherrette, but John was determined to remain true to Cathlean, his one true love whom he still wasn't willing to divorce. It was clear she had moved on, but John hadn't. Alex was still hearing of her escapades at the Booty Bunker, even something recently, about her passing out while sexing that big gorilla, Zeke. But Alex refused to let his thoughts wander down that path; Cathlean, his so-called mum, was not worth his time, and she wouldn't be spoiling his happiness anymore.

As Alex was getting a quick snack, the telephone rang. It was Sherrette calling to wish him good-night. "Hello, English," she whispered, "just thinking about you before I go to bed. What are you doing? Mother just went to bed," she continued. "I can't wait to see my baby tomorrow."

"Hullo, love," Alex responded. "I didn't expect to talk to you tonight. This is a very nice treat."

"I was thinking about you. Wish I could be in your arms right now," she purred. "You miss me?"

"Of course, I miss you. I wish we could be together right now too, but we'll have to wait until our weekend getaway." He heard a sound in the background and figured it was Miss Ida.

"Got to go, but see you tomorrow, okay? Bye!" She quickly hung up, leaving Alex smiling widely.

"That's my girl," he said. "She's mine, mine, and I love her so!" He hung up the telephone with a light heart, finished eating his snack, showered, and jumped into bed to think about her until he fell into a lust-filled sleep. Alex didn't even hear John when he came home, stumbling around about two hours later. At one point, Alex was sure he heard Tooth speaking, but then he fell into a deeper sleep and didn't stir until the next morning when it was time to get up and get ready for school.

CHAPTER 2

I t was Sherr's fifteenth birthday. Miss Ida was going to visit her sick sister again in a couple of days, at the same time that John would be going to teach a class in Hattieville. Alex and Sherrette hugged their secret to themselves; they'd decided to take advantage of the opportunity and spend some serious sexy time together at the Flores Farm. Fabian had agreed to make himself scarce and leave the lovers alone together. Alex could hardly wait as he counted the days and mentally made a list of items he needed to pick up for their little rendezvous: Mrs. B would make them a picnic basket full of sandwiches, nuts, sweet treats that Sherrette loved, and drinks. They'd have all the fresh fruit they could eat, which was a bonus. Alex had an extra skip to his usual slow walk, but he had to try to tone it down so that no one would suspect he was up to something; he just wanted the day to be perfect!

Friday dawned bright and clear. Alex jumped up and walked with John to the Mini Moke. John would be back around 10:00 p.m., or early the next day, so he and Alex embraced as they bade each other farewell. After seeing John off, Alex bounded up the stairs two at a time, then entered the bathroom where he took extra care with his shower. He also shaved off his little peach fuzz beard which had just started growing in because he wanted to be perfect for Sherrette, just as he was sure she was making herself perfect for him too.

Miss Ida's bus would be leaving at 6:30 a.m., so Sherrette would meet Alex at his house around seven. She would ride her bike to Alex's, then he would drive them to the farm. If he hurried, he could pick up the picnic basket from the restaurant while waiting for Sherrette to get to his house. That way he'd avoid gossip by not picking it up while the early risers were eating breakfast there. He quickly drove to Bluebell's, where he got the basket, then quickly returned home. His timing was perfect because Sherrette had just arrived and was climbing off her bike. He quickly grabbed her from behind and swung her off her feet, causing her to squeal happily. As he helped to transfer her little kit bag from the carrier on the back of her bike to the trunk of the car, neither could concentrate; they kept staring at each other, giddily anticipating the day ahead. In a few minutes, they were driving away on the backstreets, eager to reach their destination but careful not to be seen by too many people heading for market at that early hour. They were both quiet, not wanting to break the silence. Alex drove with his left hand while holding on to Sherrette with his right. They didn't have far to go, but they couldn't relax until they'd arrived at the farm in another thirty minutes or so.

Fabian must've seen or heard the car because he stood outside the farmhouse door with a huge grin on his face. "Al, Miss Sherrette, good to see you both. Come in, come in. Did you eat yet?" They shook their heads, so he went to the stove, scooped up eggs and sausage, and placed bread onto plates. "Here, eat up. I'll just leave you two alone. Alex, you know where everything is. Have fun, and I'll see you later, much later!" He winked, and just like that, he was gone in a flash. Alex laughed at Fabian's antics, and they hungrily dug into the fluffy eggs and warm bread. If Fabian ever decided to stop playing farmer, he could definitely open up a restaurant—the man could cook!

In short order, the lovers had finished eating breakfast, then they cleaned the kitchen up together, appreciative of the fine meal. Alex saw Sherrette trying to hide a yawn, and suddenly feeling sleepy himself, he pulled her toward the sitting room so they could cuddle up in the settee. As Sherrette started nodding off, he started tickling her until she was laughing and writhing helplessly against him, trying to escape his roaming hands. Soon, they were groaning as horseplay turned to sex play, and in five minutes, Alex was kissing Sherrette, sipping thirstily at her lips while taking both their clothes off. At the same time, he rolled a condom over his erection but had to start over a couple times, worried about tearing the condom in his haste to get their sexual action going.

Alex counted to ten in his head, making himself take deep breaths to slow himself down and caress Sherrette until she was panting and thrusting up toward him, eager for the intimate contact. As Alex soothed her and entered her, accommodating her unspoken plea, he nipped at her delicate neck, branding her with his mark and making her his own. Sherr screamed as she nipped at his pectoral muscle beautifully displayed on his chest behind a light sprinkling of hair. She loved the salty taste of his skin. "Oh, Alex," she moaned, "give it to me now, and you better come on, or I'm going to leave you behind!" Her voice was raspy and unrecognizable with passion.

"Hold on, baby," Alex said, panting. "Didn't know you were that close. Slow down." He held her hips in a strong grip as she struggled to get free. "Don't move, or it'll be over too soon," he warned, his sweat dripping onto her breasts. He reached down to lick at her skin, and involuntarily started moving again, this time with more force. Their bodies slapped against the covers spread on the settee as they started moving in earnest now. As Sherr strived for completion, Alex rubbed at her erogenous zones, each stroke hitting her just right. After another few strokes that continued to build in intensity, they both cried out lustily as they experienced the ultimate explosive climaxes together.

Sherr was still spasming and trembling as Alex disengaged from her and headed for the bathroom to get a warm, damp towel, with which he tenderly wiped her off. He was always so caring of his lady love; she thanked him with a big kiss, then turned on her side and fell asleep. Alex spooned at her back, and as he fell asleep with a full heart, he silently thanked God for giving this wonderful person to his unworthy self to love. She was so trusting of him, believing that he'd take care of her completely, and he vowed that he always would; she was all he'd ever wish for in a lover.

In another hour, they woke up refreshed and made love again, but this time, they had a scare because when Alex pulled off the used condom, he found that it was torn near the top. Knowing he needed to be honest, Alex decided he'd better tell Sherrette what he'd discovered, but he was unprepared for her reaction when she burst out crying. "Oh, no!" she said, flustered. "Please don't tell me the condom broke. Am I pregnant, well, am I?" She jumped up and ran to the bathroom, trying to clean herself up as best she could. "I can't get pregnant, Alex." He knew she was stressed because she hardly ever called him Alex. He followed her to the bathroom and hugged her tightly.

"Baby, hush. It'll be okay. Besides, it isn't the right time of month anyway," he tried to assure her.

"Oh, what am I saying? You're right, it's not my fertile time." And she relaxed in his arms, then allowed him to lead her back out so they could play cards and listen to the radio. They both were still young enough to enjoy a children's variety program that played on Radio Belize every morning. Called "Funtime," it was hosted by internationally known comic Seferino Coleman, or "Se-Fe," a self-styled local announcer who was as irreverent on the air as the government would allow him to be. The show featured music, short stories, nursery rhymes, and other little segments, and accounted for the tardy arrival to school of many an unsupervised child whose parents didn't realize how late it was until "Funtime" was over, and their children hadn't left for school yet.

Though they both loved the show, Alex and Sherr couldn't enjoy it often enough because it only came on during weekdays, and they were usually already en route to school when it aired. Being able to listen to Se-Fe's antics and favorite songs like "The Laughing Policeman" and "There Was a Hole (in the Middle of the Ground)" and poems like "Matilda," etc.; today was a rare treat that they both appreciated. The comedic interlude did much to reassure Sherrette and put her pregnancy worries to rest. So they decided that their day would be perfect; they wouldn't worry about anything at all. They would just exist in the moment and enjoy themselves! They'd eat, drink, have mind-blowing sex, and then go home holding memories of their getaway dear to their hearts till they could be together again sexually.

After "Funtime" ended, the couple played ball outside, then went fruit-picking. As they lay under a mango tree and Alex fed Sherr fruit, they enjoyed each other immensely. Things got hot and heavy at one point, and Alex wanted to make love out in the sunshine, but Sherr was inhibited, insisting that they go inside to consummate the act. Alex teased her about being a little prude, but she didn't care. This time, she aggressively initiated their sexual romp as soon as they entered through the kitchen door, causing him to revise his opinion of her being a prude. His girl was well on her way to being a sex freak; he just warned her to slow down so they wouldn't have another broken condom accident.

Sexually sated, they returned outside to eat a late picnic lunch under a leafy rose apple tree, the subtle, perfumed fragrance of the blossoms a pleasant assault on the senses. As they dozed in the sunshine, they spoke of their plans for the future, a future that now seemed to automatically

251

include both of them being together. They had the same values and found that their beliefs also synched up in many important ways. Around 4:00 p.m., they reluctantly started packing everything up to prepare for their return to town. They would leave Fabian their uneaten treats and sandwiches, grateful to him for having prepared them breakfast and allowing them this precious time to enjoy each other.

Miss Ida would be back by 6:30 p.m., and John by 8:00 p.m., if he was coming home that night, so they needed to get going right away. After they loaded the refrigerator with their donations to Fabian, Alex wrote him a quick note of thanks, and they motored back to town in rush-hour traffic, "rush hour" meaning that there were about ten cars and twenty bikes on the road. Sherrette was home by 5:00 p.m., and Alex was lying in bed reflecting on the incredibly beautiful day he and Sherrette had shared on her birthday. One moment causing him concern was the broken condom, but he was not going to think about it anymore.

"Never borrow trouble," Grampa Elton always said; Alex would heed that warning.

CHAPTER 3

O ver the next few weeks, Cathlean was having a hard time hiding her heart condition, but she still didn't want to let people know she was sick. She also didn't want to have to go back to Belmopan again, as people would wonder what was happening and why a repeat visit was necessary. Cathlean just happened to be heading for market with her friend, Betty, late one morning when who should she run into, but her aunty Shula, cousin to the current Buyei who presided over *Dugú* ceremonies at Dabúyabah. Cathlean had never had much use for this aunt, but ever the opportunist, she decided that today was the day when she would check things out, to see what Aunty had to say about Cathlean's idea of consulting with Buyei Lenny to try to heal her heart ailment.

"Mornin', Aunty," Cathlean greeted jovially. "How are you today?" She took Shula by the arm.

"Hello, darling," Aunty Shula responded, somewhat surprised that stuck-up Cathlean was greeting her. She blinked through thick glasses. "Well, my niece, haven't been seeing you, especially since I hear you left that nice Mr. Putnam and your li'l bwai. And you moved into that Bunker Whore House or whateva you call it. You know that's nothing but Satan at work, but your mum spoiled you rotten, bless her soul." She made the sign of the cross and, in a quick motion, pulled a small bottle from inside her sleeve and doused Cathlean with holy water. "Whatchu need from your old auntie, Miss High-and-Mighty?"

Cathlean cringed, hating the old sanctimonious bitch. "Who said I needed anything? Can't I say hello to my aunty?" Cathlean shook the holy water off, trying to make herself appear as innocent as possible. "We-e-ll, there's a small matter." She held her thumb and index finger a few inches apart to indicate size. "I need an appointment with the Buyei. I have to have a healing Dugú ceremony, and I know you have the right connections!"

"Mm-hmm, I just knew you wanted something! You always were conniving and think you're too good to deal with common folk. Besides, you don't follow traditional Garífuna ways at all, so a Dugú won't save you if you don't believe in it!" She smirked at Cathlean, eagerly awaiting the response.

"I do believe. It's just that I've been scared to go near the Dabúyabah because I heard that if you go there or anywhere nearby to spy, the spirits will pull you in. Before you know it, you're inside dancing in a frenzy with people in front of the Buyei, but you don't know how you got there." Cathlean often scoffed at the notion of the Dugú ritual, assorted gossip about Dabúyabah life, and the goings-on there, but now, she found herself in a very desperate position, hoping she could get in.

"*Now-fu-rie,*" she said, using the Garífuna word for "aunt," "please talk to him for me. I need this because I'm having serious heart problems. I think a *gubeeda* (evil spirit) has possessed my body." Cathlean didn't often grovel or beg, so, for once, she found herself in an extremely uncomfortable position. "Also, can you find out how much this will cost? Once it is all set up and ready to go, can you please send word to me? If I don't hear from you, I'll assume you didn't care to help me." She swallowed, then continued defiantly, "Whether through you or someone else, I'll see the Buyei!" Hugging Shula once more, she walked away, proud head held high. She wasn't going to beg anymore; it was draining and left a bad, embarrassing taste in her mouth.

Aunty Shula shook her head wondering as she watched Cathlean sashay away. *Dat gial,* she thought. *Wonder what she's up to or if she's really sick. I'll talk to Buyei, but I'll find out what's going on. She's not going to embarrass me or my family in front of a temple full of people—heck, no!*

CHAPTER 4

Shula hurried through her shopping, buying fruits, vegetables, cassava, plantains and bananas, coconuts, fish, beef, and lastly, she placed an order for a few crates of live chickens, and a whole pig, which would be delivered to the Dabúyabah later that day. One family had just finished their Dugú, so it was time for the next one to take up residence in the Dabúyabah; everything had to be restocked. Poorer families or those who owned farms brought in their own produce to feed the Dugú participants and those who permanently lived in the Dabúyabah, including assistants and high priests. Year-round, it seemed like there was always a large group of inhabitants at the Dabúyabah.

Families who couldn't bring their own food and supplies other than bed linens and newly sewn clothing for each stage of the ceremonies were levied large sums of money with which required items for Dugú were purchased. Many Dangrígans were poor, but in addition to items for food preparation, like those already mentioned, families were responsible for buying water drawn to Temple by mule-and-cart, paying for drums of rum to be liberally applied or consumed during the rituals, and "rent" of quarters to be occupied by the family while in residence. Dugú wasn't cheap!

In preparation for a Dugú in future years, some families even raised their own chickens and pigs years in advance of having their actual ceremony, unless illness or a *gubeeda* (spirit) visitation by a dearly departed relative demanded that the ritual take place sooner, not later. Cathlean's request would be one meant to promote healing; she was covering all bases in case her illness was caused by visitation from one of her deceased relatives; Dugú would serve as the second opinion she sought.

As one of the most high priestesses, Shula had direct access to the Buyei, so upon arriving back to Dabúyabah from the market, she immediately requested an audience with him and was granted it within the hour. Buyei Lenny was a handsome, youngish-appearing man, lean and healthy at forty-five years old, the eldest child of the Buyei Maximus, who'd died of cancer two years earlier. Nobody seemed to notice the irony that Maximus, the very one to whom they'd flocked for healing, had actually succumbed to illness from which he should've been able to heal himself! The brain-washed few who thought about it at all had decided that Buyei Max had, like a martyr, not been allowed to heal himself but was allowed to simply transcend Earth and "expire," not die like mere mortals.

Lenny had five other siblings, but he was the only one who believed in the old ways, had studied closely at his father's feet, and had been groomed since his teenage years to become the natural successor. Some of the council of Dabúyabah elders weren't too happy with the choice, thinking Lenny was too young and still worldly (he had several children with five different women, though he'd never been married), but they had to appear to be accepting of the new Buyei to keep their status and pecking order in the Dabúyabah. Besides, the secret plan was to allow him to fail and lose face in front of believers, but if he didn't, they'd have to arrange for an "accident" or some deadly way to eliminate him. For now, the council would allow Lenny to practice the ancient art of Dugú.

Shula was ushered into the Inner Temple where Lenny, dressed in a flowing snow-white robe, sat on a raised seat. Nubile young teenaged girls sat on pillows at his feet; their feet were bare, toes unpolished. They were dressed in white shifts and wore white turban-like head-dresses on their corn-rowed braids. They were being instructed by an older priestess in the art of sewing and coconut oil making, and some were peeling fruit to stew or to serve at dinner that night.

When Shula entered the hall, they gracefully got to their feet and silently exited the room. "Buyei, I have asked for an audience with you because I need a big favor." Shula had found that Lenny appreciated directness; he liked people to get to the point quickly—to say exactly what they came to say. "My niece has a *gubeeda* in her and wants a Dugú ceremony to heal her heart. Can we arrange it, sir?" She unrolled a colorfully marked calendar to check Dabúyabah dates and availability.

"Your niece?" he asked. "I know of only one niece: the one who married the English soldier."

Shula was amazed, as she usually was, at what an accurate memory the man had. She suspected that he was often able to heal people because he remembered every little detail he'd learned about them, and he could repeat verbatim the more appropriate parts that pertained to their problem or complaint. "Yep, that's Cathlean. She's still married but doesn't live with her husband. But I don't need to tell you that. I'm sure you know already." She cleared her throat. "I'll find out exactly what ails her, but I wanted to see if you can fit her in. We have the Lewises finishing their month of Dugú this Friday, so we may be able to accommodate. But it's up to you. If we can't do it, we just can't."

"Let me see that." He took the calendar. "Yes, yes, if we move this, and take that." He drew bold lines across the page. "Will Cathlean attend alone?" At Shula's nod, he continued, "Well, we have other petitioners who're solo, so we can match them up and do one group ceremony together. We'll finish up with the Lewis family, have Cathlean here by 8:00 a.m. Saturday morning. Please tell her not to be late!" And with that pronouncement, he dismissed Shula, who was about to throw herself at him in gratitude but at his stern look she slowly backed out of the room instead. She couldn't believe how easy it had been to get Cathlean a spot. Quickly, she called a boy to take Cathlean a note with instructions regarding fees, how Cathlean would be required to dress, what was expected of her while in Dabúyabah.

Cathlean's condition, meantime, was deteriorating. She wasn't taking her prescribed medication because one of the pills had caused her to start gaining weight, a no-no for a vain woman like her. In addition, the tonic that she was supposed to take three times a day was making her nauseous, especially because she was not completely staying away from alcoholic beverages as recommended for properly-intended results. Each day, she and the Bunker girls would have their mixed cocktails, Cathlean's drink of choice being One Barrel rum, straight. Also, when Zeke came around, Cathlean tried especially hard to be jovial and normal, acting like she wasn't sick; she never took medication in Zeke's presence and swore her friends who knew of her condition to secrecy, so he had no idea.

CHAPTER 5

On the afternoon that the boy arrived with the note, Cathlean hugged Betty screaming and jumping around. You would've thought she'd won the lottery with the way she was acting. "He said yes. I can't believe Aunty Shula came through for me. Buyei Larry said I can go to Dabúyabah next Saturday. Know what this means? I have to go shopping. You never know what good-looking man will be there. Please say you'll go with me since I can bring one family member. No, don't say it!" she said, as Betty was about to speak. "You may not be sick, but he can always help you catch and keep that cute Frankie that you like. Remember, girl, all our problems can be handled at the Dabúyabah."

"Cathy, you know I'm afraid to go near that place, much less have to stay there for a month. Besides, I don't have money to pay that healer, doctor, or whatever he calls himself, even if he can get me the man I want." At Cathlean's pout, she added, "But I'll go shopping with you if you got money."

"You know I still get money from John, so yes, I can handle it. If I need more, he can give it to me. The Chinese boutique's still open, so let's go shopping right now!" Typically, attendees at Dabúyabah had to get their clothes home-sewn so healing could take place in as natural and simple an environment as possible, but Cathlean wanted a store-bought outfit; she wouldn't settle for home-made. She quickly wrote a note and sent for a taxicab; as usual, Tooth was the one to arrive first.

"Tooth, I'm so happy to see you. We need to go to the store. I'll tell you about it on the way."

A few minutes down the road, she told Tooth about her expected stay at Dabúyabah, ending with, "I'm glad I can get in, and, in no time, I'll be healed from this heart problem at Dabúyabah."

"I told you that place is not for you. You should go back to Dr. Rivas!" Tooth shook his head.

"Tooth, stay out of it. I'm going, and you can't stop me." Cathlean cut her eyes at him and Betty.

"All right, all right," Tooth said. "I got nothing more to say. It's your funeral." He laughed evilly.

"Not funny. If I need your opinion, I'll ask you. Now, please let us out so we can prepare for Dugú in style!" She pushed Betty out of the unbroken car door and followed her. They both found outfits to wear: white blouses, midcalf-length skirts, white sandals, and a formal caftan to wear on the final night at Dabúyabah. Within two hours, they were back home and packing enough clothes to last for a few weeks. If Cathy's healing was slow, or if the Buyei determined that they needed to stay longer, they'd be able to manage since laundry was done each day by Dabúyabah attendants.

Cathlean was up and at the Dabúyabah by 7:30 a.m. on Saturday. She held her head up as she stepped under the receiving tent. If Betty hadn't been holding her hand, she might've run back out, but she could also feel unseen spirit forces holding her in place where she stood. Buyei Lenny approached them at precisely 8:00 a.m., his arrival heralded by the pungent smell of rum, which he drank from a clay jug, and spewed it over the bodies of the people gathered there. Besides Cathy and Betty, there were eighteen other females under the tent, all simply dressed in purple from head to toe. Cathy and Betty appeared overdressed in their store-bought clothes; the Buyei took note of it by raising his eyebrows. He made no comment other than to welcome them in native Garífuna language.

After whatever food or supplies they brought was logged, fees were collected, and each person was processed, they were shown to their sleeping area in the large tent. They settled in with the sound of drums being beaten in the background, a Garífuna choir was singing morning prayers at the tops of their voices, and the new entrants were served a simple breakfast of cassava bread, fried fish, and sugar-sweetened fever grass tea. Everyone was given a schedule which they needed to follow, and by end of day, each would have met directly with Buyei Lenny so he could assess the best course for treatment. Of the twenty people who'd checked in, the majority were sick, three of four were trying to catch a specific love interest's attention, and the others were taking part in Dugú because they'd been directed by the spirits of their deceased ancestors to do so.

259

Cathlean's appointment was at 6:00 p.m., but she would be allowed to take Betty with her because Betty was Cathlean's family representative, out to pursue and try to win her own love interest. The afternoon was relaxing; Cathlean saw people she knew, but she kept her eyes lowered the whole time, trying not to make direct eye contact. As usual, there were some gossips in the crowd, people that Cathlean would've preferred to avoid, but she had no say here, so she kept quiet and did as she was told. She knew they were wondering what she was doing there, since she'd loudly declared her unbelief in Garífuna rituals like Dugú on numerous occasions in the past. She was anxious to meet with Buyei Lenny one-on-one; she'd noted that he was attractive, so she couldn't wait to work her magic on him, to handle him like she would any other member of the male species.

At 5:50 p.m., a priestess came to lead Cathlean and Betty to the Inner Temple, where they were directed to sit below Buyei's seat. As soon as they got comfortable, he said, "Now, Cathlean, tell me what you want from me. You have a heart problem, yes?" He looked directly at Cathlean, eyes boring into her as if he could see into her soul and right into her damaged heart.

"Yes, the doctor put me on medication and on a waiting list for a new heart." She fluttered her eyelashes at him, but he appeared unmoved and uninterested. "He said I only have one year to live!"

"Well, doctors don't always know, do they? Betty, I know why you're here, but what do you think about Cathlean's problem?" He turned to Betty, who lowered her eyes, refusing to meet his.

"She's my best friend. I care about her, and I don't want her to die. I think she has a *gubeeda* on her," she wailed in an un-Betty-like manner. "Cathlean's too young, Buyei. I don't know if you know, but she has a son, a young man named Alex. Can you please help her?" she looked at him.

"Cathlean's going to have to believe and help in her own healing, but thank you for coming with her." With that said, he drank a mouthful of rum and sprayed it in a fine mist directly into their faces; they closed their eyes just in time. Next, he soaked his hands in a bowl of something that looked and smelled like blood (*Was the source human or animal?* Cathlean wondered). Betty could hear Cathlean gagging as the rank odor filled their nostrils. Soon after that, he poured more rum over his hands, dried them on a snowy white linen towel, and ended the ritual by putting on a pair of white gloves. "Now, go get some rest, both of you. Morning services at seven," he ordered. "I will see you then."

CHAPTER 6

As they were dismissed, the same priestess, whom they would later learned was named Rose, escorted them back to their sleeping area. The beat of the drums was loud, throbbing, sensual, and powerful as it pulsed in the air. Faint cries could be heard as dancers experienced *owen-hah*, a trancelike passing-out, overcome either by *gubeedas* that had taken over their bodies or by their own frenzied dancing. Rose told them they would see everything tomorrow, but for now, they needed to go to sleep early that first night. Gratefully, they did as they were told and hurried away.

"Whoo, girl, you see how good that man looked?" Cathlean whispered to Betty as they changed into nightgowns and got ready for bed. "I would love to get with him one night while I'm here!"

"Are you crazy? Have some respect," Betty said, looking fearfully over her shoulder. "That man don't want you, so let's just do what we came here for, and stay out of trouble," she begged Cathlean.

"The only reason you're not trying to compete with me is because you're here to get your man."

"But, he's a holy man, a healer, so stop lusting after him, you nasty girl. Think about your heart." She sat down on her sleeping pallet and grabbed her pillow.

"Okay. I wonder what will happen tomorrow. Did you hear those drums? Sure made me want to dance." She twirled around, arms up, performing an intricate dance step, then fell onto her thin sleeping pallet too. It looked and felt a little uncomfortable; they both hoped they'd be able to sleep, but they were excited and scared at the same time. "G'nite, Betty. Thanks again for coming with me."

They must've been tired because they slept soundly until the loud ringing of a bell woke them up. Cathlean, Betty, and the others dressed quickly and were led to a large eating area where delicious smells of breakfast favorites greeted them. Everyone was served a breakfast of bread, johnnycakes, fried or stewed fish, *pinole* (corn porridge), and cassava bread, washed down with gallons of hot tea and coffee. Diners sat in groups with their family members, dressed in clothes made from the same-colored material representing each family, those seeking the Buyei's counsel or assistance; a group comprised of males and females sat with their families but stood out because they all wore purple.

After breakfast, everyone was asked to remain in the hall, and the Buyei, flanked by his high priests and priestesses, walked to the front and took his place on a throne-like seat similar to the one located at the Inner Temple. As he clapped his hands and asked for silence, he lit a large *puro* (Spanish for "cigar"), and started puffing strongly on it, generating a huge cloud of aromatic smoke over his head. He started chanting prayers in Garífuna as the smoke welcomed the spirits and drew them in; then, he asked for their guidance and blessing in the activities to come and prayed that they would be pleased by his meager offering. At one point, he stood in front of his seat and motioned to a row of men who stood in front of crates lined up on both sides. As the Buyei's thunderous voice rose in intensity, the men leaned over and released the doors on the crates. There was loud squawking as the formerly confined chickens all tried to escape at the same time. But the men snatched them up, and in one well-choreographed motion, they twisted off the chickens' necks, causing them to snap with an audible crack! Dark blood spurted all over, covering those supplicants sitting up front.

The high priestesses grabbed basins and held them beneath the chickens to catch the fresh blood as they chanted and sang louder and louder, building to an ear-splitting crescendo. Pigs could be heard squealing loudly in their pens, as they, too, were led to slaughter. Some men were in charge of killing the pigs, but because of the expected blood and gore, their slaughter had to take place outside. People were grateful for this consideration since the stench inside was overpowering and raw; those of the weaker stomach were swallowing rapidly, trying to keep their recently-eaten breakfast down.

After the slaughter, Cathlean, Betty, and the others were led to another part of the Dabúyabah where an altar was laid with piles of fresh fruit, basins of cooked food, baskets of bread, boiled and fried fish, fried and baked whole chickens, great slabs of beef and pork ribs, and all manner of drinks, including water, juices, and rum. This was where the real feast was, but everyone was full from breakfast, so they weren't tempted to try to taste anything. The escort warned them that the food on the altar was for consumption by the ancestral spirits and must not, under any circumstances, be consumed by the worshippers. Worshippers were also told that if they touched or ate the food, their illness wouldn't be cured, they wouldn't attain the love interest they desired, or they wouldn't get what they had come to Dabúyabah for. As a matter of fact, they were warned that if they ate the food, they could die!

More priestesses were handing out hymnals because it was time for worship service. Drummers sat on the side quietly playing their drums, but at a signal from a priest, they started playing louder and louder until it seemed that everyone's heart had suddenly synchronized in time with the pounding of the music. Young girls entered the hall from the sides, dressed in long skirts and headscarves made from multi-colored material. They were singing as they walked; some were dancing, and some were throwing up their hands as they walked between worshippers stopping here and there to touch them.

Brother Isi-en, an older man, and Buyei Lenny's second-in-command, clapped his hands to silence everyone, then he lit large incense bowls as he started chanting and calling to the spirits in a loud voice. Goosebumps broke out on people's skin; they became afraid as the smoke rising to the ceiling seemed to take on strange animal-like shapes. The girls started dancing faster and faster at a dizzying speed until some of then fell to the floor in a trance. Some of the worshippers were so caught up in the frenzy that without realizing it, they'd risen from their seats and had joined the girls and the priest, and soon, they too were falling into the *owen-hah* state on the floor.

Brother Isi-en liberally sprinkled rum on the heads of those present, but he did it by hand because he wasn't authorized to sip and spray the rum by mouth like Lenny. The drums beat faster and faster, the priest chanted louder, and the worshippers were shaking, afraid to move or to do anything. A couple of hours must have passed because when the priest left the room, the worshippers who were still awake were shocked to see that it was afternoon. Betty and Cathlean were ushered from the room, shaken and affected by what they'd seen. They were told to go eat lunch, after which they'd have a cleansing session with Buyei Lenny. Cathlean was looking forward to this because the sooner she could start her treatment, the quicker she could recover and get the heck out of here—frankly, the place scared the crap out of her. For once, Miss Big Bad Cathy actually feared something!

CHAPTER 7

After lunch, Cathlean, along with other people who were there for healing, was summoned to the Buyei's presence. As she stood in front of him, he poured holy water and rum on his palms, rubbed them together, and massaged the area of Cathlean's heart right through her clothes. His touch was so soothing and impersonal, Cathlean forgot to be offended or even turned on; instead, she concentrated on his hands repairing her bad heart as he told her to envision them doing. He moved away from her after a few minutes, wet his hands again, and massaged each person in the part of their body where their illness lived. He spent an equal amount of time with each person, murmuring to them, instructing them to move in specific direction so he could "follow" the path of illness with his hands. As he called on the spirits to help with healing, he seemed to go into a trance.

Cathlean wasn't sure what she should feel, if anything, but she was disappointed that there wasn't a great earth-shattering moment when she could feel her bad heart getting better. She was also disappointed not to have one-on-one time with Buyei, but she figured she'd push for that another day. Curious and bored, she looked around to see how the others were faring: two men and two women were lying prone on the floor, tremors wracking their frames as they appeared to leave their bodies in full throes of *owen-hah*. Something got ahold of Mrs. Garcia, a stocky, middle-aged woman, solidly built, but it picked her up and threw her clear across the room! She staggered to her feet, then suddenly started speaking in a guttural manly voice in very old Garífuna, the traditional version spoken by the old ancestors when they'd first arrived on the shores of Belize.

Cathlean didn't understand what was being said, but she became very afraid as the voice rose in intensity and volume, sending chills down her spine. She looked at Buyei Lenny, as he began to answer Mrs. Garcia; he seemed to have no problems understanding her speech or its patterns, but the others who were awake all looked at each other, puzzled and afraid. Except for the occasional word or phrase, they, too, were having problems understanding what Buyei and Mrs. Garcia said.

Buyei bowed his head in prayer, filled his mouth with white rum again, and sprayed it on everyone in the room three times, and they seemed to slowly return to themselves. As he opened his eyes and looked at the group, he suddenly seemed drained. "That's all for now. Sister Eve"—he clapped his hands as another priestess came forward—"please take them to their rooms so they can rest before dinner." Cathlean was only too happy to hurry out the room. She was scared; this was more than she had bargained for . . . Just what had she gotten herself into? She couldn't wait to see Betty; maybe Cathlean could talk her into leaving.

When Cathlean arrived in their room, Betty was already there. She jumped up and approached, arms outstretched. "I'm so glad you're back. Can't wait to tell you how my day went. You okay?" she asked, concerned, seeing the look on Cathlean's face. Cathlean waited until Sister Eve left the room.

"Betty, this place is strange. I think we need to leave as soon as we can. I'm afraid to stay here."

"What? We just got here, Cath. What happened? I had a good time. They gave me a love potion to drink, and before I leave, I'll be given something to give to my man so he'll fall head-over-heels!"

"I'm very happy for you, but I don't think I'll be getting any better here. These people are scary." Her voice rose as they could hear drums starting to play out in the main hall. "See, we hear those drums and we feel soothed, like everything will be fine, but I don't believe it. There are spirits taking control of people right in front of us. You know the only spirits I like that close to me are the alcoholic kind!" She chuckled. "Do you think Buyei will let us leave early if we want to?" she asked hopefully. "Some of the people don't seem like they want to be here, yet they stay. I wonder why."

"Cathy, what are you saying? You already paid thousands of dollars to these people so you can get better, and you even paid my way for me.

There's no refund. Are you really sure that you want to give up so soon?" Betty asked incredulously. She paced back and forth, awaiting Cathlean's response.

"It's getting creepy around here. I don't care about the money. I'll just get more from John."

Betty shook her head. "Well, I want to stay. Give it a couple more days, will you?" she pleaded.

"Fine, fine, but I don't like being here. Hopefully my heart will heal really soon." Changing the subject, she said, "Hey, I heard there's a little party going on tonight and that there'll be a big one at the end of the month. That's in a couple of weeks. I think I can definitely stick around for that!" She sat down. "They want us to rest, but I don't do naps. I wish we could go exploring outside!" She got that mischievous light in her eye; Betty had learned to dread that look.

"Gial, behave," said Betty, shaking her head. "Why do you always want to cause problems?"

"'Cause I need some spirits. A stiff drink. I wonder if we can get one." She rubbed at her chest.

"Let's see if we can find one, come on!" Cathlean pulled Betty to her feet by the arm and they left.

They went down a different corridor, turned right, then found themselves in a big kitchen. It was hot and steamy, and people shuffled around preparing meat, fish, fruit, and salad for the evening meal. Betty and Cathlean could see through a window that some women were baking bread in large pots outside; as some rearranged fire-coals under and on top of the lids of the pot, others moved loaves of bread into and out of the pots, and wrapped them in beautifully embroidered towels. Betty pulled Cathlean forward intending to ask how they could help. Cathlean, the non-domestic, held back, unwilling to help with the baking. However, she would be happy to go outside for a few hours, which is where they ended up spending the afternoon until dinnertime.

Dinner was a feast of favorites: *hudút* (beaten green and ripe plantains served in coconut milk gravy), cassava, potatoes, banana dumplings, cassava bread, fried fish, chicken, vegetables, bread, johnnycakes, sweet buns, and dessert. Everyone ate until they were full, then Buyei announced that it was time for the night's entertainment. A group of dancers in traditional outfits danced elaborate punta numbers onstage, writhing and gyrating to the primal beat of the drums. Buyei and his assistant walked between the dancers and spectators spewing rum left and right; some people promptly started speaking in other-worldly voices, taken over by *gubeedas,* and going into *owen-hah* or simply passing out where they stood. Cathy was alarmed, having witnessed the voice-and-trance thing earlier, so she stood back, nervous and afraid, worried that she too would be overcome.

As they headed for bed that night, Cathlean was more determined that she needed to get out of this place; she would stick around until the end of the month, then leave, whether her heart had healed or not. If Betty wasn't ready to go, then Cathlean would leave anyway. With that decided, she fell into a deep sleep that night. She dreamed of her stepfather, how he had raped her, causing her to become pregnant with Alex. She jerked awake, frightened, and sat up for the rest of the night, afraid to fall asleep and have the nightmare return. She wondered why she was having this dream now. And why were the spirits of her dead ancestors clamoring to manifest themselves to her while she slept?

CHAPTER 8

For the next couple of days and weeks, the routine didn't vary much. Mornings started off with breakfast and prayers at seven, "heart-sessions" for Cathlean with Buyei Lenny during the daytime, then she and Betty would be asked to help with sewing, cooking, baking, cleaning, or doing other chores in the Dabúyabah. In the evenings, they would have tea with the other residents with whom they were becoming more comfortable and familiar, then they would watch the dancers' performance and the inevitable spirit manifestations that would take over as people went into *owen-hah*.

Betty's treatments continued to consist of daily servings of "love potion," but she was becoming both doubtful and guilty about needing to "direct" things so her boyfriend would fall deeper in love with her when she returned from Dabúyabah. Also, one of the priests had begun to give her the eye, and she was receptive to his attentions. Things were becoming complicated for her and Cathlean.

Friday of the third week dawned bright and clear; there seemed to be a sense of excitement in the air. This was the day that the main Dugú ceremony would be held. Hogs would be slaughtered; large sides of beef and mutton would be delivered; and chicken, fish, and all types of food would be laid at the altar for the spirits to enjoy and for consumption by Dabúyabah residents. People would wear their finest outfits, women were scrambling to get their hair braided in intricate styles, with ribbons and beads woven into the plaits so they would stand out. Cathlean and Betty had saved white silk outfits for this special occasion; they planned to outshine everyone in store-bought finery, headwraps, and fancy footwear. For women used to hanging out late but having been denied, they'd missed partying the most, so they planned on catching up and becoming re-acquainted in a big way.

Promptly at seven that night, Buyei Lenny processed in with his high priests. He was a sight to behold in his robes of deep crimson, trimmed in white; he was barefoot, wore numerous bracelets on both arms, and a crimson headwrap. He was preceded by multiple drummers who were also wearing their Sunday-best. People clamored to touch Buyei as he walked by; some fell at his feet as he patiently stopped and acknowledged everyone, much to the chagrin of the elders. The mood was festive: people joyfully greeted each other like long-lost relatives, which many of them actually were.

As the Buyei looked around him with his piercing eyes, it seemed like he never missed a thing. Cathlean squirmed where she sat, wondering if he knew that she and Betty were planning on leaving before schedule. The dream about her stepfather returned each night, but Cathlean wondered how he could be reaching out from the spirit world because, last she'd heard, that monster was still alive and well. She figured that her senses were opened to possibilities from the spirit realm because she was at Dabúyabah, causing her nightmares—one more reason for her to leave here! she decided to herself, scared but afraid to confide in Betty or her Aunty Shula.

As the music built to a crescendo, a large choir took up the beat, jamming and rocking the crowd with their rendition of old Garífuna standards and favorites. Then, the drummers started beating the drums in earnest and stimulating punta dancers to step up the pace. People jumped up, clapping and dancing in the aisles, where some were passing out in large numbers, overcome by the pounding pulse of the drumbeats. Dabúyabah attendants walked around armed with fans and bottles of rum and rubbing alcohol which they passed under the unconscious revelers' nostrils to wake them up.

Cathlean didn't know how it had happened, but she found herself on the stage, dancing uncontrollably, showing moves that even she didn't know she had. As the Buyei and priests joined the people onstage, the priests grabbed chickens and snapped their necks off, blood spouting, so that soon the stage was slippery from the spilled blood. At one point, Cathlean felt her heart pounding as if it would pop out of her mouth, and when she looked down at her beautiful dress, she saw that it was covered with blood. Somehow she didn't care; she felt spirit-possessed and free to enjoy herself very much tonight because, soon, she would be leaving this frightening place—no doubt about it at all.

Next day dawned bright and clear. Cathlean woke up, sore in her legs and parts of her body that reminded her of her uninhibited dance moves the night before. She jumped up and, having packed the night before, was ready to leave in ten minutes. She went to Betty and shook her, trying to get her to wake up so they could leave as planned, but Betty was out cold. Cathlean, not wanting to get caught leaving, decided she'd leave Betty and escape by herself because that's what it felt like to her—an escape from the Dabúyabah. At the exit gate, a fierce guard stood there; he appeared fresh and full of vitality, though Cathlean remembered him being drunk and up until very late the night before.

"Where you t'ink you goin', Miss?" he demanded, crossing massive arms and barring the way.

"Look, I have to go, so please don't stop me," Cathlean whined, preparing to charm her way out.

The other guard, one Cathlean thought was named Errol, stepped in front of her. "Okay, you can go. Bobbo, let 'er go," he ordered as the other guard started to protest. "Here, Buyei said to give this to you." He handed Cathlean a plain envelope addressed to her in a neat, distinctive cursive.

"What?" Cathlean asked with surprise in her voice. *Oh, maybe he wants me, after all,* she thought.

They opened the gate, and she left, grabbing her bag and walking as fast as she could. She didn't look back, afraid the spirits would draw her back in. She couldn't wait to quickly get out of this place. She could feel herself in a near panic as she got away; she literally felt like she was escaping evil. About a half-mile down the road, when she didn't feel like eyes were boring through the back of her skull, Cathlean saw old Mr. Caliz driving his mule-and-cart, and she waved for him to stop and pick her up. In short order, he dropped her off at home; Cathlean lugged her baggage upstairs, entered the house, and locked the door, breathing a huge, cleansing sigh of relief.

As she sat on bed her taking off her shoes, she heard the crinkle of paper and remembered the letter she'd put in her pocket. Curiously, she pulled it out and read:

Cathlean, I knew we would lose you, because your heart (no pun intended) is not in it. You don't believe in the old ways; there's nothing I or the spirits can do for you. Good luck with everything. I hope it works out.

It was simply signed "Lenny." The man, in spite of his status among his people, was always so incredibly humble.

She was disappointed that it was not a love letter that he'd written her. "How did that Buyei know I wasn't planning on staying the whole month? He must be really blessed, psychic, or too damn smart for his own good! I'll get better by myself. I don't need a Buyei, Dabúyabah, nor do I need to *owen-hah* to feel good. I may get that second opinion from a real doctor after all. I only hope Betty finds what she's looking for." She felt as if a huge load was lifted off her shoulders, as she realized she'd mentally prepared herself for battle with Lenny, but he'd fully released her. Tired from her long walk, she fluffed the pillows, stretched out on the bed, and fell into a dreamless sleep.

CHAPTER 9

Alex and Sherrette were deliriously happy. After that day they had spent together at the farm, they became even closer, spending all their school time together; they rode home from school together, and she managed to call him every night after they finished their homework. Alex's friends teased him that he was "whipped," while Sherrette's said her nostrils were "wide open" behind Alex. Neither one cared what anyone thought except Miss Ida, who'd relaxed about her daughter's and Alex's relationship, and John, who supported Alex and his happiness 100 percent. Things were going well with school too, in spite of their lack of concentration, so nobody was really worried.

About eight weeks after the lovers' last sexual encounter, Alex was studying for a biology test when he got a panic-filled call from Sherrette. This time it wasn't her usual playful "I love you, say you love me" telephone call; she wanted to see Alex in person so she could talk to him about a serious matter. "Sherr, what is this about?" Alex coaxed. "Talk to me, please. What's going on?" Hearing no response, he continued, "This sounds serious. All right, all right. When and where should we meet?" He was shoving his feet into his shoes as he spoke to Sherrette.

"I have to go to the store for my mother, so how about you meet me at Chen's?" she responded.

Alex immediately put his book down, jumped in the car, and raced to the south side of town, over the bridge in the town center. Chen's was much closer to Sherrette's house than to his, and he wanted to beat her there. He was successful because he had just parked when she approached, head down and looking lost. He quickly got out the car and held her hand. "Hey, Sherr," he said, "what's up?" She looked at him sideways but kept walking toward the entrance to the store.

"Hi, English. Let me get my mum's items, then we can talk." To Alex, she seemed a bit subdued.

They walked into Chen's together; since she knew exactly what she was looking for, they were through and at the checkout in a very short time. The suspense was killing Alex, so he led her back to the car so they could sit and talk. As he closed the doors and leaned over to hug her, he said, "Okay, I cannot wait any longer. What did you need to tell me, my love? Come on, let it out!"

"Well," she started, "I-I-I . . ." She paused. "I don't know how to say it. Please wait a minute."

"Take your time," Alex said, knowing that he didn't mean it. He wanted to hear it right now!

"I'm late." At Alex's raised eyebrows, she realized he didn't understand. "My period is late."

"What?!" Alex shouted, then, fearing he'd be heard outside the car, he lowered his voice. "I don't understand. I thought you were safe, and we always used condoms." Then he remembered the broken condom that day at the farm. "Oh, my God, you're pregnant. Sherr, what're we going to do?" The enormity of the problem hit him like a ton of bricks. "Oh, God, your mum will kill me!"

"I haven't told her about my condition. Right now, my dad's trying to come back into my life, and she's really upset. Now I have to add to her problems. English, I'm so sorry about this. Please tell me what to do." She started crying great big sobs as her shoulders shook with the force of her tears.

"Please hush. We love each other. We'll figure this out." He was scared and felt like he was going to cry too, but somebody had to be strong. "First, we'll need to see the doctor to see out how far along you are. I can drive you there sometime this week, or we can go to Saturday clinic in Belmopan. That may be better for us anyway, because Dangríga's too small, and nurses talk way too much for information about you to be kept quiet." His brain was clicking, trying to think it through.

Sherrette raised her tear-stained face to him. "Thank you for not being angry at me. Okay, I'll tell Mum that I'll visit my aunt on Saturday to see how she's doing, then we can stop at the clinic to see the doctor." She was sniffling, trying hard to be brave, but she was only a scared fifteen-year-old after all.

"All right, that's settled for now. Let me take you home so your mum doesn't come after you." Alex put the car in reverse and dropped her off one street away from home. As he continued on his way home, the seriousness of the situation hit him. "Oh, my Lord, what do we know about having a baby?" He pounded both hands on the steering wheel until they hurt. What would John say? And the bitch, Cathlean, he bet she would have a lot to say! Alex really didn't care what she thought, but he knew John would be disappointed and hurt. That's whom Alex always wanted to please and impress. He drove home wondering how he'd break the news but decided he'd wait until after Saturday clinic.

The rest of the week passed quickly, and at 5:00 a.m. Saturday, Alex and Sherrette were on the Hummingbird Highway heading for the clinic; unbeknownst to them, they were following the same route that Cathlean had traveled several months earlier. The only thing different was the location. When they arrived, they were number six in line, so at least they wouldn't have to wait long and would have plenty of time to visit with Sherr's auntie afterward. They casually glanced at the line and around them but thankfully didn't see anyone they knew.

Clinic began at 8:00 a.m., and soon they were called in around 8:15 a.m., but Alex already knew that Sherrette was pregnant because she'd thrown up her breakfast and was now standing there, pale and shaking, waiting to be seen by the doctor. Dr. Lilly Gillette was a plump, bubbly, matronly woman with a kind face and a twinkle in her eye. She laughed and joked, doing her best to make her patients comfortable at the most uncomfortable moments in their lives. As she ushered the young couple into a room, she kept up a flow of chatter, deliberately trying to keep things light and nonserious; it didn't work because Sherrette was terrified. Alex wasn't doing much better himself, but he was managing. As he was excused so Sherrette could provide a urine sample, they both knew what the test would show, and within ten minutes they had their answer, but they were still shocked anyway: Sherrette was three months pregnant!

Sherrette must've conceived prior to that day at the farm; the condom must have broken another time, probably during their second sexual encounter. Doc Shipley would hear about his bad batch of condoms because they didn't work! Dr. Lilly asked Sherrette personal questions about her home life, how the pregnancy would change things, and if she and Alex planned on getting married. She also offered the two standard responses to unplanned teenage pregnancy: aborting the fetus or carrying to term then putting the baby up for adoption. Sherrette was crying, clearly distraught, so Alex felt compelled to angrily speak up on their behalf.

"Ah, Doc, we plan on getting married one day, but this pregnancy won't force us to do it now because she's fifteen, and I'm seventeen. I will thank you to not talk to us about abortion, and adoption is definitely out of the equation. We'll continue to come to you for prenatal care, but you won't change our minds. Got that?" He spoke quietly but very distinctly, jaw tight and thrust out.

"All right, young man, okay, I get it!" Dr. Gillette said, hands held up asking for peace. "It's my job to tell you what your options are even though I see that you two are mature for your age. Fill the prescription, and come back next month so we can see how she's progressing. I'll give you my number. Call anytime." She shook their hands, briskly exited the room, and went to the next patient.

Alex and Sherrette walked out in a daze, scared and wondering what they were in for; he took her cold hand and rubbed circulation back into them. "Sherr? We've got this. Don't worry, please!"

"What do you mean don't worry? I'm having this baby, me! I'll be sixteen when it's born, and you'll be almost eighteen. What about school, and college? Ohhhh, Mum's going to kill me!" she wailed loudly.

"Shhh, please don't upset yourself. Think of the baby," he said in a coaxing voice. "I'll get a job and join the Belize Defense Force as soon as I'm old enough to. Dad will help me. Let's go see your aunt, then head back. We'll ask Dad to come to your house so all of us can talk." They headed out to Aunt Corrine's, a few miles down the road. The visit didn't go well because although Sherr tried to pretend everything was fine, she was miserable and wanted to cry when she saw how sick her favorite aunt was. Corrine was pale, weak, and couldn't really entertain company, so they soon left. Usually Corrine was very observant, nicknamed the "pregnancy detector" because she had a knack for knowing a woman was pregnant, but she must've been too sick because she didn't say a word about Sherrette's condition, something Sherrette was grateful for, as she tried to process the news.

"Well, maybe you can finish out the school year in class or at home, but as you grow larger, you might want to stay with your Aunt Corrine, if she's doing better. I'm not ashamed of our situation, but I don't want to have to hurt somebody for disrespecting you and our baby. We'll see how it goes."

CHAPTER 10

They got back to Dangríga in record time, united in their desire to make sure both Miss Ida and John could meet with them today so they could get the first hurdle out the way. Knowing Miss Ida, it was going to get very ugly. Alex stopped at home to pick up his dad, not explaining anything to John but asking him to wait for answers that he'd have in a very short while. Sherrette borrowed John's telephone to call and make sure her mother was home and able to receive company. They drove over, remaining unnaturally quiet on the way, making John leery and uncomfortable.

"What aren't you telling me? I don't want to wait too long for answers either," he grumbled.

"Hold on, please, Dad, just a few more minutes. Sherr, please don't say anything," he warned.

"Fine," said John, crossing his arms like a bratty child, but he sighed and stopped pushing.

When they arrived at Sherr's, Miss Ida was standing on the porch impatiently tapping her foot.

"Well, come on, come on, come inside. Hello, Major Putnam, how are you?" She led the way in. Sherrette pulled back in shock, a man was sitting on the settee, legs crossed, acting like he belonged there. He was brown-skinned with a curly Afro, brownish sprinkled with grey, and as he stood to his full height of six feet and approached Sherr, she recognized something familiar about him. "Who is this, Mother?" she demanded, backing away and into Alex's arms as he held on to her tightly.

"Darling, this is your father, Victor. I told you he wanted to meet you, so he came over today." Miss Ida was fluttering around like a little bird. Alex and Sherr had never seen her act this giddy.

"My father? What, where have you been all this time, and why do you want to know me now?"

"Baby, I'm sorry," Victor said. "What a lovely young lady you've grown into, lookin' just like my mother!" He reached for Sherr again, but she made no move to face him, leaning on Alex instead.

"I'm not your baby!" she snapped. "But hey, guess what, you're just in time for our news, *Daddy*." She said the word like a curse word; she was ready to spit. "Why did you let him come here, Mum?"

"Young lady, you will remember your manners, and think about who you're talking to! Let's all sit down. You too, Victor—you're not going anywhere. You did that fifteen years ago and never came back, remember? Sherrette, come help me, please." They went to the kitchen and retuned with ice-cold lemonade and glasses. After Miss Ida poured and everyone had a glass, she ordered, "Now, will somebody tell me what's going on?" She looked at Alex questioningly.

"Well, Miss Ida, Mr. Victor, Dad, we have something to tell you." He paused dramatically, waiting to get their full attention. "You are going to be grandparents in about six months. I know this is not what you wanted for us, but we'll do the adult thing and still go ahead and finish school."

"What?" screeched Miss Ida. "Alex, I trusted you with my precious daughter. I said not to touch her!" She came over to Alex, right fist balled, ready to punch him, but John jumped up to stop her.

"Now, Ida, no violence, please. I trust my boy. Alex, what happened with the condoms?" he asked.

"It broke, Dad. I used them every time. Sorry," he said as he hung his head. "But we can still graduate on time if we put in the effort. We will need to talk to Principal Diego so we can resolve all the issues. Sherr will have the baby in the fall, then she can go back to school next year in another city."

"Now look here, young man," Victor said jumping up. "What did you do to my baby girl?"

"You leave Alex alone, Victor," ordered Sherr angrily. "At least he'll be around to raise his baby."

"Apologize to your father, Sherrette," said Miss Ida, recovering her composure. "Do it, now."

"I will not. Sorry, Mother, but this man is a stranger to me. How dare he try to say anything?"

"I will not tolerate your lip!" fumed Miss Ida as she slapped Sherrette hard across the face. Her palm print stood out, red and swollen, as Sherrette burst into tears. "You think you're a woman now because you've been screwing around and now you're knocked up? What will my friends say?"

"Ida, please, let's all calm down!" John held her arm as she would've struck Sherr again. On her other side, Alex was fuming, furious that this woman had dared to hurt his baby-to-be's mother.

"I'll only say this once, Miss Ida, so listen up. Don't you ever hit Sherr again, or I will take her away from here, and you'll never see her or your grandchild ever. Victor, I am a man, and I will take care of your daughter the way you never did. We just wanted to tell you what's going on. Now, my dad and I will leave so you can talk things over, or should I take her with me?" Miss Ida shook her head. "Okay. Sherr, please call me later." He kissed her quickly on the lips and gave her a hug.

As they drove away, he still couldn't believe what he'd just witnessed. *What was the color of pain?* he wondered again. Would he always just witness its dark hues and not beautiful reds, cool blues, fiery oranges, or warm pastels? At times, he seriously doubted it. John could try to give him all the love he was capable of, but without Cathlean's, it was never quite enough; the color of pain in Alex's heart was overwhelming and crushing. Miss Ida's violence toward Sherr was dark pain, some of which Victor's reappearance in his daughter's life could possibly ease. Alex prayed that all these things would get resolved by the time his baby got here—it couldn't be born into all this dysfunction!

John was quiet for as long as he could stand it, but finally he just had to say, "Well, son, I'm sorry about your situation, but I was proud of you back there. You really handled yourself well. I'm not going to say that I'm disappointed, but you'll have a rough time because you're both so young. I'll be right here so please let me know what I can do. You know we'll have to tell your mum, right?"

"Why do I have to tell her anything? She left us. If she finds out, she finds out!" he yelled angrily.

"Well, I'll tell her anyway," John said. "I won't go to that place where she lives, but I'll see her sometime soon. Ida and Victor know, so it's only right that Cathlean knows too."

"Whatever, Dad. I know we can count on you. Your grandbaby will thank you for it," Alex said.

They both went quiet because all that needed to be said had been said. John was hoping that he could talk Cathlean into being there for their son, and in the process, maybe she'd remember how things had been for them, and she would come back home. Alex wished she would keep staying away; he didn't want his love for Sherrette and his new baby to be tainted by Cathlean's selfishness and unloving ways. At the end of the day, both hoped they'd get what they wanted; for now, Alex needed to plan for his, Sherrette's, and their baby's future.

A month later, Cathlean was back for her follow-up appointment at the doctor's. The news was not good: with the detour to the Dabúyabah for a cure from the Buyei, and her not seeking a second opinion, she'd neglected to take her medication; thus, there was serious deterioration in her condition. Dr. Rivas berated her soundly as she hung her head in shame; what made it even worse was that Cathlean's name hadn't moved up the heart-recipient list . . . it was still about a year long. A year was time that Cathlean couldn't afford since she was not expected to last that long. Dr. Rivas prescribed a new round of drugs, which Cathlean picked up before heading back home.

Meantime, Alex and Sherrette were experiencing their own brand of hell: they didn't want to share news that Sherrette was pregnant, but her sports activities had to be severely curtailed, much to the dismay of fans who knew her as an ace athlete. Sherrette was small but sturdy and healthy—the only new thing she did was to start wearing her uniform jacket and longer skirts to school, all designed to hide her little baby bump that nobody could actually see unless they looked closely or unless they really knew her. She experienced no morning sickness, took her prenatal vitamins, and generally was very healthy. She was approaching her fifth month and would actually be five-and-a-half months pregnant by the time the school year ended on June 20 of that year.

Alex gave up his after-school activities and clubs in favor of an evening job washing dishes at Yang Chew's; he needed to start making some money because even though everyone swore by reusable cloth diapers, diapers and baby clothes would not be cheap. Miss Ida was also allowing Sherrette to do some babysitting for Mr. Castillo, a young widower who lived next door whose wife had just died a few months before. The purpose of the job was threefold: Miss Ida was punishing Sherrette for her indiscretion, Sherrette would learn to take care of a baby so she could apply that knowledge when her own child was born, and she could also make money, which would go toward her baby care after it was born. Miss Ida also hoped that Sherrette would become so sick of taking care of a busy nine-month-old that she would give her baby up for adoption once it was born, but in fact, the actual opposite was occurring: Sherrette loved taking care of the little toddler and did her homework while watching him. She couldn't wait to see what hers and Alex's baby would look like.

Victor was always at Sherrette's trying to play daddy and granddaddy-to-be; Miss Ida seemed ready to forgive and forget, but Sherr didn't trust him. How long would he stick around this time before leaving for greener pastures? He also seemed to be getting closer to Miss Ida, bringing money, groceries, and professing his undying love for all to hear whenever he came over. Sherr was confused: she wanted to love this man as her dad, but she felt he could leave just when she started to care. She wanted to remain calm and unemotional during her pregnancy, so she would just wait and figure it all out later. Besides, Aunt Corrine was doing a little better right now, and the plan was that Sherr would go stay with her from the day school closed for the summer, through childbirth, and beyond. This would quiet any gossipy tongues in Dangríga when people guessed Sherr's condition.

CHAPTER 11

One afternoon in June, near the end of the school year, Miss Ida had allowed Sherr to visit Alex so they could spend some time together. Ida couldn't decide how she wanted to handle Sherr's pregnancy: she often berated and cursed at Sherr, calling her a "no-good tramp" one day, then calling her a sweet innocent baby that that English boy had taken advantage of. She didn't allow Alex to visit her home anymore; she would make negative comments about him and act rudely when he picked her daughter up for monthly checkups or other outings. Miss Ida was not pleased with Alex!

As the young couple sat on the porch holding hands, Alex was rubbing Sherr's stomach; she was five and a half months pregnant and just starting to show. As they were discussing their future, John arrived with Cathlean in tow. For a person who was supposed to be sick, Cathlean looked remarkably well put-together even though water retention from her congestive heart failure was starting to add weight to her frame. In her vanity, she still hadn't told John that she was sick. Alex jumped up quickly, almost knocking Sherr over. "What do you want?" he yelled. "Back to the scene of your crime, are you? Dad, couldn't you have warned me that Cathlean was coming here today?"

"Manners, son! I told your mum what happened, and she wanted to come meet your girl. Cathlean, Sherrette. Sherrette, this is Cathy, Alex's mother." They shook hands in a guarded manner.

"Hello, Miss Cathy. We met once before, but I'm happy to see you again," Sherrette said sweetly.

"Good to see you again too, child" stated Cathlean, coldly stepping back from Sherrette's hug. "Son, I haven't seen you in months. My, you've grown taller and more handsome! How have you been? Can I get a hug?"

But Alex pulled back abruptly, getting a whiff of her subtle vanilla perfume.

"Whose fault is it that you haven't seen me? I told Dad not to tell you anything. Go away, we don't want to see you." If looks could kill, Cathlean would be dead: instead, salty tears filled her eyes.

"Alex, I'm so sorry." She wiped her eyes with her handkerchief. "Sherrette, please talk to him."

"Don't talk to her!" snapped Alex. "Sherr, don't talk to this woman. She's like your dad, Victor. They should get together 'cause they're alike. He's just now coming around after leaving you all this time for Miss Ida to raise. Cathlean left me all these months, but she's never cared. John raised me."

"Wait, did you say her dad's name is Victor, and that he just came back to town? What's his last name?" She waited patiently for his response. The name Victor brought back too many bad memories and had her hyperventilating. Heart pounding, she was hot yet cold all at the same time.

"I don't know the man or his last name," said Alex. "Do you, Dad? Love, what's his last name?"

"Not the same as mine because I carry Mum's last name. I think his surname's Busano, Blanco?"

"No, you're not serious. Victor Busano's back?" Cathy trembled, her face as white as a sheet.

"I don't really know his last name, but you can call my mother and ask her," Sherr said. "Alex, please take me home? I'm suddenly feeling very ill." She held a hand protectively over her stomach.

"Sure, baby. See, Mother, you upset my girl. Thanks a lot! Be right back, Dad," he said to John.

"All right. Bye, Sherrette. Drive safely, son," John said, turning to help Cathy to a rocking chair.

"John," Cathy said in a quivering voice, "I need to call her mum. I have to find out right now."

John grabbed the telephone, dialed, handed it to Cathlean, then walked away to give her privacy. He watched from the kitchen as she spoke into the telephone. With each word, she seemed to draw into herself, shaking her head and crying. Then he heard her moan, "Oh, no!" as she dropped the receiver. Concerned, he jumped up and came over to hang up the telephone. Cathlean's eyes were wide and terrified, and she was sobbing uncontrollably. "John, it's not good news. Sherrette's dad is a

283

Victor Busano. I'll have to meet him, but the age and history match up. I think it's my mum's ex, the one I told you had raped me." She screamed a blood-curdling shriek full of rage. "Take me there now!" she ordered. John led the way to the car; he didn't like the sound of this. Were Sherrette and Alex possibly siblings? *No, that's impossible!* he argued to himself.

So he drove Cathlean to Miss Ida's, where Cathlean immediately got out and approached Victor who standing near the door. "It is you, you low-down snake. Under what rock did you crawl from? Ida, watch your baby girl from this sick man. He's a predator!" She stood there breathless, full of rage.

"Is it Cathlean? My, but you're so grown up, I didn't recognize you. How have you been?" He reached out to touch her, but she drew back in horror. "What's your problem, gial? You always were a strange one. Pretty t'ing, but weird. I remember your mother used to pray extra hard for you."

"Not too weird that you didn't deny yourself when you wanted a piece of me," she said bitterly.

"Ah, you know you liked it. Even at fourteen you were a hot one. You her man?" he asked John.

"What's it to you, pervert?" He held tightly to Cathlean's arm. He could feel her trembling in fury.

"Oh, what lie did Li'l Catty tell you? I didn't rape her. She just wanted to lie and hurt her mum."

"You're the liar," Cathlean snorted, "How could you force yourself on a little girl? Then you disappeared and I had to deal with the shame of having a baby by myself." Victor's eyes widened in shock. "Oh, stop! Don't tell me you didn't know I had a son. Mum said you left in the middle of the night when she threatened to tell the police and her brothers about what you did. Oh, you didn't know?" she continued, seeing the look on his face. "Our son's going to be seventeen, and you've been gone seventeen years."

Ida and John looked at the two talking, each thinking about what this revelation meant: Alex and Sherrette *were* siblings! She favored her mum, and Alex favored Victor a little, but the couple always looked good together; there was a familiar look about them because, in hindsight, they resembled each other. So Sherrette was pregnant by her brother. How complicated could this get?

"Before anyone gets too excited," John began, "I suggest that you get a blood test immediately to prove paternity of both children, Victor. Even if you're Alex's biological father, I raised that boy. I'm his dad! We'll have to tell them the truth, of course, but Sherrette's too far along to get an abortion. Ida, she needs to leave for your sister's very soon—they will need some time apart. Cathlean, let's head back to the house to talk to Alex." Cathlean suddenly looked old, bloated, and defeated; John wondered if maybe she was sick and hadn't told him. As they left, Ida and Victor started having a heated conversation; Ida was very upset because it looked like she had started falling for Victor again.

About a mile down the road, they passed Alex and Sherrette; Alex waved at them and indicated that he'd be home soon, so John and Cathlean headed home to wait for their son. Cathlean's heart was hurting; she thought for sure that this was the day she was going to die—her heart couldn't take this stress. Just as they parked, Alex pulled in behind them tooting his horn and grinning widely. John dreaded what they would have to do. It could be a long while before their boy smiled again.

They entered the house together, Alex carefully avoiding contact with Cathlean, and John happily embracing Alex. "Son, please sit down for a minute. We need to talk. No, Mum's not moving back in. Want something to drink? It's all right, I'll get it." He opened soft drinks, then sat down.

"Dad, you're scaring me. What is it?" Alex asked, alarmed at the serious look on his parents' faces.

"Well, you know Sherrette's dad, Victor, is back. Your mum knew him when she was a young girl. Also, turns out your dad didn't die as Mum had told you." He looked at her for encouragement. "Cathlean thought he had left town seventeen years ago, but apparently, he stuck around another couple of years because he impregnated Miss Ida too, then left town never to return until now."

"What's that loser's story got to do with me? Long as he's nice to Sherr, he's not my problem."

"What I'm trying to say, son, is that Victor's your biological father. It will be confirmed with a blood test—doesn't change anything, though, because I'm your dad where it counts, right here!" He pounded his chest above his heart. "Son, do you understand what this means? Sherr is your sister!"

"Impossible! Dad, I don't believe you! And you, Cathy, how could you tell me my dad was dead?"

"I-I-I," she stuttered, unable to come up with anything. She hesitated, not wanting to explain the shame of becoming pregnant by a stepfather, who'd raped her at fourteen. To Cathlean's mum's credit, she had believed her daughter and had promptly thrown Victor out of their home—and on his narrow buttocks! However, the baby had still grown to term inside Cathlean because her mother was Catholic, religious, and staunchly anti-abortion. She would find a way to raise Cathy's child herself.

"Yeah, that's what I thought. You've nothing to say for yourself. Once a whore, always a whore!"

"Alex, stop and listen to me. When school lets out for the summer on Friday, Sherr's going to her aunt's as planned. I'm so sorry, but you can't visit her. Let things cool off for a while," said John.

"I can't visit Sherr? Can I at least see her before she leaves? She's terrified of this pregnancy. Hey, does she know about this?" At John's nod, he continued. "She's my sister? This is bad, Dad."

"I promise we'll all sit down and talk about it before she leaves, but all intimacy ends now, Alex!"

"That's bull, and you know it, Dad! Just because we're fathered by a loser we don't even know?"

"Those are the rules so you can see Sherrette, take it or leave it. Now, I'm taking Mum home."

They left as Alex smacked the wall angrily. More pain in his life—would he ever get a break? How could Sherrette be his sister? Maybe that's why they clicked so well. Besides, he loved her; how did he just turn that off? And what was with Cathy lying to him about his dad? He'd never forgive her.

CHAPTER 12

T hat last week of school was packed with back-to-back finals, so Alex didn't have time to miss Sherrette. He saw her at school and though they hugged briefly on the field, it was strictly "hands-off." Alex felt lonely and abandoned, desperately needing to talk to somebody about his dilemma, but John, usually Alex's confidant, seemed to have sided with Cathy and Sherr's parents against him.

The night before Sherr was to leave town, the family sat down to a farewell dinner that felt more like a wake. John had had a medic friend from the army come to Miss Ida's to draw Victor's and the parents-to-be's blood and to rush-process it so there was no doubt that Victor had fathered the two. Cathlean had taken to her bed upon hearing the confirmation because she couldn't bear to look at Victor's face; Miss Ida just thought Cathlean was overreacting! They'd ordered food from Yang Chew's which John picked up on the way, but he should've saved himself the effort because they were now eating moo shu pork and fried rice without much interest or excitement.

Finally, John could take no more. "Uh, listen up, everyone. We're obviously not having fun, so it's best Alex and I go now. Sherrette, I'll take you to your Aunt Corrine's but you'll need to say good-bye to Alex now because this is it. Shhh, please don't cry." He hugged Sherr as she and Alex both started crying. Miss Ida stroked her daughter's hair and awkwardly patted Alex on the back.

"You're right, of course. Sherrette, let's go to your room. Victor, help John pack up the food."

"Sherrette," Alex began, sobbing uncontrollably. "I'm so sorry. I'll visit you. Nobody can stop me. Victor, not a word from you. I wish you'd crawl back into the hole you came out of. I hate you!" Victor wisely kept quiet, helping John pack up the mostly untouched food: half for Sherr to take with her, the other half to go to Alex's and John's. Alex stomped out and went to wait in the car. He felt like his heart was breaking as he looked at the lone light in Sherrette's window. He couldn't help but remember Romeo and Juliet and how he'd vowed his and Sherr's story would be different. Not!

They left for home, but when they got there, Alex asked to be left alone. In minutes, Tooth was there to take John to the saloon for his grog. This was one time that Alex wished he drank or took drugs because nothing could ease his pain. He worried about how distraught and apathetic Sherr was; the light had gone out of her eyes, and she'd lost her spunk. He was also fearful that she would lose their baby—not intentionally, but she wouldn't fight to save it. The next day, when Alex begged to go with John to see her off, he couldn't believe John wouldn't change his mind and allow Alex to go along. Sometimes John could be too honorable; while it was an admirable trait, it irritated Alex now.

"Much better to make the break clean. You'll thank me for it one day," he said to a pouting Alex as he left. He'd only be gone a few hours, so at least Alex wouldn't be alone that night; he turned and went back to bed. John, concerned about Alex, figured they would talk some more when John returned home. John himself was shocked at how things had gone so horribly wrong for the couple.

CHAPTER 13

The first month that Sherr had gone, Alex was in a state of major depression. He didn't want to go to the farm, go fishing, play sports, or go to the movies, nor did he want to spend time with Ainsworth and his other friends. He felt so mature and manly compared to them now; all they wanted to do was chase girls to score with and boast about it, hang out, sneak cigarettes, and partake in other juvenile activities that Alex had never really enjoyed even when he hadn't had a girlfriend.

Alex hadn't told any of his friends about the sad state of his and Sherr's situation because he was in denial: if he didn't acknowledge or talk about it, he could pretend everything was as it had been. Friends just assumed Sherr had gone to spend time with her sick aunt; Alex could only hope that she was taking care of herself and the baby. He knew that John checked on them often between drunken binges (he'd resumed that vice); if anything was wrong, John would tell him—at least Alex hoped so.

Cathlean was deteriorating rapidly, not enough to make a huge difference, but she still hadn't told John or anyone outside the Booty Bunker that she was sick. Instead, she used her anger at the friendship between John and Victor as an excuse to sever ties with John once again. She'd weakened so considerably that she had Zeke carve a stout cane for her from a mango tree limb because, as she explained it to him, she just wanted to practice "old age" walking. Fool that he was, he believed her, never suspecting that she was really sick and needed the cane to steady her when she walked! Betty had returned from Dabúyabah, and something about the love potion she'd been administered must have worked, because the men would not, or could not, stay away. Cathlean was happy that the Dugú had worked for her friend, but she was resentful it hadn't worked for her, Cathlean, who needed it most. What further galled Cathlean was that the Dugú had been her idea in the first place!

Alex had suddenly taken to riding his bike to The Jetty, where he tortured himself with images of Cathlean in sexual throes with Mr. Moss as he had discovered them some time ago. He couldn't explain his compulsion, he didn't ask anyone to accompany him, nor did he drive the distance to the location. Instead, he made the hard bike ride as some kind of penance he had to suffer for the short period of happiness he'd enjoyed while in love with his sister. His sister! He still couldn't imagine or call Sherr his sibling; it seemed so surreal, but blood had proven it. Now he was secretly scared that the baby would be retarded, deformed, or affected in some way since it was the product of two siblings—the ultimate taboo in spite of how innocent they'd been to the fact that Victor was their dad.

After six weeks of being apart from Sherr, Alex felt like he was going out of his mind. He'd tried to call her a few times, but she'd refused to talk to him. Her Aunt Corrine, who was much better now, guarded her telephone like a bulldog and wouldn't take pity on Alex or allow him to speak to his Sherrette, which was making him very angry. *I oughta go kill that bitch,* he thought. *How dare she keep my girl away from me? Bet she's never been in love either.* He decided that he'd go sneak a visit with Sherrette anyway, or he would go absolut-freaking-ly nuts. Besides, if he showed up, she wouldn't dare turn him away, right? They loved each other, so what was the harm, really?

With a solid plan formed in his head, Alex told John that he would be going on a day trip with Ainsworth, Fabian, and a few of their friends. However, he actually planned on going alone. John looked at him questioningly, disbelieving, but let it go. Alex needed a change of scenery; he was causing John to worry, so John was happy to see that Alex wanted to venture out. He hoped that maybe things were turning around. So Alex packed lunch with all of Sherrette's favorites; he hoped he could tempt her palate with something good so that she'd agree to start seeing him again. He didn't know about her, but this separation thing was killing him in a big way—he didn't like it one bit.

He was very happy that school was out for the summer because he would've been flunking out—he was sure of that. God, he hoped all this would be resolved by fall when school reopened because he'd be a senior then, and Fourth Form would be no joke! He'd have to buckle down to keep up his grades even though he was a shoo-in for valedictorian, but he also had general certificate of education (GCE) examinations for which he needed to prepare and had to sit. How well he did on those would determine if he would attend college in Canada, back in England, or at the University of the West Indies (UWI) in Jamaica. Sherr would be sitting out a semester, or the entire year, but they weren't really sure how that would work yet. Right now, he just needed to see her really badly!

As he drove down the highway, Alex was humming to himself. Considering how his life had turned to manure, he was amazingly upbeat, singing loudly with the radio and beating on the steering wheel. He wondered how big Sherrette had gotten. She was so small-framed that he sincerely hoped she'd be able to deliver with no problems. At the turnoff to her aunt's farmhouse, he wondered if anyone was home because things looked kind of quiet. It was after nine, yet nobody was moving about. Undaunted, he parked, grabbed the basket, and went to the door, where he knocked loudly.

CHAPTER 14

Meantime, back in Dangríga, Cathlean couldn't fool herself or anyone about her illness any longer. She had become bloated from water retention, her feet were so swollen that she couldn't walk or wear closed shoes, and Doc Shipley had had to order an oxygen tank and a wheelchair for her from Belize City. Zeke finally got a clue about how sick she was, and he ran like the coward he was, tail tucked between his legs—no surprise there. He liked Cathlean for the good times, but he hadn't signed up to take care of a sick old woman, so he got to stepping as if he were running on hot coals.

Betty was there for Cathlean, strong and supportive, even though she was busy juggling her horde of men and boy toys who kept following her like she was the Pied Piper of Hamlin. All of a sudden, Betty was getting all the action, which normally would've aggravated Cathlean, but Cathlean was too sick and exhausted to care. Her medication didn't seem to be working; homebrews and sure-fire cures were failing her, but she would not allow anyone to tell John what was going on with her health. Returning to Dabúyabah to have the Buyei lay hands on her was out of the question. Dr. Rivas had said she'd have maybe a year, but Cathlean seriously doubted that she would be sticking around that long.

One day, when Tooth was picking up a gentleman client from the Booty Bunker, he spied Cathlean sitting in a corner in her wheelchair, oxygen tank hanging from a pole. If she hadn't called out to him, he wouldn't have known it was her. Hiding his shock, he approached her. "Hey, Miss Catty," he said, "how you doing, lady?" He reached for her hand, which was soft, plump, and waterlogged.

"Tooth, I'm here, struggling, but still here. And you and your children?

No, don't name them again!" She laughed, but it turned into a hacking, phlegm-filled cough. "I think I'm dying, but you can't tell John or Alex. And definitely don't tell that stuck-up bitch, Ida, or that no-good man of hers, Victor. You weren't supposed to see me like this. Guess I'm not so sexy now, am I?" She giggled.

"You're beautiful, like always, Miss Catty." He lied. "Gotta go, but I'll come back to see you soon." He drove away, shaking his head, wondering what was going on with Cathlean. Something had happened with this family and with the boy and his little girlfriend, but though there was speculation, nobody really knew what was going on. Tooth vaguely knew Victor but heard he'd come back to town. It seemed like that was when all hell had broken loose! Tooth would find out what was going on. He wasn't nosy; people just seemed to like to confide in him so he'd know the true story very soon.

CHAPTER 15

When Alex knocked on the door at Aunt Corrine's, nothing happened. He repeated the knock and was about to leave in disgust and disappointment when a taxi pulled up, and Sherr and her aunt got out. It took Sherrette a couple of tries because she'd grown bigger, so Alex came over to help.

"Sherr, love, how are you? I'm happy to see you." He rubbed her stomach. "How's my baby?"

"English!" she shouted with genuine joy before her aunt pulled her back, quickly reminding Sherrette that she and Alex weren't supposed to have any physical contact. "Whatchu doin' here? You didn't tell us you were coming. Aunty would've mentioned it." She looked at Corrinne.

"I've been calling, but I can't talk to you, so I came anyway. I brought you lunch." "Young man, leave right now," said Aunt Corrine in her sternest voice. "She's not supposed to talk to you! Sherrette, you go inside, please." She pushed Sherrette in the direction of the door.

"Sherr, are you feeling okay? How are you, love?" Alex insisted.

"If you don't leave, I'll call the police constable," Corrine said. "Leave what you brought and go."

"Please, please, can't we just visit for a few minutes, Aunt Corrine?" begged Alex, now in tears.

"No. Go, don't come back to see your sister. Yes, you heard, your sister!" shouted Corrine, slamming the door.

Alex couldn't believe it; he'd driven all this way for nothing?! Why was Corrine being so mean? Alex suddenly felt full of murderous rage, the likes of which he'd never experienced before. He could kill the aunt and end his torture right now. How much more was he expected to take? He'd played by the rules, but what good did it do him? Seemed like he got the lion's share of pain, not because he wanted it, but just the luck of the draw. Alex was tired of it and of being pushed around. He would leave, but he would be back in six weeks; he just needed to see his baby enter this world.

As he drove away, he wondered how Cathlean was doing. Maybe if she or John had come with him, Corrine may have allowed a chaperoned visit. Hindsight had Alex considering this an option for next time he visited . . . and he would be back to see his baby born—nobody was going to stop him! He wondered why he thought about Cathlean. She was no longer Mum to him, so why did she cross her mind right then? Maybe he'd have John check on her, see how she was doing. She seemed off, no longer sure of herself now that Victor was back in town, and she'd looked tired last time too.

At the very moment that Alex was thinking about her, Cathlean was being rushed to the hospital with chest pains and breathing problems. She was retaining water in her lungs because of congestive heart failure, which was why she couldn't get enough air into them. She suspected that the events of recent weeks and months was causing her undue trauma and stress, shortening her life. Cathlean regretted Victor's return to town for many reasons: He was literally making her heart hurt and was also causing her son major pain to realize that he was in love with, and had impregnated, his own sister.

Cathlean should've paid attention to the dreams about her stepfather while at the Dabúyabah. Maybe the spirits of her ancestors had been trying to warn her of the pervert's imminent return, but her psyche had been in denial. She hoped she could live long enough to make Victor pay for his sins; she still planned to turn him in to the authorities for rape. Mr. Victor Busano was not going to be allowed to get away! Didn't matter that he hadn't known about his son, Alex, product of that rape, the only good thing to come out of that horror. Cathlean hadn't loved Alex due to the way he'd been conceived, but her Mama Bear tendencies always came out when people messed with her boy.

Alex broke speed records getting back to Dangríga, where he confessed to a bleary-eyed and hungover John about his unsuccessful trip to see Sherrette. He was spitting angry, but at least he'd satisfied his curiosity about what she looked like with a big belly; she was darn cute! In another six weeks, the baby would be arriving, so Alex was pleading with John now to be allowed at the birth event—if not in the hospital ward, then somewhere nearby. Alex promised to be well-behaved and follow the rules, but John didn't think it was a good idea. However, he did promise to think about it some more. After a few more weeks had crawled by, the answer was still no, which made Alex furious. Again, he felt that he was being dealt unbearable pain, just for being. Okay, so he and Sherr were brother and sister, and it was too late to have an abortion, but couldn't he be allowed to see this through? He was told no—hadn't he and Sherr done enough? There was no good way to fix this.

Cathlean was released from the hospital after about a week. It was obvious to everyone that she was ailing because she came home with full medical supplies: tanks of oxygen, bags of pills, and strict instructions to adhere to a salt-free diet. The puffiness wouldn't go away, but if she cut down on salt, it would be manageable. So-called friends stopped by to visit and encourage her, but she suspected they were curious to see the interior of the Booty Bunker. For Cathlean not to object and to be happy about these visitations probably showed just how sick she was, or maybe she was mellowing in her older years? Whatever the reason, people were happy with the transformation though they also pitied her.

CHAPTER 16

It was the eighth month of Sherr's pregnancy, a month before Alex would be returning to school for his senior year. He was frustrated because he was not allowed to visit even with a chaperone. From what he heard, Sherrette was as big as a house. What did people think he and Sherr would do once they were together? Jump one another's bones all day? Not at all; he just wanted some quiet time with his baby's mummy/ his sister, whatever she was, but it was not to be. He was heartsick at the unfairness.

He was denied at every step of the way, so much so that he started thinking that he if he wasn't around, nobody would notice. John still seemed disappointed in Alex, and Alex couldn't understand John's attitude at all. Cathlean had completely dropped out of sight and Miss Ida and Victor-the-loser were playing house. *If she didn't watch out, maybe she'd come up pregnant like her daughter!* Alex thought viciously. He wasn't even interested in registering for school, picking his classes, or any of the things that used to excite him about school or the start of a new school year. Sherr and the baby were everything to him, but he was nothing to anybody. As he brooded about this, he wondered where John was.

Alex really needed some father-son time, but alas, even that was not to be! Alex was getting more depressed by the minute, so he wandered to the bar and decided to pour himself a glass of John's One Barrel Belizean rum. He took a sip, grimacing as the liquor burned his throat and hit his empty stomach. How did people drink this mess? Alex couldn't understand the fascination, but he vowed to continue and finish the drink he'd poured. He turned on the radio and stated prancing around, dancing by himself, literally crying in his drink. As he stumbled around, Alex realized he was getting tipsy. Hey, this drinking thing wasn't so bad; the only thing was that it was hitting him very quickly. He thought about getting some food but decided he'd wait till John came home.

Speaking of John, how could Alex ever hope to measure up to his father's reputation? John was a distinguished soldier and would always be known for that. What was Alex? A screwed-up young man, unloved by his mother, loved by his father, in love for the first time in his life, but with whom? His sister, that's who! How'd he screw this up so badly? Alex felt the pain hit him sharp and deep in his chest. His anguish knew no end . . . how could he live without Sherr and his baby in his life? People were already whispering and almost guessing at the truth. Sherr might not ever be able to return to Dangríga where the gossips were waiting to tear her and the baby to pieces when they arrived. And Alex would never be able to publicly claim them or defend them. What kind of life was that going to be? Not a good or a promising one, that was for darned sure!

Alex stumbled around, pondering these things, when he bumped into the drawer of the table where John kept trinkets and important documents. Alex opened the drawer and saw something shiny out the corner of his eye. Curious, he moved some papers out the way and saw John's musket that he'd been given at retirement. This was the same gun with which John had shot at Zeke when he'd found that man in bed with Cathlean. Alex chuckled, imagining the scene, and weighed the gun in his hand. He flipped the chamber back, shocked to see that there were two bullets inside. "Hmm, I wonder why Dad left these in here?" he asked. He closed the chamber and cocked the gun, sighting along the barrel. *This really is a pretty piece,* he thought. *One of these bullets will solve my problem. Two will guarantee a permanent solution. Then I won't have to try to fight people when they try to talk about my woman/sister and my baby. I should just solve everyone's problem and go away.* He cocked the gun again, pointing it to his right temple first, then directly at his heart. The fuzziness of an alcohol-induced haze wouldn't let him realize the danger of the situation.

"Yes, that Cathlean bitch won't have to pretend to love me anymore. I'm tired of the color of my pain. Dad is the only one who's ever cared. The sperm donor, Victor? Definitely not! All he did was come along and cause problems. We were happy before he got here. I oughta use these bullets on his pathetic arse! Bye, Sherrette. Bye-bye, baby Alex-Alexa!" He calmly cocked the trigger and pulled twice in quick succession. He'd hit the ground by the time the second bullet pierced his heart—he would feel no more pain there, and that brilliant brain of his would never realize its full potential now.

Alex's eyes closed in sweet surrender. The color of his pain was like a kaleidoscope of bright and powerful hues! He was finally at peace, which is how he looked when John found him an hour later.

It was Alex's seventeenth birthday.

EPILOUGE

Present-Day Dangríga Belize,
Central America

Alex looked so lifelike in his pine wood coffin. His mother Cathlean sat in her wheelchair, oxygen tank at the ready, sobbingat the absolute horror of Alex's action, while John rubbed her shoulders soothingly. The irony was that she was on the donor lists to receive a heart, but she couldn't even harvest Alex's because it was ruptured so very badly when the bullets ripped through it. Victor, his birth dad, stood there awkwardly turning his beat-up fedora over and over in his gnarled hands; he reeked of alcohol and marijuana. The few who knew who he was would not satisfy the curiosity of those clueless to his identity. Sherrette, Alex's love and sister, stood near the coffin; she was hollow-eyed from crying and appeared broken and in shock. Her hugely protruding belly reminded her that she would be having Alex's child by herself in a few short weeks. She prayed that it would be healthy, with no disabilities or deformities because, after all, she *was* carrying her brother's child. She hoped she'd have a boy who looked exactly like his father, but girl or boy, she would name it Alexander, Alexandra, or Alexa, and call it Alex.

Tooth stood on the side, sorrowful and lamenting the waste of such a young life that had showed so much promise. He'd finally told John about Cathlean's heart issues and the fact that she was confined to a wheelchair, breathing only by means of an oxygen tank. He had wanted to prepare John for Cathlean's totally changed appearance so John would not be in shock when he saw her. Of course, John was very angry with Tooth, berating him for not having revealed what he'd known of Cathy's health condition prior to this. Maybe if Alex had been aware of his mother's heart problems and her health issues, he may not have chosen to take his own life in such a horrible way.

Tooth accepted the lambasting from John, and as John was starting to plan his son's funeral, Tooth totally shocked John when he pulled out a wad of money and handed it to John. "John, hey, all those times you and your family offered me money for driving you and Cathlean around, for picking up your boy, for rescuing you from saloons when you were drunk, I never wanted your money, yet you always forced me to take it. Have been waiting for a time when I could give it all back to you. So, here, please take this. Dere's $2,000. Use it to send your son off in style. He was a special young man, your Alex. I woulda been proud to call him son, even with my twenty-two children." He chuckled sorrowfully. "If you have money left after paying for his funeral, please give it to his girl. I'm sure he woulda wanted dat." Tooth shuffled his feet, unsure of what John's reaction would be.

John was flabbergasted. "Tooth, man, are you serious? I'm proud to call you friend. I'm not going to insult you by turning down the money, but Cathy and I thank you from the bottom of our hearts. I can pay for my son's funeral because I've always had life insurance on him, but I'll make sure Sherr gets the money. She'll need it for herself and baby Alex." He hugged Tooth tightly, sobbing.

The wake continued much in the same way as it had been going for another day and night. On the third day, as the new day dawned, they closed the coffin and took Alex to Stann Creek Methodist Church, where he and John had worshipped, for his 9:00 a.m. going-home service.

The place was packed: extra chairs and benches had to be set up in the foyer and directly outside under leafy green trees. Microphones were strung all around so everyone could hear the sad service. Alex was a well-loved and respected young man, always well-mannered and caring. People shook their heads, still shocked at the suicide, but irritated that they were not privy to what had driven such a levelheaded, mild-mannered young man to such an extreme: to end his life so violently. Vicious rumors were swirling about a possible Obeah spell that had been put on Alex, Sherrette, and her pregnancy. People were putting two and two together, but so far, nobody could confirm anything. Even the well-known "mourners" who always acted up and put on a show at every funeral were strangely quiet and subdued. Because Alex had died under such tragic circumstances, their usual show would not only be in poor taste here, but it would be totally unwelcome too.

Reverend Goff officiated at the funeral service, preaching a beautiful eulogy entitled "The Color of Pain," where he admonished parents about loving their children and to show it so the children could always feel safe and loved. Afterward, they took Alex and laid him in his final resting place in the Garden of Gethsemane Cemetery, right underneath a cashew tree, a fruit he'd loved so much. The color of Alex's pain had changed to the colors of love: peaceful, calming, and warm pastel hues.

GLOSSARY

Abanh   *Garífuna language; the number 1*

Bwai   *Kriol word for boy*

Buyei   *Garífuna language; healer and lead practitioner of the Dugú ceremony*

Creoles   *Mixed-race descendants of the original colonial French settlers born in Louisiana*

Dabúyabah *Garífuna language; temple in which the Dugú ceremony is performed*

Distritos   *Spanish word for districts or territories*

Dugú   *Ancient funerary ceremony practiced by the Garífuna people of Central America*

Fadiri   *Garífuna language; "Father" or "priest" as in the Roman Catholic religion*

Gial   *Kriol word for girl*

Gi-yow   *Garífuna language; non-Garífunas, i.e., Chinese, Indians, Kriols, Hispanic, Mayan*

Guate   *A native of Guatemala; abbreviation for the word Guatemalteco*

Gubeeda   *Garífuna language; spiritual being that enters and possesses a person's body*

Hee-u   *Garífuna language; sweet grated cassava-ginger drink, usually served cold*

Hudút	*Garífuna language; green or ripe (or a mixture of both) plantains beaten in a wooden mortar and served in coconut (falumoú) or brown-flour (tikíni) gravy*
Hu-ree-iu	*Garífuna language; Judas Iscariot, betrayer of Jesus Christ*
Kriol	**English-based Belizean dialect or language; the people who predominantly speak it**
Misericordia	*Latin language; petition for mercy for one's heart; part of Catholic religious prayer*
Obeah	*West Indian/Belizean term; West African religious practice, folk magic, or sorcery*
Owen-hah	*Garífuna language; trancelike state achieved by worshippers during a Dugú ritual*
Paisanos	**Spanish for countrymen; often shortened to paisa**
Pickney	**Kriol for child; believed to have originated from the American word picaninny**
Pinole	*Garífuna language; sweet porridge made from roasted, ground corn and served hot*
Quid pro quo	*Latin phrase for an even exchange of goods or services; trade-off*
Stella	*Mayan pillar planted vertically on the ground, used to depict scenes and/or tell a story*
Suruciu	*Garífuna language; naked, unclothed*
Uma	*Garífuna language; road or journey*

www.ingramcontent.com/pod-product-compliance
Lightning Source LLC
Chambersburg PA
CBHW021611120626
46545CB00001B/167

* 9 7 8 1 9 6 3 8 5 1 2 6 7 *